Multilingual Online Academic Collaborations as Resistance

RESEARCHING MULTILINGUALLY

Series Editors: Prue Holmes, *Durham University, UK*, Richard Fay, *University of Manchester, UK* and Jane Andrews, *University of the West of England, UK*

Consulting Editor: Alison Phipps, *University of Glasgow, UK*

The increasingly diverse character of many societies means that many researchers may now find themselves engaging with multilingual opportunities and complexities as they design, carry out and disseminate their research. This may be the case regardless of whether or not there is an explicit language and multilingual aspect to their research. This book series proposes to address the methodological, practical, ethical and other options and dilemmas that researchers face as they go about their research. How do they design their research methodology to account for multilingual possibilities and practices? How do they manage such linguistic complexities in the research domain? What are the implications for their research outcomes? Research methods training programmes only rarely address these questions and there is, as yet, only a limited literature available. This series proposes to establish a new track of theoretical, methodological and ethical researcher praxis that researchers can draw upon in research(er) contexts where multiple languages are at play or might be purposefully used. In particular, the series proposes to offer critical and interpretive perspectives on research practices and endeavours in inter- and multidisciplinary contexts and especially where languages, and the people speaking and using them, are under pressure, pain and tension.

All books in this series are externally peer-reviewed.

Full details of all the books in this series and of all our other publications can be found on http://www.multilingual-matters.com, or by writing to Multilingual Matters, St Nicholas House, 31–34 High Street, Bristol BS1 2AW, UK.

RESEARCHING MULTILINGUALLY: 4

Multilingual Online Academic Collaborations as Resistance

Crossing Impassable Borders

Edited by
Giovanna Fassetta, Nazmi Al-Masri and Alison Phipps

MULTILINGUAL MATTERS
Bristol • Blue Ridge Summit

DOI https://doi.org/10.21832/FASSET9592
Library of Congress Cataloging in Publication Data
A catalog record for this book is available from the Library of Congress.
Names: Fassetta, Giovanna - editor. | Al-Masri, Nazmi - editor. | Phipps, Alison M., editor.
Title: Multilingual Online Academic Collaborations as Resistance: Crossing Impassable Borders/
   Edited by Giovanna Fassetta, Nazmi Al-Masri and Alison Phipps.
Description: Bristol; Blue Ridge Summit: Multilingual Matters, [2020] | Series: Researching
   Multilingually: 4 | Includes bibliographical references and index. | Summary: "This book
   details online collaborations between universities in Europe, the USA and Palestine. The
   chapters recount the challenges and successes of online collaborations which promote
   academic connections and conversations with the Gaza Strip (Palestine) and forge
   relationships between individuals, institutions and cultures"— Provided by publisher.
Identifiers: LCCN 2020016677 (print) | LCCN 2020016678 (ebook) |
   ISBN 9781788929592 (hardback) | ISBN 9781788929585 (paperback) |
   ISBN 9781788929608 (pdf) | ISBN 9781788929615 (epub) | ISBN 9781788929622 (kindle
   edition) Subjects: LCSH: Jāmiʻah al-Islāmīyah (Gaza) | Language and languages—Study and
   teaching (Higher)—Computer-assisted instruction. | Language and languages—Study and
   teaching (Higher)—Gaza Strip. | Multilingual education—Gaza Strip. | Web-based
   instruction—Gaza Strip. | Internet in higher education—Gaza Strip. | Education, Higher—
   International cooperation. | University cooperation—Gaza Strip. | War and education—Gaza
   Strip.
Classification: LCC P53.28 .M86 2020 (print) | LCC P53.28 (ebook) | DDC
   418.0071/156943—dc23 LC record available at https://lccn.loc.gov/2020016677
LC ebook record available at https://lccn.loc.gov/2020016678

British Library Cataloguing in Publication Data
A catalogue entry for this book is available from the British Library.

ISBN-13: 978-1-78892-959-2 (hbk)
ISBN-13: 978-1-78892-958-5 (pbk)

Multilingual Matters
UK: St Nicholas House, 31–34 High Street, Bristol BS1 2AW, UK.
USA: NBN, Blue Ridge Summit, PA, USA.

Website: www.multilingual-matters.com
Twitter: Multi_Ling_Mat
Facebook: https://www.facebook.com/multilingualmatters
Blog: www.channelviewpublications.wordpress.com

Copyright © 2020 Giovanna Fassetta, Nazmi Al-Masri, Alison Phipps and the authors of individual chapters.

All rights reserved. No part of this work may be reproduced in any form or by any means without permission in writing from the publisher.

The policy of Multilingual Matters/Channel View Publications is to use papers that are natural, renewable and recyclable products, made from wood grown in sustainable forests. In the manufacturing process of our books, and to further support our policy, preference is given to printers that have FSC and PEFC Chain of Custody certification. The FSC and/or PEFC logos will appear on those books where full certification has been granted to the printer concerned.

Typeset by Nova Techset Private Limited, Bengaluru and Chennai, India.
Printed and bound in the UK by the CPI Books Group Ltd.
Printed and bound in the US by NBN.

Contents

	Contributors	vii
	Prologue. Collaborating under Siege: A WhatsApp Tale	xi
	Introduction: Can You 'Here' Me? Editors' Reflections on Online Collaborations between the Gaza Strip and the Global North *Alison Phipps, Giovanna Fassetta and Nazmi Al-Masri*	1

Part 1: English as an Additional Language and Online Technologies

1	Engineers Operating Multilingually: Reflections on Four Years of Glasgow-Gaza Pre-sessional English Telecollaboration *Bill Guariento*	17
2	Islamic University of Gaza Internationalization Endeavors at the Level of Postgraduate Programs *Sanaa Abou-Dagga*	36
3	Exploring Mobile Support for English Language Teachers in a Context of Conflict: Syrian Refugee Teachers in Jordan *Gary Motteram, Nazmi Al-Masri, Heba Hamouda and Shaiffadzillah Omarali*	56

Part 2: Finding Motivation for Language Learning in a Situation of Forced Immobility

4	Motivational Strategies and Online Technologies: Are Palestinian EFL University Students in the Gaza Strip Empowered to be Bilingual? *Abedrabu Abu Alyan*	73
5	'Really Talking' to Gaza: From Active to Transformative Learning in Distributed Environments and under Highly Pressured Conditions *Anna Rolinska, Bill Guariento, Ghadeer Abouda and Ongkarn Nakprada*	94

Part 3: Palestine and the Arabic Language

6 Gaza Teaches Arabic Online: Opportunities, Challenges and Ways Forward 117
   Giovanna Fassetta, Nazmi Al-Masri, Mariam Attia and Alison Phipps

7 (In)articulability of Pain and Trauma: Idioms of Distress in the Gaza Strip 131
   Maria Grazia Imperiale

Part 4: Making Connections

8 The Experience of the Islamic University of Gaza in Cross-border Academic Collaboration: T-MEDA Project as a Case Study 149
   Ahmed S. Muhaisen

9 From the Kitchen to Gaza: Networked Places and the Collaborative Imagination 165
   Chantelle Warner and David Gramling

Afterword. 'I am Here': Savouring the 'Selfie Moments' 190
Alison Phipps

Index 194

Contributors

Ghadeer Abouda is a PhD candidate at Hamad Bin Khalifa University (HBKU) in Qatar. Before enrolling in the PhD programme she was a teaching assistant at the Islamic University of Gaza (IUG), Palestine. She has a Master's degree from the IUG in the field of information technology. Ghadeer worked as a software engineer in Al-Aqsa University right after completing her BS degree from the Information Technology college in IUG. Ghadeer was a participant in EAST in 2015 and a volunteer for EAST 2016 which is the programme established between the Islamic University of Gaza in Palestine and the University of Glasgow in UK.

Sanaa Abou-Dagga is a Professor of Education in the area of research and evaluation, working at the Islamic University of Gaza (IUG) since 1999. She received her MA and PhD from Iowa State University, USA. At IUG she was the first female to be appointed in a senior administrative position. Throughout her administrative work, Sanaa was involved with many successful initiatives that promoted quality education change at the institution and at the national level. She managed several projects funded by international organizations which promoted knowledge exchange between the local and global communities. Her current research focuses on issues related to women, higher education change and development in Palestine.

Abedrabu Abu Alyan is an Assistant Professor in the Department of English at the Islamic University of Gaza (IUG). Currently, he is the Deputy Head of the English Department at IUG. He has taught many courses at BA and MA level. These courses include introduction to intercultural communication, teaching English as a foreign language (TEFL), oral communication skills, grammar and academic writing. Abedrabu has supervised and participated as internal and external examiner for many MA students. His research interests are intercultural communication, ethnography of communication, TEFL, computer assisted language learning (CALL) and discourse analysis.

Nazmi Al-Masri is an Associate Professor in the English Language Department, Islamic University of Gaza (IUG). He has worked in several senior academic positions, including Vice President for External Affairs at IUG. The courses he teaches include technology in TEFL, oral communication skills, curriculum development and academic reading. His main research interests include teacher training, language and intercultural communication, pedagogy and technology. Nazmi has been a co-investigator on 15 British and EU-funded research, capacity building and mobility projects in full partnership with universities in the UK, Finland, Norway, Germany, Austria, France and Spain. He has co-published several education-related research papers in international journals.

Mariam Attia is a Lecturer in the School of Education and Social Work at the University of Sussex, UK. She is interested in educational research which aims to cultivate wellbeing, support capacity building and promote the furthering of human potential. Mariam is the module leader for Fundamentals of Teaching and Learning in Higher Education, and Educational Theory and Practice: Critical Reflection. Internationally, she has worked with teachers and researchers in Egypt, Palestine, Jordan, Ghana, Nigeria, Cambodia and Japan. She is a Senior Fellow of the Higher Education Academy, and a member of the Society for Research into Higher Education.

Giovanna Fassetta is Senior Lecturer in Inclusive Education at the University of Glasgow. She is also part of the UNESCO Chair for Refugee Integration through Languages and the Arts (RILA) and of the Glasgow Refugee Asylum and Migration Network (GRAMNet). Recently, she has been Principal Investigator on two Global Challenges Research Fund (GCRF) projects in collaboration with the Islamic University of Gaza (IUG) and is currently engaged in a new series of research activities which include IUG as well as academic and non-academic partners in several other ODA countries. Giovanna collaborated on the design, development and promotion of an online Palestinian Arabic language course for beginner learners. She is interested in diversity and inclusion; multilingualism and intercultural communication; and participatory and decolonial methodologies.

David Gramling wrote *The Invention of Monolingualism* (Bloomsbury, 2016), co-wrote *Palliative Care Conversations* (De Gruyter, 2019) and *Linguistic Disobedience* (Palgrave, 2019), and is currently writing *The Invention of Multilingualism* (Cambridge University Press) and *Literature in the Linguacene* (Stanford University Press). His co-translation of Murathan Mungan's novella, 'Tales of Valor' (Cenk Hikayeleri) is forthcoming with Northwestern University Press. David is a proud member of the AHRC Translating Cultures Theme Researching Multilingually at Borders, and of the American Literary Translators Association Board of Directors, and is the outgoing Translations Editor of *Transgender Studies Quarterly* (Duke University Press).

William (Bill) Guariento is Senior Lecturer in English Language at the University of Northumbria. Until May 2020 he worked at the University of Glasgow, where he directed the Science, Engineering and Technology Summer Bridging Programme described in this volume. In addition to his work with Gaza, he has written and delivered subject-specific English for Academic Purposes courses for engineers in Libya, China and Chile, and works as a CELTA teacher-trainer and assessor.

Heba Hamouda is an English language teacher at Beit lahia Elementary Co-ed School, UNRWA, Gaza (Palestine). Currently, she is also an MA student in applied linguistics in the English Language Department of the Islamic University of Gaza (IUG). Her main research interests are pedagogy, technology for teaching English to children and language assessment. Heba has participated in several training workshops for Palestinian teachers working at UNRWA primary schools in Gaza.

Maria Grazia Imperiale is a Postdoctoral Research Associate at the University of Glasgow, UK. Her main research interest is language education in difficult circumstances. Maria conducted her doctoral studies on English language teaching in the Gaza Strip (Palestine), and after that she has worked with pre-service and in-service English and Arabic teachers, considering the link between wellbeing and language education and using creative methods in language pedagogy.

Gary Motteram is a Senior Lecturer in Education in the Institute of Education at the University of Manchester where he teaches on Master's degrees in TESOL digital technology. He has a special interest in technology-supported teacher education, an area in which he has published, and presents regularly at conferences. Gary's current funded research projects focus on teacher education in challenging contexts using digital technology, particularly mobile phones.

Ahmed Salama Muhaisen is a Full Professor in the architectural engineering department at the Islamic University of Gaza (IUG). He obtained his MSc and PhD degrees from Nottingham University (UK) in the field of sustainable architecture. He specializes in energy-efficient building design, with long academic and professional experience in this field. Ahmed has substantial experience in managing international research and collaboration projects funded by international funding programmes. He has held several administrative positions at IUG, the last of which is Dean of External Affairs, which he has occupied since 2017.

Ongkarn Nakprada received his MSc degree in information technology from University of Glasgow, Scotland, in 2018. He is currently working as a programmer for the Office of the Prime Minister of Thailand. His fields of interest include web development and machine learning.

Shaiffadzillah (Shai) Omarali is an educational technologist with a background in web development and programming for educational purpose. His current projects focus on the integration of ubiquitous computing, artificial intelligences, robotics, digital curriculum content, coding education and industry 4.0-driven technology and pedagogy into education ecosystems, particularly in line with developments in the areas of adaptive online learning, adaptive digital games-based learning and the future Industry 5.0.

Alison Phipps is UNESCO Chair in Refugee Integration through Languages and the Arts at the University of Glasgow and Professor of Languages and Intercultural Studies. She is Co-Convener of the Glasgow Refugee, Asylum and Migration Network (GRAMNET). She was Distinguished Visiting Professor at the University of Waikato, Aotearoa New Zealand from 2013 to 2016, Thinker in Residence at the EU Hawke Centre, University of South Australia in 2016, Visiting Professor at Auckland University of Technology and Visiting Professor at Otago University, NZ. She was Principal Investigator for the AHRC Large Grant *Researching Multilingually at the Borders of Language, the Body, Law and the State*, and is now a Co-Director of the Global Challenge Research Fund (GCRF) *South-South Migration* Hub. She is an academic, activist and published poet.

Anna Rolinska is an English for Academic Purposes Lecturer working at the Glasgow School of Art, previously also the University of Glasgow. She is responsible for designing, teaching on, convening and evaluating in-sessional and pre-sessional courses for international students. Anna's research interests include academic literacies, use of educational technology, formation of learner identity and agency, creativity in academia and the interplay between multimodality and academic discourse.

Chantelle Warner is Associate Professor of German Studies and Second Language Acquisition and Teaching and Co-Director of the Center for Educational Resources in Culture, Language and Literacy at the University of Arizona, USA, where she also directs the German language programme. Her research focuses on affective and experiential dimensions of language use and learning, foreign language literacy development, stylistics and literary pragmatics.

Prologue. Collaborating under Siege: A WhatsApp Tale

Over the past couple of years, a team based in Gaza and a team based in Glasgow have been working together through digital tools to design, develop and promote an online Palestinian Arabic language course. A WhatsApp group has been one of the main channels for collaboration and for exchanges between the teams' members. Below is a copy-and-paste of a chat that took place over 24 hours in early May 2019, as we were putting the final touches to the first draft of this book.

GF: We had a Palestinian Arabic lesson at the UNESCO Spring School. In it we made this display

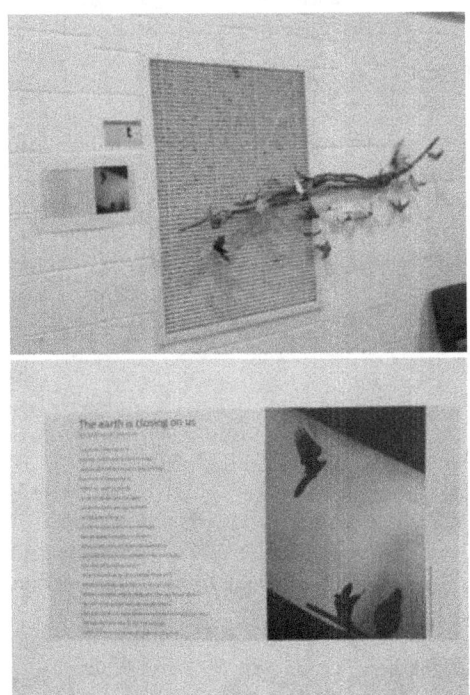

GF: HA 💗 your sister's name is next to her beautiful picture
HA: Great news and Great effort⬇️⬇️⬇️ Thanks Giovanna
HA: Oh, thank you so much. She will be happy with this. But a quick notice, it's FA not FH. But it's Ok thanks☺️
GF: Sorry! True 🙈
GF: I'll fix it!!
GF: done!
LA: Wow, great efforts! ☺️ wishing to participate with you there ☺️!
...
GF: I read about the airstrikes. I'm very, very sorry you have to live in this crazy situation! I hope you're all safe
HA: Unfortunately, there are many airstrikes. Really, it's crazy. Thanks Giovanna for thinking of us 🌷
AP: Thinking of you all and sending love and solidarity and praying the caged birds of Gaza will be safe and be able to fly free
HA: 🌷🌷
GF: I'm so so sorry to hear this! It must be so stressful and scary for you all. I pray that this will stop very soon. There are many people here thinking of you and praying you're safe 🌷
HA: Thank you so much 💗
NM: Dear Giovanna and Alison, Your kind and considerate messages are our wings that will enable us to fly high in the skies of freedom and independence, hopefully very soon. 🕊️🌷
MI: Thinking of you all 🌷❤️
HA: I hope so, but the tension becomes more and more every minute. I am sorry, but this record shows you the terrible voices that we have heard since yesterday.
HA: [Audio recording: loud explosions, people screaming, agitated voices]
AP: We are so so so sorry that this war is being waged against you; that this violence is everywhere we are with you in solidarity, writing again to our MPs and trying to be with you in solidarity and peace making
HA: Thanks. We appreciate your efforts ✿
GF: Oh, HA and all, how awful. You're my friends and my colleagues and I'm really really sorry this is what you have to go through. I pray and hope with all my might that you can soon hear birdsong and not these awful sounds. We will do all we can from here, but more than anything I hope and pray that this stops very very soon.
NM: Dear Alison and Giovanna,
With your considerate and continuing kind heartfelt messages we become stronger than the oppressors' power and our steel will becomes much stronger than the iron bars caging us. As the rockets strike all corners of Gaza every now and then, your sympathetic words compassion free us from fear and give us unlimited hope that this cloud of violence is going to end sooner or later. With humans and peace loving people like you, we will be free to fly high in peace skies regardless of pain and cries.
Today 2 wings of oppression. I and many other Palestinians suffered: air strikes that kill our bodies and siege that prevents us from flying freely. I am saying these words as I have just been prevented again from leaving Gaza after spending 10 hrs waiting and so much money but ……

	The sea of bitterness and waves of disappointment I feel will turn into flooding determination that breaks the bars of cage.
GF:	Oh, not again! I'm sorry to hear that, Nazmi. It must be very disappointing for you, but I appreciate the fact that you do not let it stop you and you keep trying. I hope this madness stops, and that we can have the pleasure to seeing you in person soon
GF:	I'm reading that there has been a ceasefire, brokered by Egypt. Inshallah it's the start of a long period of peace and of talks that can ease your suffering. Hopefully you can now rest a bit, and breathe, and enjoy your most important time of the year 🌷🌸🖤

Can you 'hear'… me?

Can you 'here'… me?

Introduction: Can You 'Here' Me? Editors' Reflections on Online Collaborations between the Gaza Strip and the Global North

Alison Phipps, Giovanna Fassetta and Nazmi Al-Masri

The chapters that are included in this edited collection recount and discuss the challenges – and the gratifications – of collaborations between higher education institutions (HEIs) in the UK and USA and the Islamic University of Gaza (IUG), a Palestinian HEI based in the Gaza Strip. The online collaborations on which the chapters are based aim to bypass borders and to keep knowledge flowing to/from the Gaza Strip[1] – despite the decade-long blockade[2] of the Strip by the state of Israel and Egypt – and to forge relationships between individuals, institutions, languages and cultures. All the chapters observe, from different perspectives, the dynamics that come into play when languages and the internet combine to become portals through which encounters can happen, and the fundamental importance this has as a form of defiance and of resistance to the physical confinement experienced by Gaza's academics, students and the general population. They highlight the limitations of multilingual and intercultural encounters when they are deprived of the sensory proximity of face-to-face situations, and what is lost in the translation of languages, practices and experiences from the 'real' to the 'virtual' world.

The United Nations Country Team in the Occupied Palestinian Territory notes that

> fifty years have passed since Israel occupied the Gaza Strip and the West Bank, including East Jerusalem; five decades of *de-development*, suppressed human potential and denial of the right to development, with an economy incapable of employing one third of its workforce and featuring extremely high unemployment among women and youth. (UN, 2017: 3, emphasis added)

As well experiencing a situation of 'de-development', poverty and high unemployment, the Gaza Strip also suffers from the isolation the blockade imposes. Travel out of the Strip is restricted, tightly controlled and costly. Travel to the Strip is highly discouraged by the UK government's official guidelines and Foreign and Commonwealth Office travel advisories.

Being able to travel to take part at conferences, to experience working and networking in other institutions as a visiting fellow and, more generally, to engage in all the face-to-face opportunities for professional and personal development: these are all opportunities that are available to – and often expected of – the vast majority of academics in the Global North.[3] As we finalise the final proofs of this book before it goes to print, all of us, globally, are experiencing limitations on our freedom of movement due to the COVID-19 lockdown. While aware of the need for physical distancing, we are also mourning the opportunities for personal interaction and travel that we had come to take for granted, the ones that enrich and expand our professional and intercultural knowledge. We soldier on and look forward to the return of those forms of face-to-face academic relations that open up new and unforeseen possibilities for collaborations and partnerships, which can impact positively on students, on a country's economy and on its infrastructures, and from which ultimately the wider society should also benefit. While we have shifted our collaborations online and learnt we can still meet and work together and that perhaps we can, in future, hold on to some form of more sustainable communication, we are still hoping and expecting that one day, not too far in the future, we will again be able to meet at conferences, become and welcome visiting fellows, visit our colleagues and be visited by them. These opportunities for academic travel, however, are unavailable to many academics from the Global South not just at this exceptional time, as they often see their visas rejected when applying for travel to HEIs in richer countries. They are almost impossible for Gaza's scholars, who experience a double set of challenges: obtaining a visa to enter a Western country and also being allowed to leave the Gaza Strip. Restrictions to travel on the scale of those imposed by COVID-19 are not new to them and will not pass with the end of the pandemic.

In 2005 Alison Phipps and Ronald Barnett co-authored a paper celebrating and critiquing modes of academic travel. Academic travel, they argued, 'indexes more than physical journeys, and physical journeys themselves point to changes in conceptions of knowledge and ideas' (Phipps & Barnett, 2005: 5). The paper pre-dated by a couple of years the beginning of Alison's partnership work with the Islamic University of Gaza. It therefore also pre-dated the experience of academic non-travel, of frustrated academic travel, of the 'Can you hear me?' greetings to colleagues, as in the title of our volume, rather than the handshake, the smile – sometimes the hug – that academics exchange when meeting at conferences. Just as academic travel indexes more than physical journeys, the prevention of academic travel indexes the political economy and political repression of scholars in different parts of the world.

The words in that 2005 paper ring hollow in light of the following ten years' work under what is now Sustainable Development Goal 16 – Peace, Justice and Strong Institutions – to develop strong and lasting academic institutions, dedicated to arts and humanities education, especially focused on languages and creativity. Phipps and Barnett (2005) argued that epistemological and ontological questions of academic travel include metaphorical movements across the boundaries of fields of knowing, but also an academic's personal journey of change, challenge and even struggle. All these forms of shift and movement, the authors posited, form a substantial element in how knowledge is created and constructed. This points to what Bourdieu (2000) calls the *Scholare* – the material base that sustains the knowledge production in academia and the fields of cultural and academic capital, together with linguistic capital, which undergird the creation of epistemologies (Bourdieu, 1988, 1993).

While the editors and authors of this volume work internationally with partners in many different international contexts and are engaged in promoting transdisciplinary modes of knowledge production across the Global South, the conditions of knowledge production within Gaza and between Gaza and their collaborators represent a particular instance of historical significance. It is not possible to produce the same generic, academic work in Gaza as in, for instance, Glasgow or Manchester. The Russell Group Universities have access to the vast resources of libraries that have been held and sustained in peace times, that have never been destroyed, unless by occasional tragic fire, and that are now stored virtually, thanks to IT capacities second only to the military. The wealth of knowledge held in these libraries is not available to HEIs in the Gaza Strip, where libraries and cultural institutions are regularly and repeatedly deprived of their treasured contents by bombing raids. Peacetime also affords the financial resources for libraries to buy access to online academic books and journals, the often exorbitant costs of which are out of bounds to institutions impoverished by the prolonged blockade which has crippled the Strip's economy to unsustainable levels. The kinds of thought which are possible when there are no drone strikes on a daily basis, and when over a half of the population of working age is not unemployed, are very different from those of a land under a severe blockade, suffering persistent conflict and occupation for over 60 years. Deprived of the 'luxury' of time, wealth and resources that only prolonged peacetime can offer, academics in Gaza must often engage in what Levi-Strauss famously terms *bricolage* (Lévi-Strauss, 1962), or forms of improvisation.

In their introduction to *Creativity and Cultural Improvisation*, Hallam and Ingold (2007) state: 'There is no prepared script for social and cultural life. People work it out as they go along.' Academic life everywhere is marked by this anthropological observation: we improvise. For those of us in the United Kingdom (at least for now), we have the help of - atleast sources at our fingertips and access to visas and passports which allow – at least during non-pandemic times – travel to more countries than almost any other nation-state enjoys. For 2 million Palestinians living in Gaza, the opposite applies: there is little or no chance of visits to archives, or for study leave, or of taking up the many fellowships and scholarships that are awarded to Gaza's excellent scholars. Throughout the making of this volume there have been regular emails, WhatsApp messages and Skype calls asking for repeated visa letters and informing of repeated visa refusals by UKVI – the United Kingdom Visa awarding body. There has been repeated last-minute news about the border Rafah (between the Gaza Strip and Egypt) re-opening for a very brief window of time, and intermittent updates from colleagues waiting there, only after 30 or even 50 hours of no sleep and little food, to hear of yet another refusal, and of more dismay, sadness and frustration.

Several of the chapters in this volume were born in a besieged condition, through an obstacle course littered with the litany of challenges that have formed the unique experience of our Palestinian colleagues and their communities. As with academic relationships with the North of Ireland/ Northern Ireland only a few decades ago, it is important to attend to the discourses that shape a nation's experiences: First Intifada, Second Intifada, Oslo, Al Nakba, the Siege, Blockade, the Gaza Strip. Some are geographical coordinates, others historical moments, but in every chapter of this book they are constant and necessary referents, as enduring and vital as those of academic referencing conventions. A book about developing multilingual educational practices online with colleagues in the Gaza Strip cannot be written without these references, and without every author having some latitude to repeat as a way of signally identification and belonging.

IUG has been very active in recent years in forging and consolidating links with other institutions worldwide. This has resulted in a large number of partnerships and collaborations, which include many countries and most disciplines. While on occasion trips to or (more frequently) from the Gaza Strip have allowed academic partners to meet, discuss, learn and share ideas and knowledge in person, more often the collaborations *need* to be carried out online. The word 'need' is emphasized here as too often the online dimension of partnerships with IUG is not the result of strategic choices to maximize reach, enhance a project or complement a programme, but simply the result of the impossibility of engaging in person. In outlining the 'capabilities approach', economist and philosopher Amartya Sen puts forward the idea that the focus of human development must be '[...] not just on what a person actually ends up doing, but also on what she is in fact able to do, whether or not she chooses to make use of that opportunity' (Sen, 2009: 235). In other words, Sen argues that being able to choose is more important for an individual – and for groups – than what is achieved, and that this freedom is the cornerstone of social justice. Even assuming that through online work IUG's scholars and students could achieve full collaboration and level partnerships (which is highly debatable), the fact that they are denied effective choice through the extreme restrictions of movement from/to the Strip also denies them substantive freedom. Thus, in putting together this book to celebrate the many online, multilingual partnerships that IUG has been able to forge and which allow 'academic hospitality' (Phipps & Barnett, 2007) despite the blockade, we also wish to openly acknowledge that these partnerships are by no means sufficient, nor a substitute for the freedom to choose.

In the next sections we will give an overview of the context of the Gaza Strip as the site of all the collaborations discussed in the chapters. We will then give an overview of the chapters and the way in which each looks at the multilingual dimensions of a specific collaboration, and at the challenges and opportunities of the online partnership(s). Before we do this, however, let us stress that the chapters were written by academics based at IUG and at HEIs in countries of the Global North. Some were written across and through borders, and the editing of these chapters by academics based in Gaza and in Scotland has been precisely an instance of the collaborations it discusses: it has suffered from those same challenges it narrates, but also enjoyed the same gratifications.

While putting together this book, we experienced delays and setbacks. In part, they were the consequence of the violent repression of protests at the borders of the Gaza Strip[4] and, as we were putting the final touches to the first draft of the manuscript, also of the bombing and shelling mentioned in our Prologue. However, delays were also caused by the need to navigate different approaches to academic writing, to reconcile different styles and different levels of familiarity with the process, and to keep each characteristic voice while also meeting the requirements of academic publishing criteria. Moreover, the book brings together scholars from a range of disciplines that are not often found side by side (e.g. second language acquisition, educational technology, sustainable architecture) and thus different disciplinary conventions have had to be negotiated through prolonged and sometimes complex online, multilingual, intercultural and interdisciplinary conversations.

The lengthy multilingual, multimedia, intercultural and collegial labour required to give this multivocal book the form it has now may remain invisible to those approaching the finished product. However, this edited collection embodies its focus: the stubborn resolve to collaborate online academics, multilingually and interculturally, *even though* some of us live in a situation of protracted crisis, but also *because* some of us live in this situation. It is a way to explore together our different approaches to academic writing in order to achieve a resonance that would do justice to our collective work, and to create an opportunity for our besieged colleagues to enter in multilingual, intercultural and interdisciplinary conversations with other academics, within the pages of this book and beyond them. It is a way to 'here' each other in the quiet space of printed pages which still reverberate with the repeated 'Can you hear me?' of our online meetings, meetings during which our collective, multilingual voices can break up into a million pieces upon crossing our screen. It is, in truth, another stubborn way to be together, despite all odds.

The Context

The term 'Occupied Palestinian Territories' refers to an area that includes the West Bank, the Gaza Strip and East Jerusalem. The Gaza Strip is a narrow ribbon of land facing the Mediterranean Sea, which borders to the north and to the east with Israel, and to the south with Egypt. Measuring 40 km in length and between 14 and 6 km in width, the Gaza Strip is a very small territory, home to almost 2 million people. It is one of the most densely populated areas on earth, with about 5,200 people per km^2, as reported by the Palestinian Central Bureau of Statistics (PCBS, 2018).[5]

While a detailed discussion on the origins of, and reasons for, the fragmentation of the Palestinian nation and its dispersal to unconnected territories is beyond the scope of this book, it is important to acknowledge that the shattering of the Palestinian nation was the consequence of the 1948 takeover of Palestinian land and villages by Israel, a time Palestinian refer to as the '*Nakba*' (catastrophe) (Tawil-Souri & Matar, 2016). The eastern and northern borders of the Gaza Strip are the result of an Israeli-Egyptian agreement, and these same borders have been virtually impenetrable for well over a decade as a result of the Israeli blockade of the Gaza Strip. Widespread restrictions to the only remaining crossing into Egypt, to the south, make movement from/to Gaza extremely difficult. The blockade, officially justified by Israel as an act of self-defence (Winter, 2015) entails, alongside the closure of all crossings between the Gaza Strip and Israel, a naval blockade, which imposes severe limitations to fishing rights, as well as limited access to fuel and electricity (Erakat, 2012).

According to UNWRA's figures for 2016, approximately 70% of the 1.9 million population of the Strip are of refugee origin (see https://www.unrwa.org/where-we-work/gaza-strip); that is, Palestinian families were forced to leave their homes during the *Nakba* in 1948. Only about 360 km^2 in size, the Gaza Strip is the site of a set of appalling statistics. In the words of Tawil-Souri and Matar (2016):

> More than two-thirds of the population is made up of refugees; 70% live in poverty; 20% live in 'deep poverty'; just about everybody has to survive on humanitarian handouts; adult unemployment hovers around 50% give or take a few percentage points; 60% of the population is under the age of 18. This is the Gaza where on a good day there is no electricity 'only' 20 hours a day; where, before the latest Israeli military operation, in summer 2014, there was already a shortage of 70,000 homes; where 60% of the

population suffers from food insecurity; where 95% of piped water is below international quality standards; where every child aged 8 or [older] has already witnessed three massive wars. [...]. One can be dumbfounded by Gaza's sheer statistical impossibility. (Tawil-Souri & Matar, 2016: 3)

Severely constrained by the blockade, the population of the Gaza Strip survives on carefully monitored supplies (of food, fuel, construction material, medicines, etc.) that are allowed into Gaza, their quantity calculated to be just sufficient to keep the population alive, but never enough to allow for the building up of reserves, and thus constantly one step away from shortage (Winter, 2015). Because of the blockade and of the 'statistical impossibility' it creates, the Gaza Strip suffers from a range of social, economic and humanitarian problems. These are further exacerbated by the huge death toll, the individual and collective trauma and the destruction of infrastructures which, in recent years, have been caused by intense bombing on the part of the Israeli army.

The restrictions imposed on access to natural resources, the lack of material and infrastructure for production, and the regular destruction caused by bombings have had, inevitably, dire consequences on the Strip's economy. A 2015 report published by the United Nations Conference on Trade and Development notes that:

> three Israeli military operations in the past six years, in addition to eight years of economic blockade, have ravaged the already debilitated infrastructure of Gaza, shattered its productive base, left no time for meaningful reconstruction or economic recovery and impoverished the Palestinian population in Gaza, rendering their economic well-being worse than the level of two decades previous.

More recently, the UN Office for the Coordination of Humanitarian Affairs (OCHA, 2018) reports that 'over 68 per cent of households in the Gaza Strip, or about 1.3 million people, are severely or moderately food insecure'. The 2015 report by the UN Conference on Trade and Development warned that, as a result of the dire situation it faces, the Gaza Strip could very soon become 'uninhabitable'.

Deprived of employment opportunities and of mobility, the population of the Gaza Strip depends heavily on aid and humanitarian relief provided by the international community to mitigate the consequences of the blockade and wars. While this is essential to the survival of the population, extensive and prolonged dependence on international aid alone cannot redress the challenges the Strip faces, nor is it sustainable in the long run. However, the people of the Gaza Strip have no choice but to inhabit this nearly uninhabitable land, trapped in a situation of forced immobility by the blockade. As well as financial consequences, the situation in Gaza has huge repercussions on individuals' mental health and wellbeing. As an UNRWA Gaza Situation Report highlights: 'wide-spread youth unemployment in Gaza can lead to frustration and depression' (UNWRA, 2016).

As noted earlier, while only a complete and permanent lift of the blockade can significantly improve the situation in the Strip and reverse the current trend of de-development, small opportunities to 'escape' its confines are made available by the increasing reliability and ubiquity of online and mobile technologies. Online collaborations can thus become precious opportunities for Gaza's academics to engage in scholarly intercultural and multilingual work with colleagues worldwide, and to maintain a visible (and audible) presence within the global community. In the next sections we give an overview of chapters in this collection, which discuss some of the ways in which online tools have allowed IUG to increase its collaboration with HEIs in several countries around the world and to expand its internationalization efforts.

Overview of this Edited Collection

All the chapters in this collection discuss online collaborations with/from the Gaza Strip. They are from academics based at IUG, but also at the University of Glasgow and the University of Manchester in the UK, and the University of Arizona in the USA. The collaborations and projects illustrated in each chapter come together from a range of different academic subjects, spanning disciplines such as applied linguistics and education but also including contributions from academics with expertise in information technology and engineering. Regardless of their disciplinary backgrounds, the chapters discuss what were, inevitably, multilingual and multicultural encounters carried out for the most part in the virtual space. To aid the reader, we have grouped the chapters into four broad topics, according to the main focus of their content. The headings for each topic are: *English as an additional language and online technologies; Finding motivation for language learning in a situation of forced immobility; Palestine and the Arabic language; Internationalization and imagination.*

Part 1: English as an Additional Language and Online Technologies

- Chapter 1. *Engineers Operating Multilingually: Reflections on Four Years of Glasgow-Gaza Pre-sessional English Telecollaboration* – B. Guariento
- Chapter 2. *Islamic University of Gaza (IUG) Internationalization Endeavors at the Level of Postgraduate Programs* – S. Abou-Dagga
- Chapter 3. *Exploring Mobile Support for English Language Teachers in a Context of Conflict: Syrian Refugee Teachers in Jordan* – G. Motteram, N. Al-Masri, H. Hamouda and S. Omarali

Guariento's chapter discusses the *English for Academic Study Telecollaboration* (EAST) project, a collaboration between the University of Glasgow and the Islamic University of Gaza. Now in its fourth year, this collaboration is attempting to overcome this subject-specific shortfall while providing graduate-attribute skills of benefit to all participants, both in Glasgow and Gaza. The real-life challenges provided through the online collaboration have proved highly motivating for IUG and UofG pre-sessional students, improving their experiences and expanding their knowledge and language skills.

The chapter by Abu-Dagga outlines the structure of IUG graduate programmes (Higher Diploma, MA, PhD), their main processes and outcomes and the strategies adopted to ensure their expansion, in the face of the severe challenges experienced by the Gaza Strip. The chapter looks at language requirements and at the use of English as a medium of instruction and assessment in different graduate programmes that also use multilingual textbooks and references.

Motteram *et al.* discuss an ethnographic study that involves using mobile technologies and field visits to identify the professional needs of Syrian English teachers in Jordan and to develop online materials to enhance the teachers' pedagogical competence. Sponsored by the UK Economic and Social Research Council (ESRC), the study is part of a joint project between the University of Manchester and the Islamic University of Gaza, in cooperation with the British Council in Jordan, and with the International Association of Teachers of English as a Foreign Language (IATEFL). The chapter highlights the challenges faced by the project in relation to access and questions of immobility.

Part 2: Finding Motivation for Language Learning in a Situation of Forced Immobility

- Chapter 4. *Motivational Strategies and Online Technologies: Are Palestinian EFL University Students in the Gaza Strip Empowered to be Bilingual?* – A. Abu Alyan
- Chapter 5. *'Really Talking' to Gaza: From Active to Transformative Learning in Distributed Environments and under Highly Pressured Conditions* – A. Rolinska, B. Guariento, G. Abouda and O. Nakprada

Motivation is the focus of Abu Alyan's chapter, which discusses its crucial importance for learning outcomes in IUG's EFL students. The chapter illustrates views of effective motivational strategies held by Palestinian university teachers and students. It focuses in particular on the motivational strategies used with EFL students, whose opportunities for travel outside the Gaza Strip – and therefore for using English in a range of contexts and for face-to-face interactions – are very limited.

Rolinska *et al.* outline the original 2015 pilot EAST Project between the Islamic University of Gaza and the University of Glasgow, focusing on the active learning precepts that underlie its pedagogy. Using the post-course student survey, the chapter looks specifically at students' progress made in terms of communication, team-working and problem-solving skills, representative of the 3D Global Engineering Competencies proposed by Patil and Codner (2007). It examines in detail two case studies (one each from Gaza and Glasgow), providing exemplars of potentially transformative outcomes which emerged from the active learning precepts of the course.

Part 3: Palestine and the Arabic Language

- Chapter 6. *Gaza Teaches Arabic Online: Opportunities, Challenges and Ways Forward* – G. Fassetta, N. Al-Masri, M. Attia and A. Phipps
- Chapter 7. *(In)articulability of Pain and Trauma: Idioms of Distress in the Gaza Strip* – M.G. Imperiale

In the Arabic language section, the chapter by Fassetta *et al.* argues that the global and increasing demand for Arabic language teaching, combined with the opportunities offered by online communication tools, can offer opportunities for online employment to large numbers of unemployed Palestinian graduates. The chapter highlights how the internet represents, for the people in the Strip who are trapped by the blockade, a far from ideal but yet important way to engage with the rest of the world, and it makes recommendations for ways in which this can be capitalized on and expanded.

The chapter by Imperiale illustrates an online research project investigating idioms to express distress in the Arabic language that were adopted by the Gazan population during the large-scale bombings that hit the Gaza Strip in the summer of 2014. Grounded in the concept of 'languaging' and of metaphorical images and drawing on the literature on idioms of distress, the chapter brings into dialogue works in critical applied linguistics and in global mental health, in order to frame and to develop an intercultural understanding of localized ways of expressing pain and suffering.

Part 4: Making Connections

- Chapter 8. *The Experience of the Islamic University of Gaza in Cross-border Academic Collaboration: T-MEDA Project as a Case Study* – A.S. Muhaisen
- Chapter 9. *From the Kitchen to Gaza: Networked Places and the Collaborative Imagination* – C. Warner and D. Gramling

The chapter by Muhaisen opens this section by outlining IUG's experience, in particular its faculties of Engineering, Nursing and Law, of participating in a multidisciplinary, international project called 'T-MEDA'. The main aim of the project, which was funded by the EU through its Tempus programme, was to build a new framework to create academic curricula based on tools developed by the Bologna process. For this purpose, institutions from 17 different countries, speaking at least eight different languages, participated in the project. The paper illustrates how, although they could not participate personally in any of the organized meetings, the IUG team successfully managed to take an active part in the project via online communication technologies.

Warner and Gramling from the University of Arizona combine a prose essay and poetic reflections in their chapter, to think about the experience of participating in the Researching Multilingually at the Borders of Language, the Body, Law, and the State Project as one of the two non-European hubs with IUG. The authors engage with spaces of encounter, including the home kitchen where they drafted many of their contributions, and the hotel where a meeting of the project team was hosted in the last year of the project. At the latter meeting, the lead collaborator from the Islamic University of Gaza was also present in person. In the chapter, Warner and Gramling contrast the forms of collaboration and conversation that emerged in face-to-face interactions with the events in which they participated remotely.

'Here-ing' You

Technology has offered us all a way of bypassing the isolation and the separations from colleagues which the blockade of the Gaza Strip and the visa regimes of the UK and USA have imposed in the last 12 years. The chapters in this book present research undertaken across borders, under vastly differing conditions and with vastly unequal access to resources, an attempt at decolonizing multilingualism, including Palestinian Arabic, working online to tackle the staggering rates of youth unemployment which hamper the futures of Gazan young people and graduates. It does so without the usual ways of building relationships open to academics who might travel in the ways Phipps and Barnett outlined in 2005. These assumed an ever greater opening of borders and of new 'contact zones' (Pratt, 2008) to enable renaissances in knowledge production, assumptions that are now (temporarily) put into question by the exceptional circumstances imposed by COVID-19.

Revisiting the conclusion of 'Academic travel: Modes and directions' (Phipps & Barnett, 2005) is a sobering endeavour. In the 15 intervening years, the modes and directions of academic travel have lost some of the utopianism of an open borders dream and, for the academics collaborating in this volume, have hit literal and metaphorical buffers. The final sentence of that paper, however, still resonates, if not as originally conceived: 'academic travel turns out to offer, even if as an unintended consequence, no less than a revitalization and a reframing of academic life itself' (Phipps & Barnett, 2005: 13). The 'revitalizations' in this volume are those of an activist academia determined to pursue original contributions to knowledge out of precarious conditions. It is about the determination not to allow protracted conflict to stand in the way of the peace-seeking activities of knowledge creation in universities, and about the relationships and friendship which sustain them.

The reframing of academic life this entails relies on not allowing some forms of knowledge, to use Butler's (2004) term, to be 'more grievable' than others. Thus, in the pages of this volume are the uneven, sometimes even lumpy differences in style, in expectation, in academic training. Rather than trying to homogenize these to pretend a uniformity that is not there, the editors have chosen to let the different styles and approaches stand as interdisciplinary contributions but also as contributions which allow the contrasting situations to be seen and heard.

In his book *In the Shelter*, which reflects on the Good Friday Agreement of 1999 and the subsequent Peace Process in Ireland and Northern Ireland, Pádraig Ó Tuama (2015) cites a poem by David Wagoner entitled 'Lost'. In this poem Wagoner refers to 'here' as to a 'powerful stranger' and Ó Tuama notes that:

> The Truth of this poem is an old truth. There are the places you wish to go, there are the places you desperately wish you never left, there are the places you imagine you should be, and there is the place called here. (Ó Tuama, 2015: 130)

Here is the place we don't know, a powerful stranger, as Wagoner calls it, a place that finds us when we are lost. The 'here' of the sound of voices saying 'Can you hear me?' is an auditory place, before even being visually pixilated, sometimes dropped, then connected again. There is a visceral experience of language, of languages and of language learning which flows through the chapters in this volume. In this context, 'hearing' also means 'here-ing' – it means that despite lost connections, and the blockade, and the visa refusals, and the enormous resource inequality, and the drones with their bombs, we can meet one another as 'powerful academic strangers'.

It would be wrong to suggest that this meeting is an easy encounter similar to other academic encounters that happen in settings where largely cultural, linguistic and even political affiliations are well rehearsed and interculturally nuanced. Here, in the encounters between academics in Gaza and their colleagues in Glasgow, Manchester, Arizona, or on engineering programmes in Asia, there are significant intercultural challenges. How we do 'critical thinking' in relation to our practices and institutions, the ways in which we show rigour in academic writing, the ways in which we communicate online and its etiquette, the accommodating of different days of rest and work and the flurry of messages on the 'wrong days' – all of our different practices nest into, challenge and disrupt our 'normal' rhythms of academic life. The discomforts and also the joys these bring with them let us know that 'we can hear you', because we are 'here-ing' you – because you are here, present, and we are doing academic work together, regardless. This 'hear-ing' is ontological and epistemological; it is affective and embodied. Technology, then, is anything but 'remote'. 'Can you "here" me' is the challenge for revitalizing and reframing our work through a scholarship formed interculturally, under siege.

Notes

(1) The name Gaza Strip refers to the strip of land that, together with the West Bank and East Jerusalem, constitutes the Palestinian Territories occupied by Israel since 1967. In this book we will use the terms 'Gaza Strip', 'the Strip' and 'Gaza' interchangeably, as required by style and according to authors' preferences. The name 'Gaza city' will be used to refer to the Strip's main urban area, where the Islamic University of Gaza is located.
(2) The United Nations Office for the Coordination of Humanitarian Affairs defines the restrictions to movement imposed on the Gaza Strip by Israel as a 'blockade' (see https://www.ochaopt.org/theme/gaza-blockade, accessed 27 September 2018). The Cambridge Online Dictionary defines a 'blockade' as: 'the situation in which a country or place is surrounded by soldiers or ships to stop people or goods from going in or out' (see https://dictionary.cambridge.org/dictionary/english/blockade, accessed 27 September 2018). The Gaza Strip is 'besieged' as a consequence of the blockade. According to the Cambridge Online Dictionary, in fact, to 'besiege' means 'to surround a place, especially with an army, to prevent people or supplies getting in or out' (see https://dictionary.cambridge.org/dictionary/english/besiege, accessed 27 September 2018). However, the word 'siege' is widely used both in the Gaza Strip and internationally to refer to the blockade and it is now almost synonymous with it. As a consequence, we have kept each author's preference in relation to the use of siege and/or blockade.
(3) Throughout this book, the terms 'Global North'/'Western' and 'Global South' will be used to refer to economic and geopolitical constructs rather than geographical regions. This distinction takes into consideration historical and socio-economic relations of inequality and power imbalances that are largely the result of colonial pasts and neo-colonial presents.
(4) These ongoing protests are called the *Gaza Great March of Return* by the Palestinians. According to the UN Relief and Works Agency for Palestine Refugees (UNWRA), in the one year since the protests began at least 195 Palestinians (including 41 children) have been killed and close to 29,000 people injured (see https://www.unrwa.org/newsroom/press-releases/great-march-return-scores-people-killed-and-injured-over-one-year, accessed 27 May 2019).
(5) By way of comparison for scale, consider that the population density in the UK is 275 persons/km^2; in Italy it is 201 persons/km^2 (StatisticsTimes.com, 2018).

References

Bourdieu, P. (1988) *Homo Academicus*. Cambridge: Polity.
Bourdieu, P. (1993) *The Field of Cultural Production*. Cambridge: Polity.
Bourdieu, P. (2000) *Pascalian Meditations*. Cambridge: Polity.
Butler, J. (2004) *Precarious Life: The Power of Mourning and Violence*. London: Verso.
Erakat, N. (2012) It's not wrong, it's illegal: Situating the Gaza blockade between international law and the UN response. *UCLA Journal of Islamic and Near Eastern Law* 11, 37–84.
Hallam, E. and Ingold, T. (2007) Creativity and cultural improvisation: An introduction. In E. Hallam and T. Ingold (eds) *Creativity and Cultural Improvisation* (pp. 1–24). Oxford: Berg.

Lévi-Strauss, C. (1962) *La Pensée Sauvage*. Paris: Plon.
OCHA (United Nations Office for the Coordination of Humanitarian Affairs) (2018) Food insecurity in the oPt: 1.3 million Palestinians in the Gaza strip are food insecure. See https://www.ochaopt.org/content/food-insecurity-opt-13-million-palestinians-gaza-strip-are-food-insecure (accessed 25 May 2019).
Ó Tuama, P. (2015) *In the Shelter: Finding a Home in the World*. London: Hodder & Stoughton.
Patil, A. and Codner, G. (2007) Accreditation of engineering education: Review, observations and proposal for global accreditation. *European Journal of Engineering Education* 32 (6), 639–651.
PCBS (Palestinian Central Bureau of Statistics) (2018) On the occasion of the International Population Day 11/7/2018. See http://www.pcbs.gov.ps/post.aspx?lang=en&ItemID=3183# (accessed 24 May 2019).
Phipps, A. and Barnett, R. (2005) Academic travel: Modes and directions. *Review of Education, Pedagogy, and Cultural Studies* 27 (1), 3–16.
Phipps, A. and Barnett, R. (2007) Academic hospitality. *Arts and Humanities in Higher Education* 6 (3), 237–254.
Pratt, M.L. (2008) *Imperial Eyes: Travel Writing and Transculturation* (2nd edn). New York: Routledge.
Sen, A. (2009) *The Idea of Justice*. London: Penguin.
StatisticsTimes.com (2018) List of countries by population density. See http://statisticstimes.com/demographics/countries-by-population-density.php (accessed 24 May 2019).
Tawil-Souri, H. and Matar, D. (eds) (2016) *Gaza as Metaphor*. London: Hurst.
UN (United Nations Country Team in the Occupied Palestinian Territory) (2017) Gaza ten years later. See https://unsco.unmissions.org/sites/default/files/gaza_10_years_later_-_11_july_2017.pdf (accessed 25 May 2019).
UNCTAD (UN Conference on Trade and Development) (2015) Report on UNCTAD assistance to the Palestinian people: Developments in the economy of the Occupied Palestinian Territory. Trade and Development Board, Sixty-second session, Geneva, 14–25 September. See http://unctad.org/meetings/en/SessionalDocuments/tdb62d3_en.pdf (accessed 25 May 2019).
UNRWA (UN Relief and Works Agency) (2016) Gaza situation report 132. See https://www.unrwa.org/newsroom/emergency-reports/gaza-situation-report-132 (accessed 15 June 2019).
Winter, Y. (2015) The siege of Gaza: Spatial violence, humanitarian strategies, and the biopolitics of punishment. *Constellations* 23 (2), 308–319.

Part 1

English as an Additional Language and Online Technologies

1 Engineers Operating Multilingually: Reflections on Four Years of Glasgow-Gaza Pre-sessional English Telecollaboration

Bill Guariento

The Siege of Gaza, and the isolation, war damage and shortages that it has engendered, have brought about many compensatory strengths within Gazan society in general, and its higher education sector in particular. The collaboration outlined in this chapter has been built on two very specifically Siege-related attributes found among students and staff at a Gazan university: expertise in online platforms that can help overcome the isolation, and a keen interest in exploring potential engineering responses to the destruction and the shortages that have resulted. Each of these have in turn been built on the Palestine-specific characteristic of '*sumud*', which can be translated as '[...] personal and collective resilience and steadfastness' (Marie *et al.*, 2018: 20); working on our pre-sessional English language course in far-away Scotland, we have had many opportunities to appreciate (and to benefit from) this unwillingness to bow down in the face of immense challenges, the 'stubbornness' that the editors note in their Introduction. This opening chapter outlines the stages of a successful online collaboration between students on science, engineering and technology (SET) Master's courses at the Islamic University of Gaza (IUG), and pre-sessional international students hoping to embark on SET-related Master's courses at the University of Glasgow – the English for Academic Studies Telecollaboration (EAST) Project. It also looks at one, less successful, attempt to broaden this endeavour to embrace biomedical science (Biomed) students at each institution, and draws some conclusions from this relative failure. The chapter offers an overview of the four years of the collaboration to date, examining how the overall project was structured and funded, the organizational, financial and technological challenges that were overcome, the lessons that have been learned, the challenges that remain, and the benefits to both institutions that have resulted. It also reflects on the political economy of the collaborative work, and its relationship to ideologies of global mobility and immobilization.

The Initial Rationale for Setting Up an Online International Link-up

The UK is the second most popular destination in the world for overseas study, with 458,000 international students in 2017/18 (Universities UK, 2019). The University of Glasgow, like all UK universities, has seen a growth in the number of international students; in the academic year 2016/2017 (the most recent year for which statistics are available at the time of writing), slightly over 5000 of the 28,600 students at the university were from outside the UK/European Union (EU). But a better idea of the significance of this group can be gained from the fees they are charged. Many of the students reported on in this chapter were studying for an MSc in electronics and electrical engineering; taking this as an example, while home and EU students will pay £8000 per year, those from overseas will be paying over £21,000 to access the very same course (University of Glasgow website, 2018). Overseas students clearly have an economic significance for the institutions that host them that goes well beyond their numbers, but they often lack the language needed for entry to their chosen postgraduate courses. Many students opt to take a secure English language test (such as IELTS), whereas others instead choose to attend a pre-sessional summer course at their university, a bridge to matriculation that provides (beyond the key language skills) the added value of acculturation, taking 'culture' both in the most generally accepted sense, but also to signify learning about the workings of a UK university, i.e. the 'culture of academia'.

In the larger universities, there is often a subject-specific element to the tuition that is provided. However, these summer pre-sessional courses are held at a time when faculty tend to take holiday, and are delivered by English language teachers who are recruited just for the summer months and who, as a rule, lack subject-specific knowledge. The dearth of meaningful engagement with content that results can in part be overcome via published courses (and a really extensive range of subject-specific textbooks has emerged), but there remain many UK university courses that target niche areas of SET, or interdisciplinary degrees (crossovers, for instance, between engineering and management studies, or engineering and accountancy) that have yet to benefit from a course book. An even more fundamental problem with the provision of appropriate content, however, is the fact that these are by definition disciplines that evolve very quickly indeed, and published materials can be considered dated within a few short years or, as in the case of electronics and electrical engineering or information and communications technology, much faster.

Teaching materials must also be paid for, and this can be quite expensive for institutions. One response to this is to produce materials in house, but the production of a well-researched and attractively presented in-house course will also incur significant costs for a university; even a five-week course will necessitate many weeks of staff time, depending upon the experience of more established staff members who tend to be at the higher end of the pay scales. Moreover, as with the course books, every year these materials will need to be revisited and, if necessary, updated or replaced.

At the University of Glasgow's English for Academic Study (EAS) unit, we felt that these top-down solutions were unwieldy, resistant to change and costly. At the same time, as trained teachers of English, we had our own opinions as to how effective learning could best be fostered, and how the university's graduate attributes definition of the effective communicator – i.e. one 'able to articulate complex ideas with respect to the needs and abilities of diverse audiences' and 'to communicate clearly and confidently, and listen and negotiate effectively with others' (University of Glasgow Graduate Attributes Matrix) – could best be met. We were aiming to create a much more authentic course than could be provided by a textbook or through in-house materials, one whose emphasis 'should primarily be on meaning and communication and which replicates communication in the real world' (Guariento & Morley, 2001: 350).

In particular, we knew the classroom value of the 'information gap', a central tenet of the communicative language teaching methodology that has driven developments in English language instruction over the past three decades. An information gap occurs when your interlocutor possesses information that you require in order to complete a task, which in turn leads to an authentic reason for speaking (or writing) in order to overcome the gap. We wondered whether a cross-border response building on students' personal content-interests could be fashioned, and whether a methodology channelling the motivational power of the information gap might be achievable online. To enable this, we needed access to an overseas partner.

Genesis and Basic Design of the Project

There is a history of fruitful collaboration between the University of Glasgow's School of Education and the IUG, dating back to 2007. In 2015 staff from English for academic studies within the School of Modern Languages and Cultures in Glasgow (from now on, for the sake of simplicity, just 'Glasgow') approached the Vice-Dean for Internationalization at the IUG (from now on, 'Gaza') with a view to engaging their students as partners on the project work element of the culminating five weeks of Glasgow's pre-sessional SET course.

We started with a simple premise. One (or sometimes two) Gazan students would form a 'team' with two (in some cases three) Glasgow-based pre-sessional students, providing a range of engineering-related challenges facing those living in the Gaza Strip. The Glasgow-based students would choose a project title from this list, one which they considered relevant to their coming studies, and gather information, working towards a 1500-word written project and a presentation, each for submission in the final week. The written project would be researched jointly by the Glasgow-based students, then written up individually. The Gazan students, having provided the initial Gaza-specific engineering problem to be analysed, would subsequently provide content feedback on their Glasgow-based partners' responses over the five weeks of the EAST Project, via Facebook, email, Skype and WhatsApp, analysing in particular whether these responses were feasible, given the geography and the massive resource constraints under which Gazan engineers must operate.

Worth emphasizing at this point is the multilingual nature of these teams. As many as 60% of pre-sessional students in Glasgow speak Mandarin as their mother tongue, while maybe 20% are Arabic speakers, as a rule from Saudi Arabia, and the Glasgow-based groups were formed with the aim of maximizing the mix of L1 speakers. Due to the prevalence of students from China, some uniformly Chinese groupings were unavoidable, but in all cases, the resulting interactions obliged *all* participants to use English as a lingua franca (ELF); any temptation to use L1 intra-group (Glasgow-Glasgow) would usually exclude a team member, and any similar temptation to use L1 inter-group (Glasgow-Gaza) would *invariably* exclude a member of any given team. This was a fundamental strength of EAST as it came to develop, and has been key to its longevity.

Partners? Running a Project with an Inherent Power Imbalance

An important element of the role played by the Gazan students was the need to provide content feedback alone, without any suggestion of help in actually writing the written project, and this raised an important ethical issue from the outset. Lorente (2010), writing about the Philippines, outlines government policy aimed at preparing prospective migrants for the remittance-gathering overseas employment which is so key to overall Philippines GDP and (controversially) choosing to categorize the language needs of each according to their professions/skills. Was it acceptable to similarly limit the role and expectations of the Gazan participants? Were we fashioning, via these limitations, something akin to what Lorente terms 'scripts of servitude'? The importance of fostering creativity and imagination in networked interactions is developed in Part 4 of this book, and some of the Gazan participants in fact found the confines of their assigned role to be frustrating, as we can see from end-of-course student comments (unabridged), such as:

> Ensure the sustainability of collaboration by request an extra joint-research or press article. (Gaza student)

May be if we swap the role so Gaza students give the presentation and Glasgow ask questions and giving feedback. (Gaza student)

However, the 'gatekeeping' (Roberts, 2010) function of the pre-sessional English course needs to be borne constantly in mind as a factor that has conditioned the evolving collaborations in the past four years. As we have seen, the Glasgow-based students come from a range of countries. These students choose the pre-sessional course as an alternative entrance route to a secure English language test. However, they still need to pass the examinations in Listening and Reading at the end of the course, and to obtain a pass grade for their 1500-word essay (linked to project work) and similarly a pass grade for their end-of-course oral presentation (likewise linked to project work), in order to access their Master's programmes. Thus, although the project forms only about 25% of the total time commitment of the final five-week course, it is a key contributor to the end-of-course assessment of the Glasgow-based students' linguistic readiness for university study.

Regarding the Glasgow-based students, as organizers, we felt that incentives were not lacking. The proposed link-up to engineering students in Gaza would provide:

- meaningful practice in all four skills, including Speaking and Listening (which are harder to practise outside class);
- access to authentic engineering and IT challenges;
- opportunities for developing the skills inherent in teamwork;
- the chance to gain subject knowledge;
- the opportunity to build intercultural awareness.

However, while we liked to think that the Glasgow-based students would buy into the project (and, as we shall see, feedback was favourable) for these *intrinsic* benefits, at root they had no choice; either they performed, or access to their Master's courses would be denied. In other words, the gatekeeping nature of the pre-sessional course meant that involvement in the project was obligatory for the Glasgow-based students. The gatekeeping aspect of the course for these participants (and the total and unfair absence of any such incentive for the Gazans) was an immutable feature of whatever collaboration we would be able to produce.

We thus had a reasonable idea of what would incentivize the Glasgow-based students, and we imagined that, to a degree, the Gazan students would also be incentivized by the same opportunities that the online collaboration would afford. First, although we asked administrators in Gaza to find students with an overall IELTS equivalent of 6.0, but ideally with an equivalent of 6.5 in Speaking (crucial for meaningful synchronous oral communication), there would still be opportunities for enhancement of language skills. Beyond this core issue, we also hoped that the Gazan students would, like those in Glasgow, benefit from the chances to develop team-working experience, to gain subject-specific knowledge and to work with people from other cultures. An end-of-course certificate of participation would also be provided, and these perceived benefits were explained via initial contacts with the prospective Gazan participants.[1]

We also hoped that the intrinsic value of education in Palestine would be a significant driving force, an impression based on the organizers' previous knowledge of the Palestinian context and experience gained from previous interinstitutional collaboration, but in addition we went into the project aware of other factors, which might be termed structural imbalances, likely to incentivize Gazan involvement. For example, might institutions (and the students within them) agree to participate in order to break out of the psychological isolation resulting from longstanding and ongoing blockade, i.e. might a force motivating Gazan participants (both administrators and students) be the knowledge that they have few alternative modes of interaction with the world beyond the Strip? Was this a fair premise on which to base a partnership, and (given the very significant power imbalance) could it be termed, in any true sense of the word, a collaboration? If this was one concern, we also worried further that participation in the project might result from a hope that any involvement in an international collaboration could potentially increase the likelihood of actual travel beyond the Gaza Strip (something over which we had absolutely no control). These fears regarding manifestations of symbolic power in such a crude manner were present from the very start of the project, have never left, and will be returned to in the conclusion.

Response to Power Imbalance

To reiterate, in simple terms, we started our project with an understanding of a really significant power imbalance, namely that the key arbiter of Glasgow-based students' commitment was the fact that successful completion of the five-week pre-sessional course would open the road to their future Master's studies, an objective that was unavailable for the Gazan participants.

In partial response to this structural imbalance, we decided to offer a two-week course in the provision of constructive feedback, to be delivered to the Gazan students before they teamed up online with their Glasgow-based partners. This course (available via creative commons, https://goo.gl/ifxdh7) takes a three-stage exploration-integration-application approach (Garrison & Arbaugh, 2007) to the issue of providing constructive feedback, with each stage being progressively more complex, challenging and open-ended. It was designed to develop the Gazan students' ability to guide the Glasgow-based students towards content knowledge in a manner combining efficiency with diplomacy, and to ensure that they understood the need to avoid providing language assistance (see Guariento *et al.*, 2018, for a detailed description) in order to maintain the 'gatekeeping' nature of the Glasgow pre-sessional.

The constructive feedback course was designed to ensure that the project was as effective as possible in terms of delivering useful feedback to the Glasgow students, but it also provided workplace skills that we hoped would be valuable beyond the immediate confines of the telecollaboration, of potential value in finding future online employment. The World Bank (2018) itself labels an unemployment rate of 60% among 15- to 29-year-olds in Gaza as 'staggering', and as a result the Ministry of Education has been proactive in searching for ways to improve the digital literacies of Gazan students (and thereby their chances of accessing remote work).

In terms of resourcing, writing the pre-project Constructive Feedback course involved extra work for the Glasgow-based staff but, after an initial plenary session, much of the actual course was delivered asynchronously, in a way that required regular monitoring and some group and individual feedback, but that avoided serious rescheduling of other commitments. From the Palestinian perspective, pre-course, the IUG allocated a staff member to take on the tasks of publicizing the collaboration and of selecting students; in view of anticipated audio-quality issues, a minimum Listening/Speaking ability of IELTS equivalent 6.0 was stipulated (selection to be undertaken by IUG). The Writing/Reading stipulation was less rigorous, as it was felt that the asynchronous nature of reading/writing interactions would allow for querying and clarification in the case of ambiguity (as did, in fact, transpire). The final task of the administrator in Gaza was in following up locally on any online participation issues flagged up by her colleague in Glasgow.

EAST 1

The first iteration of the project (EAST 1) ran for five weeks, from the end of July to the end of August 2015. In a plenary session on the very first day of the pre-sessional course in late July, students newly arrived to Glasgow (from China, Indonesia, Saudi Arabia, Brazil, etc.) learned about the project, and were asked to choose a topic that interested them from the list sent from Gaza and to find two partners interested in the same topic. The majority bought into the authenticity of the five-week project from the outset, and understood the need to maximize the time available on a short course. Not all could find topics directly related to their coming studies, although almost all acknowledged that this willingness to accept an external brief foreshadowed likely post-university work scenarios.

Interestingly, a significant number of the non-Arab students had never heard of the Gaza Strip, so there was also a need to provide background information regarding the geography and politics of the area. The short explanation, on day 1, proved insufficient, and later iterations of the project brought various responses to overcome this lack of information (see EAST 4, below).

The Glasgow-Gaza groups were set up on this first day, and ensuring timely initial contacts was the next administrative task; this needed to happen within 36 hours and had to involve a face-to-face element in order to create a Glasgow-Gaza 'bond'. The organization of this link-up was left to the students, but by EAST 4 we had decided that this stage was so key that it needed to be done in-class, to ensure that the ice was broken and true ownership created. Another crucial administrative task during these first two days was the need to set up Facebook groups for each Gaza-Glasgow pairing, which a Glasgow-based staff member was able to undertake on a teaching load reduced by 40% over the final five weeks of the pre-sessional course (regular subsequent monitoring was also necessary, to ensure online interactions were ongoing).

In terms of progress with the content of the projects, monitoring in weeks 2, 3 and 4 fell largely to the five class teachers, who had been inducted over a two-day period prior to week 1. On the final Monday of the five-week course, the Glasgow-based students handed in their individual 1500-word projects, and the Glasgow-Gaza groups jointly delivered their closing presentations. Each participant, whether in Glasgow or Gaza, was able to speak for five minutes, after which questions were taken from a live audience in both institutions. Internet connectivity varied over the two days of the presentations, but was much improved by the end, as organizers learned how to maximize quality by avoiding audio feedback. An unexpected issue was that of audio interference from the (obviously crucial) air-conditioning in Gaza; this made it difficult for the Gazan audience to follow the presentations, and the only remedy was to turn off the air-conditioning for as long as was bearable (this brought home to the organizers an unexpected drawback of needing to hold the course in the very hottest month of the year – the problem of air-conditioning background noise was even present in Glasgow, in a country not noted for high temperatures). Gazan students were asked to upload video-versions of their talks beforehand, to overcome any interruptions to the live link resulting from electricity cuts, but in the main these back-ups were not needed, and Gazan students were able to present 'live', and to participate actively in the subsequent Q & A sessions.

In Glasgow, the cost implications of adding this international link to the pre-sessional course were fairly small, beyond allocating a reduced teaching load to one staff member, as some form of project would have run anyway, regardless of any involvement with an overseas partner. This was not the case in Gaza. During the course itself, although the Skype/Facebook/WhatsApp interactions could in theory take place from home, the reality of life in Gaza (sometimes with as little as four hours' electricity per day) meant that funding was needed to open the university facilities during their holiday period, in order to take advantage of the institution's back-up generator. A small sum, remaining from a previous project in Glasgow, was made available to Gaza to offset some of these costs, and for the administrative load mentioned above. Thirty-seven Glasgow-based students, in groups of three, linked up with 20 Gazan students, in pairs. Participants at both institutions were monitored pre- and post-project on their perceived levels of confidence, according to: ability to communicate orally in English; problem solving; teamwork; intercultural awareness; content knowledge; and digital literacies (see Guariento et al., 2016, for a detailed description of these data).

EAST 2

Student reaction, post-EAST 1, was positive at both institutions across this range of criteria, and the decision was taken to expand provision in 2016 into a second strand of the Glasgow pre-sessional course. A Biomed cohort was chosen, providing roughly similar numbers of students in Glasgow as the successful IT/SET cohort of 2015, and being an area in which Gaza is again strong. As we have seen, feedback from Gaza demonstrated a desire for an expanded role for their students, i.e. a change from mentor to co-researcher, and EAST 2 followed this more horizontal relationship for the Biomed cohort (while the IT/SET cohort continued with the EAST 1 organizational principle, i.e. with Gazan students as 'content providers'). The Biomed students at Glasgow still needed to write their final 1500-word essay on their own, for the 'gatekeeping' stricture already mentioned, but the Gazan Biomed students were also given content-specific (i.e. Biomed) feedback on an end-of-course 750-word summary and oral presentation. This content feedback was provided by PhD students working within Glasgow's School of Medicine and, as this involved working outside Glasgow's School of Modern Languages and Culture, there were cost implications. For Gaza, running EAST 2 was costed at a higher (and more realistic) figure than the EAST 1 pilot, even taking into consideration the expanded student numbers involved (a Gaza/Glasgow ratio of 21:31 for the SET cohort and of 20:24 for the Biomeds, i.e. a doubling overall). This money was sourced via a successful application to the British Council's ELTRA Programme, which provided £7500 to cover costs in Gaza and £700 to cover the costs of paying the Glasgow PhD biomedical students. Participants at both institutions were again monitored pre- and post-project on their confidence levels according to the criteria adopted for EAST 1 (for a detailed description of the EAST 2 data, see Rolinska et al., 2017).

This student feedback evaluated the SET course more highly than the Biomed. The decision by EAST course organizers to ask the cross-institution Biomed researchers to investigate generic health issues (rather than the Gaza-specific issues facing their IT/SET counterparts) was, in retrospect, probably the main contributory factor here. The rationale was that Gaza-specific health issues might be of too limited an applicability beyond the Gaza Strip, but the result was two Biomed groups, nominally paired, but actually working in parallel on generic health issues, i.e. without the 'information gap' concerning Gaza which had generated high levels of communication during EAST 1. The following comment exemplifies the resulting challenges, related to the broad nature of the brief:

> 'When we have different ideals about the topic we will take a long time to make a decision' (Glasgow student).

There was also the problem that the Biomed students in Gaza had more pressing outside commitments during the course, such as family commitments (the Gaza Biomed students were, on the whole, slightly older) or the need to carry out paid work (unemployment among health practitioners in Gaza is, relatively speaking, lower). As a consequence, Gaza Biomed students were less able to link up with their partners in Glasgow with regularity. For EAST 3, the decision was therefore made to revert to an IT/SET-specific cohort.

EAST 3

EAST 3 ran for five weeks astride July and August 2017. There were 81 Glasgow-based IT/SET students, an unexpected increase.[2] This growth in numbers resulted in some instances of 4:1 Glasgow:Gaza pairings. In terms of maximizing Gazan 'reach' overseas this was a positive development but, organizationally, a 4:1 partnership is rather vulnerable; if a Gazan student had dropped out for any reason, it would have left the students in Glasgow without their *in situ* 'expert'. This did in fact happen in two cases (the students in Glasgow were able to continue with their project, although the project became perforce more generic in nature, and course organizers had to factor in their lack of access to local feedback at the assessment stage). Care was taken to ensure that Arabic speakers within the Glasgow cohort were spread across the groupings. An unforeseen increase in student numbers across the entire pre-sessional course in summer 2017 also meant staffing shortfalls, and course administrators in Glasgow had to step in as teachers. Although the course received positive generic feedback on the final day, we were unable to administer the pre-/post-course data comparisons of EAST Projects 1 and 2, and in the end-of-course presentations, participants were only able to speak for three minutes each (when combined with ongoing observation over the five weeks of the pre-sessional course, still ample for the purposes of evaluation).

In terms of cost, EAST 3 was run by Gaza with no external financial input. By this time (March 2017), Glasgow had made a successful bid to the EU's Erasmus+ International Credit Mobility (ICM) programme, securing a grant of €240,000 to bring 12 students from Gaza to Glasgow for six- or 12-month study-abroad visits. Using this funding, students from Gaza are able to gain credits towards their home degrees while taking courses in Glasgow. With another bid for €355,000 ongoing while

EAST 3 was being organized, organizers in Gaza were able to make the case to their own finance office for a continued involvement in the EAST Project even without the external funding that had been sourced for EAST Projects 1 and 2. Although participation in EAST did not provide a direct route into ICM funding for Gazan students, the inclusion of EAST within the ICM bid had certainly strengthened it, and this would presumably remain the case for future bids.

EAST 4

This ran in July and August 2018, and was once again restricted to SET/IT students. To overcome the fact that many students knew little or nothing of Gaza on arrival, students were shown a *Guardian* video-clip (Greenwood *et al.*, 2018) outlining the breadth of engineering-related issues facing residents of the Strip, and asked to reflect on potential social and health effects. As organizers, our experience on EAST Projects 1 through 3 has shown that fruitful collaboration has depended on the forging of solid Glasgow-Gaza 'bonds' early on, and (despite a busy timetable) a week 1 slot was released to ensure that Skype/WhatsApp contact took place within class time, i.e. a compulsory ice-breaker.

The significant 2017 growth in Glasgow student numbers continued into summer 2018, with over 160 students participating (cf. 37 in summer 2015). Interest in participation from Gaza also grew, with expressions of interest from 80 students (90% of whom met the overall IELTS equivalent stipulation); this level of demand can probably be linked to the two successful International Credit Mobility bids mentioned above and the desire among Gazan students for an opportunity to study at the University of Glasgow. It ought to be restated here that access to ICM opportunities is not dependent upon Gazans' participation in the EAST Project. These mobility packages are open to *all* students at the IUG who can find credit-bearing courses in Glasgow related to their own courses; of the first group of eight Gazan scholars who successfully reached Glasgow on the ICM-financed programme in January 2018, only three had participated in a previous EAST Project.

Organizers in Glasgow are keen to find out whether the success of the Glasgow/Gaza relationship can be replicated with another overseas partner. Any future collaborating institutions must be able to furnish (like the IUG) committed staff and students, availability in August, solid connectivity and a workable time-zone difference (to enable synchronous sessions). For EAST 4, a new link-up was piloted with a university in Chile (INACAP), limited to just 16 IT students, and paralleling the ongoing participation from Gaza. As coordinating online contact between Glasgow, Chile and Palestine requires extensive logistical organization, no Chile-Palestine contact was attempted, although the longer term aim is for a 'triangle' of this nature, one that could put Gaza in a key position as an experienced administrator, and which would be a significant further step in breaking Gaza's academic isolation. Chile, a country with a sizeable Palestinian community and one placed workably in terms of time zones, would be well placed for a longer term expansion of this nature.

Alongside the exploration of links with other international partners, organizers in Glasgow are also keen to see whether the EAST model can be replicated with other disciplines within the IUG or perhaps other universities in Gaza; they held a post-EAST 4 webinar (in February 2019) in order to explore this objective. This invitation was sent out via the British Association for Lecturers in English for Academic Purposes listings, and expressions of interest were received from the following universities: Manchester Metropolitan, Leeds, Canterbury Christchurch, Southampton and Coventry. It is also hoped to visit Gaza to help move forward any possible collaborations that may result. This visit can take advantage of funding already forming part of the two Erasmus+ bids, although the reluctance of the University of Glasgow to provide insurance for a trip to an area of the world on the Foreign Office 'no-visit' list must still be overcome.

Finally, the organizers are keen to further explore the role of motivation. Previous iterations of EAST have prioritized language ability as the principle criterion for selection of students from Gaza, but positive experience from EAST 4 suggests that Gazan students who are particularly eager to participate may in fact prove equally valuable interlocutors. Eagerness is a less easily quantifiable criterion for selection, but on all projects to date we have seen some evidence of relatively weak linguists who have contributed to work of high quality; hence our interest in this area. What features of 'eagerness' made these weak linguists so effective as partners? How are they translanguaging? What resources do they bring to the interaction that are not merely about narrowly conceived linguistic proficiency in English?

Having given an overview of the four projects held to date, and our hopes for the future, the chapter will now move on to summarize the main successes that have resulted and the challenges that remain. We are aware that unsaid but present (and growing) political economy and power-imbalance concerns underlie each of these successes.

Successes

An analysis of the data available from EAST Projects 1 and 2 clearly showed students' positive assessment regarding the value of the course in terms of enhanced communication skills, teamwork, problem solving, digital literacies and intercultural awareness. This held true, although less markedly, for the EAST 2 Biomed cohort. Comments were positive from both Glasgow and Gaza but, in all cases, feedback from Gaza was the most positive.

Focusing first on the language benefits of the project, the following comments from participants are illustrative:

> Our group was formed by 3 students of different nationalities. So we needed to speak just in English and be as clear as possible. (Glasgow student)

> I think the way it improve my communication skills like when i say that i moved from the intermediate level to advanced level. (Gaza student)

> For example, we said hello at the beginning and use suitable words like 'could you please'. Also, considering about the special situation of them, we avoid asking questions which have some relationship with the sensitive aspects. (Glasgow student)

> I have overcome my fear of communicating with english speakers and enjoy it. (Glasgow student)

> I think I have courage now to try speaking English without spend a lot of time to order the words in my mind or be afraid of grammars faults. (Gaza student)

> It was my first experience to talk with others in the English language therefore as an incentive for me in order to work on improving my experience in communication, since the only communicative for me was between family and friends … there these give me more daring and self-confidence. (Gaza student)

The comments suggest various positive outcomes from the online project work, from a fairly direct appraisal of a perceived improvement in language proficiency to more nuanced developments, such as the pedagogical value of mixed-nationality groupings that the project engendered. The need to pay attention to quite complex politeness strategies stemming from the 'need to compromise' and the 'sensitive aspects' of life in Gaza suggests that the project's value touched on pragmatic and intercultural issues that, we hope, both stretched and stimulated participants. Interestingly, the final three comments all talk of a really meaningful chance to overcome affective issues ('fear', 'courage', 'daring'); it seems that these were issues faced by both student groups.

To focus on a benefit specific to Glasgow, a gratifying gain has been students' understanding of the value of the process set in motion by the way in which the EAST was conceptualized. This is particularly important since most pre-sessional students come from educational trajectories that prioritize product (for instance, essays and certificates) over process. Despite the gatekeeping function of the five-week pre-sessional course, the nature of the project brought home to many an understanding of how knowledge and experience can be gained incrementally:

> Actually, I think the topic doesn't have much relation to my subjects, but I found an article using the latest technology-data mining to solve it. I learn a lot and i know once are you thinking, anything has a relation to each other. (Glasgow student)

Similarly, teachers in Glasgow have considered involvement on the course very favourably:

> I can't think of a course I enjoyed teaching more. The link to Gaza is of real value to staff and students and gives a sense of working on a real, applied project rather than an abstract project, which is important in SET. (Post-course teacher feedback, August 2017)

The final success noted by participants, less tangible but probably the greatest overall, has been the bringing together of students who previously knew little of the other's culture. The Glasgow-based students particularly appreciated the opportunity to learn in depth about a new country, and to do this indirectly by working together to try to overcome real-world challenges its people were facing. Discovering the value of this inductive method of learning about another culture (see Bikowski, 2011) has been one of the key successes of the projects to date. For the students in Glasgow, many from relatively privileged backgrounds, it was often a first contact with people living in much more challenging circumstances than their own:

> I just knew that there were wars in Gaza, but I didn't know to what extent they influence in daily life of the people there. (Glasgow student)

For the Gazan students, many noted their happiness at being able to break their feelings of isolation, even if only in virtual terms, and to tell others about life in Gaza:

> Listening to other people from other nationalities thinking with our problems and solve it is very supportive. Of course, we communicate with other students from different nationalities. I also participate in raising cultural awareness about my country and its problems. (Gaza student)

For both groups, a great value of the projects has been in enhancing human contact:

> When I dealt with others with each one has its own culture, my view of the subject really changed ... i actually get to know some cultures and really impressed by some. (Gaza student)

> In this project, we learn to distribute the jobs, and share the ideas. And sometime even learn to compromise. (Glasgow student)

However, there remain many challenges to overcome, which are discussed below.

Challenges

To start with the core linguistic issue, there were also a couple of less positive comments from students which must be highlighted:

> The project was very useful although if the project was with other universities inside the UK might be more useful rather than Arabic country,

> because they can correct some mistake in term of speaking. (Glasgow student)
>
> Maybe contacting native speakers would be more effective on our communication skills. (Gaza student)

Both comments express an overt preference for a native (presumably British) interlocutor, and both are revealing. Braj Kachru (1986) divided World Englishes into three basic categories. Although the neatness of this division has since been questioned, the basic premise of concentric circles denoting Inner (using English as a native language), Outer (as a second language) and Expanding (as a foreign language) users of English is of clear relevance to the EAST Project, which depends for its success on communication between speakers from countries where English may have some official role, but is of very limited daily use in most domains. In EAST 4, we attempted to address the issue by making explicit reference on day 1 to the fact that the majority of encounters in English now involve ELF contacts, i.e. between non-native speakers outwith Kachru's Inner Circle (this ties in explicitly to issues of motivation, mentioned in Chapters 4 and 5 of this book). More challenging, there seems to be a disconnect regarding just what makes up an effective communicative act; to paraphrase Canagarajah (2018: 272), our Glasgow and Gazan students may be overestimating text as their 'unit of analysis', and thereby in turn overestimating the value of the native speaker as the carrier of this text. Canagarajah's avowal of text plus *context* (he cites the centrality not only of setting, but also of social networks) seems particularly apposite to the EAST Project; within an already crowded course, we need to find materials that move beyond the global employability aspects of English language proficiency to look at examples of successful (and less successful) engineering interactions in cross-cultural settings. Analysis of such interactions will generate valuable language practice opportunities, but (more fundamentally) may serve to convince our students to value an L2 speaker as interlocutor and, by so doing, to value *their own* potential as communicators.

Academics in Gaza were themselves divided about whether interactions with international students were an advantage. One academic was in clearly favour of ELF interactions as currently practised in EAST, in particular through an intercultural lens:

> Contacting international students will open the space for more cultural exchange between the pairs that would increase their awareness and respect to other cultures, perspectives, ways of thinking, etc. and make them more open-minded.

A second academic, focusing on the language benefits, was equally clearly in favour of the involvement of native speakers:

> [...] because this will enable them to learn the right pronunciation and the appropriate use of words.

A third expressed a more nuanced viewpoint:

> Communicating with British students may improve IUG students' pronunciation and speaking skill through being exposed to native speakers. Additionally, meeting their expectations is likely to strengthen their motivation and contribution in the EAST activities. However, speaking to international students provides IUG Students with a variety of accents (and) with a variety of ways of thinking and learning styles as well as giving them an opportunity to communicate with students from different linguistic, cultural and educational backgrounds

Although the academics' comments reinforce the perceived intercultural value of EAST, they also suggest language-related issues that could make an in- (rather than pre-)sessional link-up potentially attractive from the Gazan perspective. In short, in language terms, the pre-sessional set up is one that could usefully evolve.

A second challenge, the difficulty inherent in online interactions ('*Can you hear me?*') does have to be acknowledged, too. The IT links at the IUG have been prioritized (despite resource shortfalls), as they must be in a country almost 100% dependent upon the internet for its links with the wider world, but electricity cuts have an unavoidable impact on student-to-student interactions. These can be overcome,[3] particularly as the majority of contacts are asynchronous, but it is crucial that the Glasgow-based students are, from the outset, aware of the difficulties under which their Gazan partners are operating, and the addition of the *Guardian* video in week 1 (which outlines the pernicious effects of the blockade on Gaza) during EAST 4 was an attempt to ensure this awareness.

Organizationally, the experience with the Biomed cohort during EAST 2 was instructive, and suggests that any future expansion into other disciplines (maybe back into Biomedicine) needs to replicate the Gaza-specific 'information gap' that has, we believe, been such a central contributor to the success of the IT/SET collaborations to date. It would be wonderful to experiment with other disciplines from other Glasgow pre-sessional strands, but Gaza to Glasgow links for, say, management or for accounting would be more challenging both from a qualitative and quantitative perspective, and would require staff and resources in Glasgow that are unavailable.

Beyond language, IT links and the logistics of project organization, there is of course the issue of finance. If funding can be sourced it is of course a boon, but we have succeeded in embedding the EAST Project work within the Glasgow pre-sessional course without any significant cost implications (beyond the 40% reduced teaching load for one staff member). The cost implications in Gaza are higher, as the IUG has needed to open its facilities during their summer holidays, but IUG has been willing to do this in view of the increased international links (including funded links) that have resulted. Applying for such funding requires patience, and probably requires a Gazan partner able and willing to run a pilot on a self-funded basis (unless the UK institution can provide this financing). It also calls for considerable time spent post-project, in the autumn, to put together a funding application for the following year. Such applications need to show evidence of solid UK-Gaza coordination, but we have happily found plenty of goodwill at British Council and EU levels for Gaza-based initiatives.

At the University of Glasgow, similar levels of goodwill have been demonstrated by support bodies, but a wider institutional commitment, beyond the English for Academic Study Unit (which has provided the space for experimentation with these projects) has been somewhat disappointing. In part, this may be due to organizational difficulties accompanying working with Gaza that simply don't exist anywhere else in the world.[4] In part there may be residual reluctance to move beyond the one-dimensional image of Gaza as depicted by many news providers. Only once did a University of Glasgow staff member explicitly voice concerns of this nature, questioning whether sending funds to a Gaza-based institution would fall foul of anti-terrorism laws, but one does wonder whether similar concerns are silently shared by others, leading to a reluctance to engage in or to take what are perceived to be potentially risky decisions. It is rather dispiriting to note that such reluctance never really needs to rise to the level of open questioning in order to be very effective in dissuading partnerships. Finally, there may in part be an organizational preference towards targeting more obvious sources of international student recruitment, countries and regions with greater financial resources and with the infrastructure already in place (agents, recruiting events) to send students to Glasgow.

Conclusion

As we have already noted, the evolution of the collaboration, from online mobility to actual mobility over four years, is in itself a development with major political, moral and economic implications. Is there a hope among participants in Gaza that participation will lead to overseas travel? Are organizers in Glasgow (and in Gaza) comfortable with the fact that student involvement in a project may be based on such a hope, one moreover dependent on successful funding applications? Even if funding for travel *can* be accessed, are organizers comfortable with having to make gatekeeping decisions regarding, for instance, assessment of language level that may follow? The issues of symbolic power, whether related to dreams of mobility or actual mobility, require really serious reflection and consideration.

Yet the evolution from online to actual mobility has without doubt been a source of great satisfaction to the organizers in Glasgow and, judging by what our Palestinian colleagues say, in Gaza, too. During EAST 3,

Glasgow-based Thai and Chinese students worked with two partners in Gaza to research telecommunication engineering strategies to address the absence of addresses in the Gaza Strip (see Rolinska *et al.*, this volume, for further details). To witness in January 2018 the same Thai and Chinese students meeting in person one of their former Gazan online partners, now an International Credit Mobility funded student in Glasgow, was very moving indeed.

There is a fear that working with Gaza may prove emotionally overwhelming for some of our Glasgow-based students but, on day 1 of future projects, alongside the *Guardian* video outlining the vast scale of challenges facing Gaza, we also plan to show videos from previous student projects. One of these videos, entitled 'EAST Project – Road Traffic Problems in Gaza', can be found on YouTube. It was shot by an engineering student in Gaza to demonstrate how the parking of cars, the dumping of construction material and the encroachment of shops and cafés renders long stretches of pavement inaccessible to pedestrians, causing serious safety issues in the Strip's main cities. The video shows the strength in adversity of those living in Gaza, but is an illustration not only of '*sumud*' (the collective resilience and steadfastness of the Palestinian nation mentioned in the Introduction), but also that, in everyday life, what frustrates Gazans is also what frustrates Brazilians, or Indonesians, or Glaswegians. As the video (and the wider EAST telecollaboration) shows, there is far more that unites than divides us.

Notes

(1) For a further discussion of issues relating to motivation in the face of forced immobility, see Chapter 5 in this volume.
(2) A real challenge on pre-sessional courses is the unpredictability of student arrivals. If organizers could know who was coming to Glasgow beforehand, a great deal of useful preparatory work could be done in a way that parallels the preparation with the Gazan students, but this is unfortunately not the case
(3) See Chapters 2 and 3 in this volume for further analysis of EAL pedagogies using online media.
(4) After a slow start, the commitment of the university's marketing and recruitment arm has been exemplary. However, after months of work had gone into preparing solid and fully funded exchanges, many recipients (both staff *and* students) were refused travel – some by Israel, some by Egypt, some by internal Rafah/Hamas related issues at the border crossing, and some by the UK's own visa-issuing authority.

References

Bikowski, D. (2011) Review of 'Online Intercultural Exchange: An Introduction for Foreign Language Teachers'. *Language Learning and Technology* 15 (1), 24–28.

Canagarajah, S. (2018) Materialising competence: Perspectives from international STEM scholars. *The Modern Language Journal* 102 (2), 268–291.

Garrison, D.R. and Arbaugh, J.B. (2007) Researching the community of inquiry framework: Review, issues, and future directions. *The Internet and Higher Education* 10 (3), 157–172.

Greenwood, P., Balousha, H., Susman, D., Khalili, M., Michael, C., Mahmood, M. Caller, P. and Jenkins, A. (2018) Even the firehoses leak: How Gaza deals with urban destruction. *The Guardian*, 5 April 2018. See https://www.theguardian.com/cities/video/2018/apr/05/inside-gaza-how-a-city-under-siege-prepares-for-war-video (accessed 28 November 2018).

Guariento, W. and Morley, J. (2001) Text and task authenticity in the EFL classroom. *ELT Journal* 55 (4), 347–353.

Guariento, W., Al Masri, N. and Rolinska, A. (2016) Investigating EAST (a Scotland-Gaza English for Academic Study Telecollaboration between SET Students). In *Proceedings of American Society for Engineering Education* (Paper 14492). Washington, DC: ASEE.

Guariento, W., Rolinska, A. and Al Masri, N. (2018) Constructive content-based feedback in EAP contexts. *Higher Education Research & Development* 37 (3), 514–532.

Kachru, B. (1986) The power and politics of English. *World Englishes* 5 (2–3), 121–140.

Lorente, B. (2010) Language in the making of global workers. Paper presented at *Language, Migration and Labour* Conference, University of Freiburg, Switzerland, 28–29 January.

Marie, M., Hannigan, B. and Jones, A. (2018) Social ecology of resilience and 'Sumud' of Palestinians. *Health* 22 (1), 20–35.

Roberts, C. (2010) Language, migration and the gatekeepers. *Language Issues* 2 (21), 4–18.

Rolinska, A., Guariento, W. and Al Masri, N. (2017) Establishing and sustaining EAP student partnerships across borders. British Council ELT Research Paper. London: British Council.

University of Glasgow (2018) University of Glasgow Graduate Attributes Matrix. See https://www.gla.ac.uk/media/media_183776_en.pdf (accessed 20 May 2019).

Universities UK (2019) See https://www.universitiesuk.ac.uk/International/Documents/2019/International%20facts%20and%20figures%20slides.pdf (accessed 1 May 2020).

World Bank (2018) Palestine's economic outlook. See https://www.worldbank.org/en/country/westbankandgaza/publication/economic-outlook-april-2018/ (accessed 21 November 2018).

2 Islamic University of Gaza Internationalization Endeavors at the Level of Postgraduate Programs

Sanaa Abou-Dagga

Introduction

Many higher education institutions (HEIs) worldwide are moving towards internationalization. Internationalization is a complex, multifaceted concept and has been one of the most widely asserted and researched policy trends (Renc-Roe & Roxå, 2014). Among the most common definitions of internationalization in higher education is that developed by Knight (2004: 11), who defines it as 'the process of integrating an international, inter-cultural or global dimension into the purpose, functions or delivery of post-secondary education'. A more enhanced definition that focuses on being inclusive and intentional in addressing learning outcomes for all students was produced by De Wit *et al.* (2015). They define internationalization as the *intentional process* of integrating an international, intercultural or global dimension into the purpose, functions and delivery of post-secondary education, to enhance the quality of education and research for all students and staff and to make a meaningful contribution to society. This definition is adopted by the International Association of Universities (IAU) and by many universities worldwide – including the Islamic University of Gaza (IUG) – as it underscores that internationalization is not a goal in itself, but a means of enhancing the quality and excellence of the HEI and research. In addition, internationalization serves societal needs by focusing on culture, rather than solely on economic rationales and returns.

Research in the field (e.g. De Wit *et al.*, 2015; Hoang *et al.*, 2018; Sanders, 2019; Shahijan *et al.*, 2016; Zhang, 2018) shows the existence of several internationalization approaches, strategies and models worldwide, with every experience being a reflection of its context and a way to meet the context's specific needs. Since there is no 'one size fits all' model or approach for internationalization, HEIs can benefit from the best thinking model and good practice from other institutions around the world (IAU, 2019).

The aim of our chapter is to delineate some of IUG's internationalization strategies for postgraduate level programs in the specific context of siege and occupation, strategies which help lessen IUG's isolation from the global academic community. In particular, it will discuss two strategies utilized in postgraduate programs: (a) the use of multilingual education and communication, more specifically English and Arabic; and (b) the use of up-to-date technologies, especially information and communications technologies (ICTs) and related infrastructure for teaching, researching and implementing collaborative international projects in postgraduate programs. This will also be done with reference to the use of technology and language for an international project entitled 'Strengthening Higher Education Capacities in Palestine for Gender Equalities' (SHE-GE),

The chapter will first give an overview of current trends in higher education in Palestine, focusing on IUG's internationalization efforts at both institutional and postgraduate program levels. The discussion is based on a desk study of published materials, a literature review and institutional policy documents. Following this, the chapter briefly outlines the specific context of internationalization of the SHE-GE Project, exploring the learning processes and the challenges and using interviews with IUG academics.

Current Developments in Higher Education

Current trends in the development of HEIs worldwide, along with emerging ICTs and increasing global access to the internet, have made universities more responsive to the educational needs of students and staff, since easy communication and rapid access to information have opened the gate to more collaboration and cooperation. Collaboration is usually seen as a process leading to jointly constructed artefacts or achievements, while cooperation is defined as the process leading to an assembled product. As Dillenbourg (1999: 8) puts it: 'in cooperation, partners split the work, solve sub-tasks individually and then assemble the partial results into the final output. In collaboration, partners do the work together.' Online collaboration and cooperation are possible nowadays between educational institutions, as long as the institutions involved have the intention to do so, as well as having the necessary resources, among which are multilingual skills for staff and students and the technological infrastructure required.

One of the academic phenomena most connected with current developments in the higher education sector are multilingual and multicultural collaborations between universities. As a term, multilingualism conveys the ability of an HEI to have regular use of more than one language in their daily activities over space and time (McCloud, 2015). Specifically, it has been used to describe the situation where 'staff, teachers and students, despite their similarities, have different first languages, none of which need to be the language of instruction' (Lauridsen & Lillemose, 2015: 9).

The promotion of multilingual education, including the use of the English language in the international context, is essential for academic and scientific cooperation in teaching, research and community activities. In fact, one of the most significant phenomena regarding the internationalization of higher education around the world is the wider use of English for research, scientific study and graduate education (Gonzalez, 2017). The use of the English language facilitates cooperation and collaboration between academics and gives access to the benefits of a wealth of resources. In Gaza, the English language has not only been used for academic exchange purposes, but also to convey to the world the hardship that Gazan universities have been experiencing, in addition to conveying their hopes and aspiration for a better future. Imperiale *et al*. (2017: 36) discuss the values and goals of English in the context of the occupation, pain and pressure of the Gaza Strip and conclude:

> In Gaza English language education has a vital role: despite the forced immobility and the consequent enforced monoculturalism and monolingualism that the siege imposes, participants aspire to open up spaces for intercultural curiosity to be explored and fulfilled. The online space opens a fast-developing means to use English language for intercultural exchanges and establishing relationships with the international community when immobility prevents face-to-face encounters.

The provision and use of ICTs is vital to facilitate communication and cooperation between HEIs, particularly in places that are characterized by isolation and restricted mobility such as the Gaza Strip. However, online collaborations are not unproblematic, and another study, looking at online training for teachers of Arabic to speakers of other languages in the context of the siege of the Gaza Strip, discusses the many challenges that were encountered throughout the delivery of the course, mainly technological and linguistic ones. As the authors note, it is also essential to learn to incorporate challenges into interactions and to '[...] accept them as a "normal" part of the online exchange' (Fassetta *et al*., 2017: 148).

Higher Education in Palestine

Higher education in Palestine has encountered many difficulties since it was established in the early 1970s. Many Palestinian universities were established after the Israeli occupation of the West Bank and Gaza in 1967, as a means of resisting efforts to obliterate Palestinian culture and national identity. As Abu-Lughod (2000) notes, Palestine's institutions of higher education were developed under the most trying social, political and economic circumstances, the result of a military occupation determined to disempower Palestinian society. As Moughrabi (2015) stresses, any society that has undergone such a massive and debilitating assault should have collapsed long ago. Palestinian HEIs play a great part in preventing such a collapse.

The Palestinian higher education system is rich and challenging in its experiences. It is rich because of the motivation and eagerness of the Palestinians to learn in spite of all the difficulties, to get connected with people in other places and to share their experiences with them (Saffarini, 2010; see also Phipps *et al.*, this volume). It is challenging because the Palestinian higher education system is in the crosshair of the Israeli occupation, and the Palestinian government with its deep financial constraints and lack of legislative oversight (Bahour, 2016). In fact, Palestinian people consider their enrolment in HEIs as their main asset. In the absence of natural resources, education plays a vital role in developing the economic, political and social conditions of the Palestinian people.

Higher education in Palestine presents students with specialized disciplines that qualify them for employment. One of the sector's aims is to enhance cooperation between HEIs locally, regionally and internationally in accordance with national needs and priorities. Since its establishment, the Palestinian higher education sector has undergone rapid expansion and diversification. Universities are using emerging technologies to create learning environments to stimulate students and prepare them for lifelong learning (see also Abu Aylan, this volume). E-learning has grown rapidly, and almost all universities offer some type of virtual education in addition to using online facilities to get connected with the outside world. Arabic language is the official language for instruction in Palestinian universities, but Palestinian HEIs teach some courses and programs – especially in the science and technology fields – using the English language as a medium of instruction.

There are three types of HEIs in Palestine: (a) 'government institutions' administered by the Ministry of Education and Higher Education (MoEHE); (b) 'private universities'; and (c) 'public universities', which are mainly privately financed but receive limited funding from the government in addition to being heavily regulated by MoEHE. The majority of the 49 Palestinian HEIs in the West Bank and Gaza Strip are relatively young, and the oldest has only been in existence for 48 years. According to the 2017 MoEHE Annual Report (the most recent at the time of writing), there are 15 universities, 17 university colleges[1] and 18 community colleges in the West Bank and in Gaza. According to the latest figures available, Palestinian universities have a total student population of 136,459 students, comprising 27 PhD students and 8692 Master's and Higher Diploma students, while the rest are bachelor's degree students. To these, 56,027 students enrolled in Al-Quds Open University[2] need to be added. Moreover, the MoEHE Annual Report (2017) shows that annual new admissions stand at 34,003 students in the universities plus 14,476 in the open education system. Graduates in 2015/2016 were 27,231 from universities and 10,764 from open education. There were around 27,231 faculty members at universities with 6% at the rank of full professor and 9% at the rank of associate professor; 60% of the faculty are PhD holders.

Postgraduate programs in Palestinian universities are relatively new (the first Master's program started in the 1976/1977 academic year), compared to their undergraduate counterparts. The opening of postgraduate programs at Palestinian universities helped to meet the needs of the Palestinian community by providing qualified scientific cadres in the various fields of knowledge, able to conduct research and to teach, in addition to contributing to the production, transfer and development of scientific and cultural heritage. The postgraduate degrees granted by Palestinian universities, according to MoEHE (2018), are divided into:

- *Higher diploma* (30 credit hours). This can be pursued after a bachelor's degree and students have the right to progress to undertake Master's studies.
- *Master's degree* (36 credit hours plus a thesis or comprehensive exam). The length of study is two years. The student can embark on an academic career and progress to undertake PhD studies.
- *Doctorate* (minimum 48 credit hours plus thesis). The length of study is three years, and students have the right to teach at the university and pursue an academic career.

In general, universities in Gaza are struggling to perform their developmental roles. Jebril's (2018) study underscores the impact of 'de-development'[3] on Gaza's universities, showing that the occupation and the changes in the Arab World have repercussions on the educational context in the Gaza Strip that are more complex than previously thought. Jebril (2018) notes that the tightened siege on Gaza has incapacitated and demobilized universities, sometimes putting them in the position of having to prioritize immediate, operational needs over pursuing quality and prospects.

Among the many restrictions and challenges that students and staff in the Gaza Strip face are obstacles to travel to other Palestinian universities in the West Bank. Moreover, universities in the Gaza Strip experience challenges when traveling into and out of the Strip, with the consequence that: academics are unable to attend conferences, undertake research, upgrade qualifications and maintain contact with scholars abroad; foreign academics and scholars face great challenges in visiting Gaza universities (see also Phipps *et al.*, this volume); there are obstacles to the import of books, equipment and materials; and it can sometimes lead to the arbitrary arrest and detention of Palestinian academics while travelling. As a consequence, faculty seeking to attend even the briefest event abroad must allow additional days to ensure timely arrival at their destinations and to return home. This imposes substantial additional costs, not least because the likelihood of delays or refusals means that air tickets cannot be booked in advance. Unsurprisingly, this discourages travel, leaving faculty, administrators and students virtually isolated from the international community and less able to pursue research, and it seriously damages students' and staff's morale.

IUG: An Overview

Despite all the aforementioned difficulties and the isolation imposed on the people of the Gaza Strip, including its academics, universities have been able to survive. Some institutions even manage to compete regionally and worldwide, using available ICTs to replace face-to-face communication. As several other contributors to this volume also note, although demanding and sometimes frustrating besides being expensive, this kind of virtual collaboration is a choice that Gaza's academics (including IUG's academics) and their counterparts outside Gaza city have to make in order to confront and bypass the problems of entering and leaving the Gaza Strip.

IUG is one of the biggest and oldest HEIs in Palestine. It is an independent[4] academic institution supervised by MoEHE and managed by a board of trustees composed of experienced professionals in different fields. Raising the levels of educational programs based on quality standards and enhancing partnership and cooperative relationships with local, regional and international organizations are the goals IUG is striving for. IUG has 11 faculties: Medical (Medicine, Nursing, Medical sciences), Technical (IT and Engineering), Arts, Education, Commerce, Islamic Teaching (Osuol Al Dine), Shariaa & Law, and Science. IUG has 18,000 undergraduate and postgraduate students enrolled in about 130 programs in the different disciplines. About 60% of the students are female and almost one-third of IUG staff obtained their postgraduate degrees from 25 countries who used or at least were exposed to a dozen different languages. As noted earlier, the main language of instruction is Modern Standard Arabic, with the use of English for teaching some specializations at the undergraduate and postgraduate levels. In addition, IUG uses sign language for deaf students and Braille language for visually impaired students (IUG, 2018a).

Over the past decade, IUG has succeeded in building and expanding multilingual international networks and partnerships with many local, regional and international institutions, and has developed partnerships with more than 130 European universities. It also has research partnerships located in 21 EU countries as part of participation in 40 EU-funded multilateral and bilateral programs, including TEMPUS, Erasmus Mundus, Erasmus+, Al Mqadisi (France), APPEAR (Austria), HEI ICI

(Finland) and Horizon 2020 (IUG, 2018b). Moreover, IUG has partnerships with more than 66 Palestinian and Arab universities in Jordan, Lebanon, Syria, Egypt and Tunisia. Additionally, IUG is a coordinator of three EU-funded projects under Erasmus+ and APPEAR programs.

IUG's Internationalization Efforts at the Institutional Level

In 1991/1992 IUG started its first graduate program in the Faculty of Education with a general Higher Diploma in Teacher Education. In 1992/1993 the Master's program in Education was opened. In 1994/1995 Master's programs were opened at the Faculty of Islamic Teaching (*Osuol Al Dine*), followed by Sharia and Law, Engineering and Science, Arts, Commerce, Health Science, Nursing and Information Technology. At present, IUG is considered the largest institution in Palestine in terms of postgraduate programs, as it hosts 33 Master's programs in different disciplines in addition to five PhD programs.

To survive the challenges that Palestinian HEIs face and in order to internationalize in a context of occupation and siege, IUG adopted a range of polices and strategies that support postgraduate programs. This is in addition to the provision of some facilities for incoming and outgoing students in terms of credit recognition and support units. This provision is made in the anticipation (and hope) that the siege will end, so that more of IUG's students will be able to travel freely abroad, while international students will be able to choose IUG for their studies.

Two of the strategies adopted were: (a) mobility for staff and students; and (b) the use of the English language as medium of instruction and assessment in most postgraduate programs. In addition to these, it also adopted strategies that facilitate the use of ICTs for teaching, assessment and research.

With regard to mobility, IUG has provided its postgraduate students and staff with many opportunities for international mobility over the last seven years through international credit mobility programs. Such programs allow students to study courses/modules related to their specializations for one or two semesters in an international university with which IUG cooperates at the postgraduate level. Although mobility for most Gazans is challenging, a few postgraduate students and staff were able to participate in mobilities within the Erasmus Plus (E+) EU program and then return to Gaza. To date:

- 26 postgraduate students have participated in International Credit Mobility;
- 12 IUG academic and administrative staff have participated in E+ International Credit Mobility programs.

Below is an overview of some of the strategies and procedures that IUG adopts to support of the use of ICTs and the English language as a medium of instruction and assessment. The overview is based on document analysis and interviews conducted by the chapter's author. The interviewees were two selected male faculty members working at the Research and Graduate Deanship, and a female colleague based at the external affairs office who was also involved in the SHE-GE Project.

The postgraduate programs structure

To open an academic program at Palestinian universities requires submitting the proposal in line with the guidelines of MoEHE and the Accreditation and Quality Assurance Commission (AQAC). Proposals for accreditation of postgraduate programs are usually written in English, especially those in the Applied Sciences discipline. Usually the reviewers offer comments and feedback in English, as some of the external reviewers may be academics working outside Palestine. This process is in congruence with national policies towards being connected with the international academic community.

In 21 of IUG's programs in the Applied Sciences (Science, Health Sciences, Nursing, IT, Engineering) in addition to specific programs in the Human Sciences (e.g. Master's in Applied Linguistics & Translation), evidence of English proficiency is required in order to join the program and/or for the doctoral thesis. In the three doctoral programs that are delivered in Arabic (i.e. PhD in the Arabic language, PhD in Education and PhD in Islamic Teaching – *Osuol Al Dine*), applicants are requested to prove their English language proficiency by providing the results of an English test, This is required in order to ensure that doctoral students are able to locate and engage with resources written in English. In some of the Master's programs in the Faculty of Commerce (i.e. Business Administration, Accounting & Finance, Development Economics, Regional & International Studies), which are delivered in both Arabic and English, applicants are required to provide TOEFL results. Similarly, in the Master's program in Crisis & Disaster Management, applicants are required to present evidence of English proficiency.

Cooperation between local and international universities is highly encouraged by the Palestinian MOEHE and AQAC, especially during the process of developing MA and PhD programs. Appendices 1 and 2 at the end of this chapter provide detailed information about English language requirements for postgraduate programs in the Humanities and Applied Sciences Faculties at IUG.

Teaching and learning processes

Fourteen of the postgraduate programs at IUG at MA and PhD level are taught in English. Instructors sometimes use Arabic, besides English, to present course material that may need further explanation, and both

English and Arabic are used for Master's theses in some courses, depending on students' and instructors' proficiency and preferences.

International guest speakers from outside Gaza whose native language is not Arabic are invited to deliver seminars on specific topics using online communication tools such as Skype. Most of the guest speakers are colleagues of IUG's faculty or distinguished scholars who have been invited through international collaborative projects. As well as using ICTs for knowledge exchange opportunities, staff at IUG use blended learning for their classroom teaching, combining traditional methods with digital media. Such an approach to teaching offers students an opportunity to explore online resources that may be in languages other than their mother tongue.

Assessment is usually in English and it includes a variety of techniques such as the use of quizzes, exams, presentations, assignments, written papers and projects. As an optional choice, some faculty use Moodle as an interface for teaching, learning and assessment.

Course resources and required reading materials such as textbooks and scientific articles for most of the 14 postgraduate programs are in English, and IUG's central library has access to databases such as EcoLink, JSTOR, HINARI, Elsevier Science Direct and Emerald. Moreover, the library policy is to support faculty members with all necessary resources for each academic year by ordering textbooks from worldwide online stores. However, delivery can take more than six months as the process is monitored by the Israeli authorities.

Thesis writing and defense

In almost all the English-based postgraduate programs at IUG, the thesis is written in English with students using IUG's general guidelines for writing theses. Besides, the thesis is usually defended either publicly or privately (mostly this depends on the student's choice after consulting with her/his advisor) in English. In some cases, the thesis may be supervised cooperatively by a foreign supervisor who speaks English, as IUG regulations at the postgraduate level allow for cooperative online supervision.

In the last five years, about 100 oral defense sessions for IUG theses were organized via video-conference facilities or Skype, as external examiners were participating from different places worldwide (Jordan, Egypt, Algeria, Tunis, Morocco, Saudi Arabia, England, Germany). Moreover, several IUG students studying abroad as part of their program of study defended their theses using IUG virtual facilities with an interview panel at IUG, as they were unable to travel back because of the siege. For example, in 2017 an IUG (MA) student enrolled in the College of Education defended her thesis from Germany with an interview panel at IUG, as she was not able to return to Gaza, and was awarded her MA. In addition, several Gazan PhD students enrolled in universities outside Gaza defended their theses online as they were not able to travel back to the country where they studied. For example, in early 2018 a PhD student (also an IUG staff member), enrolled in the education program at Tunis University, held her oral defense from IUG's premises using Skype, while all the committee members were at Tunis University. The discussion continued publicly for two hours and at the end of the defense session the student was awarded her PhD.

Thus, IUG's adoption of online communication tools, coupled with English language use in the graduate-level programs, opened a window for Gazan academics and their students to communicate with the world outside the Gaza Strip and go beyond the physical limits surrounding Gaza. They were able to engage and exchange knowledge, attitudes and expertise, to appreciate different cultures and to understand realities in different contexts. Most importantly, Gazan academics and students were able to send a message to the outside world saying that Gaza is alive and full of hope despite all the hardship it has to endure. The experience is described as valuable by IUG faculty members. Being connected to the world outside through positive experiences makes them feel, as one faculty member put it, 'lively and part of the academy'.

The IUG environment in favor of internationalization is strengthened through: (1) clear procedures and policies; (2) the existence of supporting structure such as the External Affairs Office; (3) flexible administrative procedures to implement international projects; (4) positive culture towards international academic collaborations; and (5) the diverse background of IUG staff, as many have received their graduate degrees from well-recognized universities worldwide. It is important to note that IUG's mission is about nurturing education, culture and civilization within the Palestinian community, keeping up with current trends in higher education and technology advancements, encouraging scientific research, and contributing to building future generations and developing the society in a framework of Islamic values (IUG, 2018a).

IUG Efforts of Internationalization through Collaborative Projects

IUG has been awarded several international projects that currently contribute to the development and enhancement of many of the postgraduate programs at IUG. Below are examples of some international projects during the last two years (IUG, 2018b):

- 'Promotion of Energy-efficient Buildings towards Developing Sustainable Built Environment in the Gaza Strip', funded by the Austrian Partnership Programme in Higher Education & Research for Development (APPEAR – academic partnership phase) – Austria;
- 'Educational Empowerment of Deaf Students', funded by APPEAR (preparatory phase) – Austria;

- 'Promotion of Energy-efficient Buildings towards Developing Sustainable Built Environment in the Gaza Strip', funded by APPEAR (preparatory phase) – Austria;
- 'Capacity Building for Energy-efficient Buildings towards a Sustainable Built Environment in the Gaza Strip – Palestine', funded by APPEAR (advanced academic partnership phase – Austria;
- 'Strengthening Higher Education Capacities in Palestine for Gender Equality', funded by APPEAR (academic partnership phase) – Austria (which will be discussed more in detail in the next section);
- 'Joint MSc in Software Engineering', funded by the EU through the TEMPUS Programme; consortium consists of members from Palestine, Italy, Germany and Slovenia;
- 'Research Output Management through Open Access Institutional Repositories in Palestinian Higher Education', funded by the E+ Programme funded by the EU; consortium consists of members from Palestine, Austria, UK and Italy;
- 'Develop Business and Economic Research Centers Capacity at Palestinian Higher Education Institutions', funded by the E+ Programme funded by the EU; consortium consists of members from Palestine, Spain, UK, Italy and Sweden.

The enhancement of the quality of postgraduate programs has been the focus of international collaborations. Most of the above international academic projects played an important role in the internationalization of IUG postgraduate programs as the implementation of projects' activities are usually done by the projects' teams, which consist of both IUG staff and their international counterparts. For example, a joint Master's degree program was developed within the framework of the 'Joint MSc in Software Engineering', funded by the EU through the TEMPUS Programme.

It is worth noting that there are challenges that IUG has yet to overcome, such as the relatively low involvement with international cooperation on the part of some staff. The reason behind this reluctance, as mentioned by the Dean of the External Relations Office at IUG, may be attributed to several factors, such as: lack of sufficient experience in managing international projects; low fluency in the use of the English language for writing and conversational purposes; lack of awareness of the benefits of international projects, academically as well as financially; and lack of appreciation of the value of being open to other cultures. While any of these factors (in different combinations) may have a part in the low involvement in international cooperation on the part of some academics, research is needed in order to highlight the specific issues that prevent further engagement.

One of the pioneering international projects with which the author of this chapter is closely involved is entitled 'Strengthening Higher Education

Capacities in Palestine for Gender Equalities' (SHE-GE). This three-year project is the first of its kind in Palestinian universities in the Gaza Strip and will be illustrated in the next section, as an example of the way in which international collaborations are contributing to enhancing and diversifying IUG's postgraduate programs of study.

The SHE-GE Project

The SHE-GE Project is an international collaboration between IUG and Graz University (UniGraz) in Austria and was funded in 2017 by the international Austrian APPEAR programme. The overall aim of the SHE-GE Project is to enhance gender equality and equity. It contributes to women's empowerment in Gaza through the establishment of a Women's Studies Centre (WSC) at IUG. This is an umbrella unit for the development of a broad knowledge base on women and gender issues (IUG, 2017b). Four objectives were envisioned for the Centre:

- Enhancing the capacity of the IUG faculty in women and gender studies through different activities, such as academic visits between IUG and UniGraz, online courses, workshops, seminars, lectures, mirror MA theses[5] (students at both universities), research, curriculum enhancement, joint conferences, enhancing library resources in the field and training for community.
- Developing IUG's institutional teaching through an MA programme in Women Studies and by building research capacity in the field.
- Enhancing awareness of women and gender issues outside the universities of IUG and UniGraz by reaching out to the local community and women's groups.
- Promoting regional and international networking for knowledge and intercultural exchange.

The academic work and communication between project team members is done in English, but dissemination, knowledge exchange and community engagement in Gaza and Austria require the use of Arabic and German. The multilingual approach incorporates several benefits, such as intercultural and international awareness, knowledge exchange, appreciation and understanding of different cultures, and the enhancement of communication skills, with some students also showing interest in learning the partners' languages.

Some activities of the SHE-GE Project contribute to the internationalization efforts of IUG at the level of postgraduate programs. Such activities include: the development of an MA programme in Women Studies at IUG; MA mirror theses (where MA students from IUG and UniGraz write on the same topic); enhancement of IUG's Human Rights course by adding a component about women's rights; and the development of an 'Online postgraduate module in interdisciplinary gender studies'.

In the following section, the Online postgraduate module in interdisciplinary gender studies is delineated, to illustrate the richness of the experience. This module was planned during the preliminary stage of the project, when both the IUG and UniGraz teams agreed to replace a planned month-long visit for two IUG project team members to UniGraz with this specialized online module. Travel to UniGraz was not possible for IUG's team members, due to the siege imposed by Israel and further exacerbated by restrictions imposed by the Egyptian authorities on single passengers crossing (Rafah), and by Palestinian internal political divisions.

The Online Module in Interdisciplinary Gender Studies

Overview

The online module is designed for the enrolment of IUG staff and students and UniGraz postgraduate students, and its content was developed in the light of consultation between IUG and UniGraz. The module consists of 16 ECTS[6] and was organized by UniGraz. It comprises the following:

- Core course (4 ECTS) where participants study 'Theories of Gender'.
- Specialized courses (4 ECTS each) where participants choose one of the following two courses: 'Gender in the Technological World' or 'Gender Governance and Gender Mainstreaming'.
- Research project (8 ECTS) which is mandatory for all participants.

The technology tools used for module delivery are Moodle and Wiki, plus a face-to-face component through Skype, in addition to the use of emails. To date, the online courses were attended by international exchange students enrolled at UniGraz as well as IUG staff interested in the topics of the project. As an example, 35 students in the academic year 2017/2018 attended the 'Theories of Gender' course, which included six participants from IUG. The UniGraz participants were from several European countries, South Korea and Australia. The student body of the course was culturally diverse, and they used English to communicate. It is worth noting that, as related by the Austrian course instructor, this course is among the courses favored by Erasmus and other international exchange students studying at UniGraz.

Several virtual meetings/consultations (group or individual) using Skype in English were conducted between course participants and the courses' instructors. Participants had to register via Moodle for a slot to do the consultation, which focused on the understanding of some course materials and topics. This was available to both IUG and UniGraz participants. Course instructors provided participants with electronic reading materials and resources (e.g. books, journal articles, YouTube videos, international reports and professional websites). Most of the materials were in English; however, some of resources were in German for UniGraz participants who spoke German, and some were in Arabic for IUG participants.

As part of the design of the online courses, multicultural reflection was included in the course assignments and activities. Therefore, a reflection from the participants' experiences and points of views in relation to women and gender issues was part of the weekly online discussions and the courses' reports, papers and projects.

The experience

Six participants from IUG and 29 from UniGraz enrolled in the first year of the project. Eight participants from IUG and 35 from UniGraz enrolled in the second year of the project. The difference in intake between the two universities is due to the fact that at UniGraz the course is part of an MA programme, while at IUG is it part of a project and the concept of women studies is still new to IUG's students and staff.

According to their feedback, IUG participants experienced a 'lively' learning environment where they got a chance to interact virtually with participants from different cultures and countries. When interviewed for this chapter, one of the IUG participants noted that the 'modules gave them a good chance to share and exchange ideas and information'. This is particularly important in a field of study that is described by specialists as 'controversial' in relation to stereotypes (Connell & Pearse, 2015; Cundiff & Vescio, 2016). The Moodle platform, in addition to the course instructions, allowed course participants to exchange knowledge and communicate weekly to reflect on the course's materials.

Although English language levels were uneven among the course's participants, all IUG participants engaged in the weekly virtual discussions according to their ability. The variety of contributions of perspectives on gender and women issues was beneficial to the participants as it offered a chance to confront various cultural assumptions and consider various perspectives and experiences. As the instructor of one of the courses noted, 'there are more frequent synergies of opinion across cultures throughout the course than at the beginning'.

The challenges

The level of English language was uneven among IUG and UniGraz participants, and so sometimes participants struggled to find needed words to present their opinions and perspectives. However, the course instructors played a role in guiding participants to articulate their thoughts. Similarly, the level of competence in the use of technology was uneven among IUG participants, and it took time for them to get used to the Moodle interface and to use it properly.

Different and specific needs (e.g. deadlines for some assignments that came during holidays and religious occasions) arose from the participants, which added pressure on the management team at both universities as they had to communicate with the course instructor and convey their specific needs. Moreover, the technology sometimes failed to work and, as a consequence, the management teams at both universities struggled to implement some of the activities.

The solutions

In the first course of the module, readings reflected different perspectives and there were weekly planned sessions for IUG participants to discuss some of the reading materials. For example, participants whose English language and technology skills were self-assessed as 'good or very good' helped colleagues by illustrating how to use Moodle effectively in addition to summarizing the main points in the articles. It was interesting to observe communication between IUG participants from different academic backgrounds around women and gender issues. Additionally, an Arabic translation of the instructions for some of the unfamiliar assessment activities was provided to facilitate some of the course participants. Moreover, Arabic translations of some of the course materials were located and distributed to those who needed them. The schedule time for submission of assignments in Moodle took into consideration holidays in both countries, and management team members in the two universities were flexible and prepared always to have plans B and C in case something did not go as expected.

The lessons learnt

Reflecting on the experience briefly outlined above, it is clear that online courses that are shared between universities in different countries can be useful tools in the internationalization efforts, provided that they are planned and implemented thoroughly with a clear vision towards outcomes. Participants in the module got a real chance to communicate and interact, which gave them the opportunity to appreciate different cultures, and to express how they feel, and why they feel so. The process of managing such online courses is challenging but enabling, as demonstrated by a SHE-GE Project team whose level of expertise in dealing with the complexities and challenges is on the rise. Professionalism, dedication and flexibility are vital in order to be aware of needs and gaps and to act to redress them. This was demonstrated, for example, by providing IUG course participants with Arabic resources related to the course topics and readings, to complement the materials in English and to allow understanding of the subject and thus active engagement in the activities even by participants less proficient in the English language.

In-depth future research is needed to find answers to questions that were raised throughout this experience, such as the following:

- How beneficial is the multilingual and multicultural online experience in terms of the learning outcomes for participants at the two universities?
- How beneficial is the multilingual and multicultural online experience in terms of minimizing the cultural gap connected to the course's topics?
- How does this kind of learning differ from face-to-face learning?
- What can we improve to fully achieve the learning outcomes of the course?

Conclusion

Universities in the Gaza Strip are struggling to perform their developmental roles, as many restrictions and obstacles face their students and staff with regard to mobility. These have a negative impact on the participation of Gaza's HEIs in the worldwide academe. However, Palestinian institutions of higher education in the Gaza Strip are able to find ways to get connected to the world despite the challenges they experience. As a case in point, procedures towards internationalization at graduate level at IUG focus on the use of the English language and of appropriate online communication technologies. These, together with a culture of strengthening international collaborations, have opened windows for IUG's staff and students for international knowledge exchange in the different disciplines, contributing to IUG's mission to be open to the world and to support future generations who can appreciate different cultures besides their own.

The challenges are still many, and they are dealt with by IUG management through clear policies and procedures. The university's hard work to achieve its mission can be described in connection with two statements from two different faith/culture traditions. The first comes from a Hadith of the Prophet Mohammed (peace be upon him) which says: 'verily actions are by intentions, and for every person what s/he intended'.[7] This Hadith is key to Islamic thought, culture and understanding, highlighting the balance and connection between one's internal and external states. It emphasizes the importance of having an intention for every physical act that we do, and the importance of having a purpose for every action. It also foregrounds the need to become aware of one's intentions. The second statement is the old English proverb, 'where there's a will, there's a way', which means that if someone is determined enough, s/he can find a way to achieve what s/he wants, even if it is very difficult. The Hadith and the old proverb jointly summarize the spirit and attitudes of academia in the Gaza Strip, which have resulted in achievements under the most difficult circumstances.

The central questions that remain are: How long will the current situation last? How will the internationalization experiences of Gaza's universities evolve out of this context in the future? Are the experiences going to assist Palestinian universities authentically in achieving their missions in teaching, research and community service considering protracted siege and occupation? Will these efforts of international collaboration and cooperation continue? No-one currently has an answer to these questions. However, being optimistic is something that characterizes the Palestinian people. As Said (1998: 158) says: 'I have never met a Palestinian who is tired enough of being a Palestinian to give up entirely.'

Appendix 1: English Language Requirements in the Humanities Faculties at IUG

Faculty/ college	Program (MA/PhD)	Language of study	Language of thesis	English proficiency evidence
Arts	(1) Applied Linguistics & Translation (MA)	English	English	The student is required to provide an IELTS score of 6.5 or TOEFL (IBT) 90/TOEFL (PBT) 550
	(2) Arabic Language (PhD)	Arabic	Arabic	The student is required to provide his/her department with a result of English level test.
Education	(1) Education – Curriculum & Instruction (PhD)	Arabic	Arabic	The student is required to provide his/her department with a result of English level test.
Osuol – Al Dine	(1) Osuol Al Dine (PhD)	Arabic	Arabic	The student is required to provide his/her department with a result of English level test.

Appendix 2: English Language Use and Requirements in the Applied Sciences Faculties at IUG

Faculty/ college	Program (MA/PhD)	Language of study	Language of thesis	English proficiency evidence
Science	(1) Mathematics (MA & PhD)	English	English	(1) The student is required to provide an IELTS score of 6 or TOEFL (PBT) 500.
	(2) Physics (MA) (3) Biology & Medical Technology (MA) (4) Chemistry (MA) (5) Environmental Sciences (MA) (6) Biotechnology (MA)	English	English	(2) The student is required to provide his/her department with a result of English level test.
	(7) Crisis & Disaster Management (MA)	English/ Arabic	English/ Arabic	The student is required to provide his/her department with evidence of English proficiency.

(Continued)

Health Sciences	Medical & Laboratory Sciences (MA)	English	English	The student is required to provide his/her department with a result of English level test.
Information Technology	Information Technology (MA)	English	English	The student is required to provide his/her department with evidence of English proficiency.
Nursing	Community Mental Health Nursing (MA)	English	English	The student is expected to have a decent level of English proficiency.
Engineering	(1) Water Technology (PhD)	English	English	The student is required to provide an IELTS score of 6.5 or TOEFL (PBT) 550.
	(2) Electrical Engineering (MA) (3) Architectural Engineering (MA) (4) Computer Engineering (MA) (5) Civil Engineering (MA)			The student is required to provide an IELTS score of 6 or TOEFL (PBT) 500.
Commerce	(1) Business Administration (MA) (2) Accounting & Finance (MA) (3) Development Economics (MA) (4) Regional & International Studies (MA)	English/ Arabic	English/ Arabic	The student is required to provide a TOEFL result of 500 points.

Notes

(1) University colleges offer academic bachelor's and technical diploma degrees. Programs are more technically oriented.
(2) Al-Quds Open University adopts a blended education system that combines the traditional education system and the e-learning system.
(3) Roy (1978) defined de-development as 'a process which undermines or weakens the ability of an economy to grow and expand by preventing it from accessing and utilizing critical inputs needed to promote internal growth beyond a specific structural level'.
(4) It is private but non-profit.
(5) The idea of mirror MA thesis in this project is to have a Wiki platform for students to share research experience between the two countries and cultures. One student from each university will work on the same umbrella theme, but with a supervisor from their home university, perhaps from a different disciplinary background and/or with a different methodology.

(6) ECTS is a European Credit Transfer and Accumulation System. It is designed to make it easier for students to move between different countries.
(7) 40 Hadith Nawawi. English translation, Hadith 1 (https://sunnah.com/nawawi40/1).

References

Abu-Lughod, I. (2000) *Palestinian Higher Education: National Identity, Liberation, and Globalization*. Durham, NC: Duke University Press.

Bahour, S. (2016) Palestinian universities on the frontline. See https://epalestine.blogspot.com/2016/10/palestinian-universities-on-frontline.html (accessed 14 April 2019).

Cambridge Online Dictionary (n.d.) See https://dictionary.cambridge.org/dictionary/english/ (accessed 17 May 2019).

Connell, R. and Pearse, R. (2015) *Gender: In World Perspective* (3rd edn). Cambridge: Polity Press.

Cundiff, J.L. and Vescio, T.K. (2016) Gender stereotypes influence how people explain gender disparities in the workplace. *Sex Roles* 75 (3–4), 126–138.

De Wit, H., Hunter, F., Howard, L. and Egron-Polak, E. (2015) Internationalisation of higher education: A study for the European Parliament. See https://www.europarl.europa.eu/RegData/etudes/STUD/2015/540370/IPOL_STU%282015%29540370_EN.pdf (accessed 19 July 2019).

Dillenbourg, P. (1999) What do you mean by collaborative learning? In P. Dillenbourg (ed.) *Collaborative Learning: Cognitive and Computational Approaches* (pp. 1–19). Oxford: Elsevier.

Fassetta, G., Imperiale, M.G., Frimberger, K., Attia, M. and Al-Masri, N. (2017) Online teacher training in a context of forced immobility: The case of Gaza, Palestine. *European Education* 49 (2–3), 133–150.

Gonzalez, R.G. (2017) Internationalization at a German university: The purpose and paradoxes of English language Master's and Doctoral programs. *International Education Journal: Comparative Perspectives* 16 (2), 49–62.

Hoang, L., Tran, L.T. and Pham, H.H. (2018) Vietnamese government policies and practices in internationalisation of higher education. In L. Tran and S. Marginson (eds) *Internationalisation in Vietnamese Higher Education* (pp. 19–42). New York: Springer.

IAU (International Association of Universities) (2019) Internationalization. See https://www.iau-aiu.net/Internationalization (accessed 15 October 2019).

Imperiale, M.G., Phipps, A., Al-Masri, N. and Fassetta, G. (2017) Pedagogies of hope and resistance: English language education in the context of the Gaza Strip, Palestine. In E.J. Erling (ed.) *English across the Fracture Lines* (pp. 31–38). London: British Council.

IUG (2017a) *Graduate and Research Deanship Report*. Gaza: Islamic University of Gaza.

IUG (2017b) Strengthening Higher Education Capacities in Palestine for Gender Equality (SHE-GE). Project funded by APPEAR. See http://shege.iugaza.edu.ps (accessed 3 June 2019).

IUG (2018a) About IUG. See http://www.iugaza.edu.ps/en/About-IUG (accessed 15 December 2019).

IUG (2018b) About international relations. See http://exrelation.iugaza.edu.ps/en/External-Relations/International-Relations/About (accessed 15 December 2019).

Jebril, M.A. (2018) Academic life under occupation: The impact on educationalists at Gaza's universities. Doctoral thesis, University of Cambridge. See https://doi.org/10.17863/CAM.18900 (accessed 19 December 2019).

Knight, J. (2004) Internationalization remodeled: Definition, approaches, and rationales. *Journal of Studies in International Education* 8 (1), 5–31.

Lauridsen, K.M. and Lillemose, M.K. (eds) (2015) Opportunities and challenges in the multilingual and multicultural learning space. Final document of the IntlUni Erasmus Academic Network project 2012–15. See http://intluni.eu/uploads/media/The_opportunities_and_challenges_of_the_MMLS_Final_report_sept_2015.pdf (accessed 15 May 2019).

McCloud, T. (2015) Multilingual and multicultural identity exploration. Honors College Thesis 11, University of Massachusetts Boston.

MoEHE (2017) *Higher Education Statistical Yearbook 2016/2017*. Ramallah, Palestine: Ministry of Education and Higher Education. See http://www.mohe.pna.ps/services/statistics (accessed 25 May 2019).

MoEHE (2018) Higher education system. See http://www.mohe.pna.ps/moehe/ministerialsystemsandregulations; http://www.mohe.pna.ps/Higher-Education-/Higher-Education-System (3 April 2019).

Moughrabi, F. (2015) Palestinian universities under siege. *International Higher Education* 36, 8–9. See https://ejournals.bc.edu/ojs/index.php/ihe/article/viewFile/7435/6632 (accessed 15 March 2019).

Renc-Roe, J. and Roxå, T. (2014) The internationalisation of a university as local practices: A case study. *Education Inquiry* 5 (1), 24048.

Roy, S. (1978) The Gaza Strip: A case of economic de-development. *Journal of Palestine Studies* 17 (1), 56–88.

Saffarini, G. (2010) Higher education and research in Palestine. Paper presented at the 2nd EMUNI Research Souk, Euro-Mediterranean Student Research Multi-Conference on *Living Together in the Multi-Cultured Society*. An-Najah National University, Nablus, Palestine, 14 June.

Said, E.W. (1998) *After the Last Sky: Palestinian Lives*. New York: Columbia University Press.

Sanders, J.S. (2019) National internationalisation of higher education policy in Singapore and Japan: Context and competition. *Compare: A Journal of Comparative and International Education* 49 (3), 413–429.

Shahijan, M.K., Rezaei, S. and Preece, C.N. (2016) Developing a framework of internationalisation for higher education institutions in Malaysia: A SWOT analysis. *International Journal of Management in Education* 10 (2), 145–173.

Zhang, Z. (2018) English-medium instruction policies in China: Internationalisation of higher education. *Journal of Multilingual and Multicultural Development* 39 (6), 542–555.

3 Exploring Mobile Support for English Language Teachers in a Context of Conflict: Syrian Refugee Teachers in Jordan

Gary Motteram, Nazmi Al-Masri, Heba Hamouda and Shaiffadzillah Omarali

Introduction

This chapter illustrates and discusses the experience of collaborating across borders during the *Supporting and Developing Teachers in Contexts of Conflict and Disturbance* (SDTCCD) Project, funded by the UK's Economic & Social Research Council (ESRC). The project drew on expertise in transformative online education (Motteram, 2017; Motteram *et al.*, 2006, 2007) developed at the University of Manchester (UoM) and on the expertise of the Islamic University of Gaza (IUG) and UNRWA schools[1] in Palestine, which had developed pedagogical and technical skills to provide quality education services to Palestinian refugee teachers and children in a context of war, blockade and conflict (UNRWA, n.d.). The collaboration drew from the skill sets of both partners to identify the needs of Syrian English language teachers and trainers working in Jordanian refugee camps and to design and test materials for distance and mobile language learning. It was anticipated that the project partners could offer complementary skills, knowledge and practices in relation to language, pedagogy, technology and online learning in situations of protracted crisis.

The SDTCCD Project had been planned to include three exploratory field visits to Syrian refugee camps in Jordan, to help achieve the purpose of the project. The plan had anticipated that, alongside other expertise, the IUG partners would also provide bilingual language support

(Arabic-English) to the UoM team. However, despite every effort made to overcome travel restrictions imposed by the blockade on mobility from and to Gaza, none of the IUG team was able to visit Jordan during the running of the project. As a consequence, online collaboration became a central feature of the project, as the content of the project itself, but also as the means to ensure effective teamwork in the absence of opportunities for face-to-face meetings.

Over the course of one year (from January to December 2017), the SDTCCD Project investigated ways of translating knowledge about online educational practices developed in UK higher education contexts and at IUG into practices for the new domain of a refugee camp. It also looked at ways to make best use of digital technologies to support English language teacher development in contexts of conflict and disturbance. The communication tools used for the project and for the teamwork were Skype, email and WhatsApp. These brought together the Syrian teachers with colleagues from the British Council in Jordan, IUG (Palestine) and the UoM (UK) to collaboratively identify and produce relevant pedagogic materials that would be useful for the Syrian language teachers and also for groups of teachers working in other in fragile and conflict-affected countries. This chapter thus presents two interlinking narratives: that of the ongoing project with the Syrian teachers and trainers on the one hand and, on the other, the technological methods employed to get around the fact that the IUG team were not able to visit Jordan in person and meet the Syrian teachers.

In the next section we explore more of the background context in which the SDTCCD Project took place, before describing the dynamic collaborations of the group as they worked with mobile technology, as one possible solution to some of the issues of access and sustainability they were encountering. Into this we interweave the ways in which the IUG partners contributed to the project as co-creators of the materials developed and as cultural and linguistic mediators (Arabic-English).

The Syrian Refugee Crisis

The UN High Commissioner for Refugees, Filippo Grandi, has stated that 'Syria is the biggest humanitarian and refugee crisis of our time, a continuing cause of suffering for millions which should be garnering a groundswell of support around the world' (Grandi, 2016, para. 2). Since the war began in Syria in 2011, over 6.6 million Syrians have been internally displaced and over 5.6 million people have fled Syria seeking refuge and safety, mainly in Jordan, Turkey and Lebanon (UNHCR, 2018).

The Jordan Response Plan for the Syria Crisis (JRPSC) 2018–2020 showed that 'Jordan currently hosts more than 1.3 million Syrians, including 655 thousand registered refugees' (JRPSC, 2018: 7), and that they face challenges in several areas, including education, health, housing, water and electricity supply. The plan underlined multifaceted collaboration strategies to handle the challenges related to education services offered to Syrian refugee children, and noted that:

> Overall Syrian refugee students, particularly those living in camps, are performing well below the national average. Syrian refugees have specific challenges related to access to formal education, which is often linked to the lack of recognition of prior learning and financial vulnerabilities that might lead to child labor and child marriage. Furthermore, distance from school, poor learning environments, insufficient and underqualified teachers, inadequate teacher training, and outdated curriculum and pedagogy also contribute to the risk of drop-out. (JRPSC, 2018: 21)

One of the ways of meeting the needs of Syrian refugee children is to enhance the skills of Syrian language teachers and trainers working in refugee camps in Jordan. The SDTCCD Project discussed in this chapter focused on a refugee camp in Jordan (henceforth 'the camp'), and drew on existing expertise in relation to education in situations of protracted crisis in order to develop the competence of Syrian language teachers.

An area of priority in the camps is that young adults who are no longer in school (if they have been in school) need to develop skills to succeed in education, to work and to strengthen resilience and hope, or simply to improve their livelihood and wellbeing, as will be detailed below. A second priority area is the provision of support for younger children who are not coping with the education provided in formal schools that are run by the Jordanian authorities, hence the focus on 'informal schools' as they are locally known (see discussion below). A further challenge is the employment of underqualified teachers who are inadequately trained, which is an issue highlighted by some teachers in refugee camp schools who said that 'they did not receive any teacher training, and only had to show they had graduated from university' (Human Rights Watch, 2016).

A review of effective practices and interventions that promote quality education and wellbeing in conflict and post-crisis contexts emphasizes '[investment] in research on mobile learning and teaching platforms' (Burde *et al.*, 2015) as one of its priority recommendations. Given the shortage of resources and opportunities in the refugee camp we worked in, we wanted to explore whether mobile learning, supported at a distance via social media tools like WhatsApp, might be a viable solution for teachers in the camp.

Education in Jordanian Refugee Camps

In the camp, two school systems operate side by side: the formal schools run by the Jordanian education authorities and the informal schools run by refugee teachers. The formal schools are a version of the Jordanian school system and are taught by Jordanian teachers. The teachers enter the camps in the same way in which the UoM academic did – through the security gates. They might live locally or come in from Amman every day with other NGO workers. These schools follow the Jordanian national curriculum, and the children who want to go on into further or higher education need to pass the Tawjihi, a high-stakes, end-of-school examination that is considered tough even for Jordanian children. As with so many education systems in the world, English plays a significant role in the passing of the Tawjihi. The informal schools attempt to fill the gaps for the Syrian children between where they are and where the Jordanian system expects them to be. This gap is considerable in most cases, as the Syrian children have missed a lot of schooling even before they arrive in the camp. The gap is not just in English language, but in all subjects. The informal schools run in the opposite half of the day to the formal schools. The boys go to the Jordanian schools in the morning and the informal schools in the afternoon. Teachers and students use Jordanian textbooks in the formal schools, but the Syrian teachers in the informal schools do not have access to textbooks, nor would they be allowed to use them even if they did. They are expected to create their own materials as best as they can.

At the time of the SDTCCD Project, new materials for the teaching of English had recently been developed through a cooperative effort between a number of charities and some of the teachers who work in refugee camps. However, none of the teachers that we were working with had collaborated in drafting these materials. These materials were comprehensive in that they covered all of the levels of the English language curriculum, but there were only enough copies for the Syrian teachers to use them as reference books for lesson planning; there were no class sets. At the time of the final visit, the main resource from these materials that the Syrian teachers used was the flash cards, which they said they found helpful.

The Importance of English Language Proficiency for Syrian Refugees

While most humanitarian institutions focus on providing refugees with three basic survival needs (food, shelter and health), Machel (2001) explored the importance of offering education as the fourth focus of humanitarian aid. The right to education for Syrian refugees has also been emphasized in the three *JRPSC* (2015, 2016–2018 and 2018–2020) by the Jordan Ministry of Planning and International Cooperation, which discuss education as a main priority, especially for Syrian refugee children, who represent 51% of the refugee population in Jordan (UNHCR, 2016). As Alexander *et al.* (2010) note, the role of education is fundamental to building hope for refugee children and young people, and also for their families and communities.

Offering refugee children and youth quality foreign language programmes is one of the skills that might give them access to further and higher education both in Jordan, which is partially English medium (Alhababha *et al.*, 2016), but also outside Jordan. The SDTCCD Project was attached to the British Council's LASER Project,[2] whose aim was to provide refugees with sufficient English language skills to access higher education in Jordan and online courses run in English from a variety of countries (e.g. India, the UK and the USA). This, it was hoped, would open opportunities for refugees to go on to study further in Europe, Canada or the USA.

Learning other languages can also strengthen resilience and hope and potentially creates more opportunities for employment and a better life for communities in contexts of conflict and emergency. The fact that the people we worked with spoke English meant that they had day-to-day employment. In addition, proficiency in a range of foreign languages enables refugee children to tell their story multilingually outside the camps, and allows them to enhance their intercultural understanding (Capstick & Delaney, 2017) by expanding their opportunities for interaction.

Mobile Technologies and Education in Refugee Camps

Due to the steep increase in the numbers of forcibly displaced people, initiatives focusing on educating and training refugees and asylum seekers are currently taking place worldwide. Moreover, a number of studies show that mobile technologies can provide sustainable multi-purpose support to people in contexts of emergencies and crisis, especially in relation to education, psychosocial support, humanitarian services, communication and increased cultural awareness (e.g. Bachore, 2015; Brinkerhoff, 2009; Charitonos & Kukulska-Hulme, 2017; Harney, 2013; Jungbluth, 2017; Kukulska-Hulme *et al.*, 2015; Thompson, 2009; Vernon *et al.*, 2016). Hannides *et al.* (2016) suggest that mobile connectivity alone can provide refugees with psychosocial support so that they feel less vulnerable and can be more resilient. UNHCR (2016) reveal that mobile connectivity is critical to refugees' safety and security and for keeping in touch with loved ones in the isolation of camp life (see also Xu & Maitland, 2015). Wall *et al.* (2015: 13) assert that for transnational populations, such as Syrian refugees, mobile phones potentially enable 'social and economic networks to remain strong, be repaired, or developed anew'.

Charitonos (2018) reports on several events and projects that explore the central role of digital and mobile technology in educating displaced populations, such as the British Open University Project 'Citizenship and Governance SRA' (see http://www.open.ac.uk/research/themes/citizenship-governance) and the British Council Project on 'Mobile Pedagogy for

English Language Teaching' (see https://englishagenda.britishcouncil.org/research-publications/research-papers/mobile-pedagogy-english-language-teaching-guide-teachers). One of these projects is the Teachers for Teachers initiative, launched in Kakuma Refugee Camp, Kenya (2015–2017), which supported refugee teachers through offering them on-site and online tailored training to improve teaching and learning in the camp. This project used online coaching and mobile mentoring through WhatsApp. One of the major outcomes of this project is the creation of six sets of open-source training materials for primary school teachers in crisis contexts, including *Mobile Mentoring for Primary School Teachers in Crisis Contexts* (see http://www.tc.columbia.edu/refugeeeducation/resources/).

The Project

Data and aim

The SDTCCD Project used observation, interviews (through online tools and in person) and archival research to identify the needs of English language teachers in a Syrian refugee camp and to explore possible solutions using mobile tools. Alongside this, the project also carried out a desk-based review of the available literature, collected field notes made during three week-long visits to Jordan by the UoM team, and kept a record of emails, Skype meetings and online conversations made using WhatsApp. The project meetings included teachers and international humanitarian staff working in the camp, as well as teacher trainers working for the British Council in Jordan (from the LASER Project – see above). Smaller meetings of the project team were also held regularly and recorded.

The project looked at the interaction between four linked communities: the teachers who work in the refugee camp in the informal schools with school-aged pupils; the trainers[3] who work with youths and young adults in vocational education; the NGOs they work for, or which manage the teaching activity; and the research team based at IUG and UoM. There were 27 Syrian teachers/trainers, four NGOs, and two teams of two people at each university.

By drawing on the complementary knowledge, skills and experience of the IUG and UoM members of the team, the SDTCCD Project wished to explore the feasibility of creating a model of mobile teacher education that could be used in a wide range of contexts to supply training and/or materials for different teacher groups, but primarily for those who work in places that are hard to reach. The study worked specifically with the 27 English language teachers/trainers, who were selected to follow a language and pedagogy training course run in the refugee camp.

The site could have potentially been anywhere, but the British Council in Jordan, who facilitated our access to the teachers, were planning to run a face-to-face training course on behalf of a number of NGOs, and the camp offered us the limited access conditions we were looking for. We could have picked a less challenging context in which to run the process, e.g. refugee groups living and working in Amman, but we did not believe that this would help us to get a clear understanding of the difficulties involved.

Accessing the refugee camp: Challenges and solutions

We had been warned that wireless internet access in the camp would be limited and previous studies had also highlighted this issue (Xu & Maitland, 2015). As a potential solution, we had prepared materials that could be used offline, while hoping to maintain contact with the teachers via a mobile tool like WhatsApp (which uses low bandwidth) and through personal visits, although a key goal was to set up a process where visits would ultimately not be necessary. In order for a project like this to be scalable and sustainable in the future, it needs to confront the reality of the situation that teachers working in refugee camps face and make use of distance learning models. We had made contact with a small start-up company based in the Middle East (Ustad Mobile) who had created an Android-based mobile app that was a delivery shell for materials authored using a variety of open source tools. This fitted in with one feature of our model, namely making it possible for anyone to use our materials development pathway at a later stage. Our aim was to work with this particular teacher community to discover their needs and then to use this information to source relevant materials for English language teaching. We were also hoping that this would be a collaborative and joint process to which the teachers would contribute, and that we would not simply 'supply' a course to them.

There is a considerable wider political dimension to what we were trying to achieve. The Jordanian government are keen to make sure that this particular community stays where it is (i.e. in refugee camps) and then goes back across the border to resume their lives at some point. As the Zaatari Camp Management Council (2017: 11) note: 'The Jordanian government does not want to allow the establishment of permanent schools as it would give the impression that the camp is more of a permanent settlement rather than a temporary placement.' This approach is also part of the wider regional strategy to keep Syrians in the region rather than having them travel onwards to Europe or further afield (Achilli, 2015). These policies seem to be in line with what the vast majority of Syrians also desire since, according to research conducted by Bubbers (2016), 85% of 2200 Syrian families interviewed in Jordan and Lebanon said they yearn for their homeland and would return within six months once the war ends. However, with the continuing lack of security in the region it is possible that these views may have changed, and most of the teachers who were engaged in the SDTCCD Project – those with whom we are still in contact – are still in the refugee camp.

Crossing boundaries and barriers – both physically and virtually – was a key feature of the project. This refugee camp is often described as a 'makeshift city in the desert' (Bulos, 2014) and the 'fourth-largest city in Jordan' (Lee, 2018), and while it is set up to provide humanitarian relief for Syrian refugees, it is also tightly controlled by the Jordanian authorities. There is a fear that radical elements may be living in the camps and internet access is tightly controlled (see below) to try to prevent any external radicalization of the community (Turner, 2015). Outsiders require permits to get in and out and move around the camp, and this process mirrored the situation for colleagues at IUG who, despite great efforts by the team, were not able to leave Gaza as, during the lifetime of the project, Gaza was closed for exit and entry. However, through mobile communication during the field visits to the camp, the team members who were able to visit the camp sent regular updates via mobile devices, and there were regular discussions among the team using online and mobile technologies.

The teachers' views and practices

The first face-to-face focus group was run during Visit 1 (April 2017) by the UoM team member who was able to visit Jordan. The focus group discussed with the teachers the following topics: what makes a good teacher; how people learn languages; learning independence; and classroom management. Possible topics had been identified during online discussions by the whole project team prior to the visits and were honed further during the actual visits. The UoM team member who travelled to Jordan kept in regular contact with IUG team members and the other member of the Manchester team via WhatsApp, email and Skype, and the whole team worked on the protocols for the focus groups via these internet-based tools.

Discussing what makes a good teacher allowed the Syrian teacher group to reveal some of their attitudes towards teaching, to show their knowledge of language teaching terminology and to discuss ideas about their practice. Talking about language demonstrated their knowledge about the importance of language learning and about how languages are learned. Discussing independent learning enabled them to talk about how they viewed the learner and the learner's role in the learning process. Conversations on classroom management revealed their practices as teachers and their methods of engagement with teaching and the students; it also helped to highlight some of the areas that they were interested in working on, topics that were important to them in their context. The focus groups were also important ways to start getting to know each other and to establish a rapport and these conversation points seemed like a good place to start as they were of relevance to everyone concerned. Discussions were conducted in pairs in Arabic and English, but all summaries were presented in English as the UoM researcher was not bilingual.

Throughout the project we looked at ways in which we might get around the fact that IUG team members could not leave Gaza. Arabic was sometimes used in the WhatsApp group chats with the teachers as a support language, although the English teachers did not really need Arabic since their English proficiency was very good. The use of WhatsApp, or other similar forms of digital communication, would have been beneficial while visiting the camp as it would have offered a form of language support with administrative staff who are not so proficient in English. However, internet and phone access while in the camp was very limited. The team also tried to find ways of making Skype work, but the internet connection was not stable enough for regular video conferencing. We did manage one Skype discussion during the last camp visit, during which an IUG team leader spoke in Arabic to the trainers who worked for an NGO, which the trainers really appreciated. We also spent a long time trying to persuade the other NGO – who managed the English teachers – to allow us to use Skype meetings with the teachers for development sessions. However, we were not successful in persuading them that this was a good idea. The NGO appeared only to want to continue working with Skype with students and not with teachers. This may have been because of a lack of time on the teachers' part, or it may simply have been that they did not believe that Skype-based training was a good way forward. Despite asking, however, a clear reason was never given.

The needs analysis that was conducted in the early stages of the project revealed a number of topics that also came up in the online discussions on WhatsApp and during the focus groups. As can be seen in Figure 3.1, lack of resources was the top concern, followed by lack of appropriate facilities and class size.

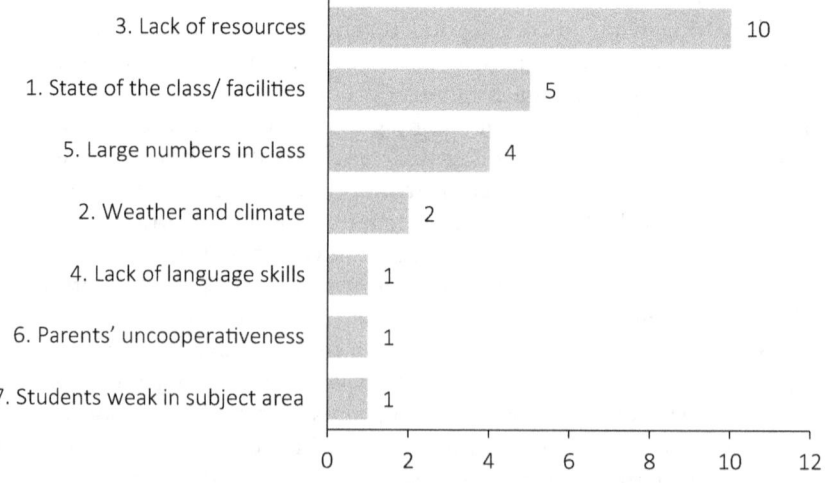

Figure 3.1 Data from initial needs analysis conducted by the project team

However, class observations showed that the language teachers made good use of the limited resources they had, and we never observed classes with more than 30 students. There were no textbooks for the children in the sense that there were no class sets of books, and the teachers relied mostly on using a blackboard/whiteboard as the focus of the lesson. As noted above, however, during the last visit in August, a new primary level English language course was provided by the NGO they worked for, and the teachers made good use of the new flash cards that had become available to them.

Because all the teachers had access to mobile phones (although not all had smartphones), when they had access to online data, which varied, they could download materials from the internet and make use of some of these in the classroom. Two teachers used mobile phones to play English songs for the children, chosen because they were related to the curriculum areas. By many standards, these classes could have been seen as well equipped, particularly for the younger children. However, the online discussion shown in Table 3.1 gives a more nuanced view of what resources are needed (we report these conversations exactly as they were typed in the WhatsApp group and we have not made any corrections to the language).

The issue of differentiation of teaching and materials to respond to a wide range of levels in each class was one that was raised very frequently. While the outside observer might see a well conducted and organized lesson with a reasonable level of resources, the teachers' insights provide a much more nuanced picture. T1 is concerned with the issue of how to manage lower level learners without disadvantaging the higher level learners. T2 asks how we might assess levels of proficiency during the running of the class, and then goes on to propose the idea of multilevel textbooks. This highlighted the teachers' awareness of the specific needs of their context and allowed us to understand more about the needs for resources than was obvious from the observations we made which had actually surprised us in the resources that appeared to be available.

Table 3.1 Lack of resources to differentiate within classes

04 May 2017	18:56	T1	I have many levels in one class .how I can help the weak students with out effect the good students
04 May 2017	19:11	T2	I think we need more than one way to deal with that problem.
04 May 2017	19:24	T2	We need an active way to classify students in the class
07 June 2017	14:49	T2	Right .mutli- level classes need muti- level books
07 June 2017	15:00	T2	In fact Ido that but I need higher level books cos they can help my

The Project's Outcomes

The combination of data sets, needs analysis, discussions about teaching and discussions via WhatsApp informed the project team's decision on the teaching materials to be included in the Ustad Mobile app. The project had been designed to include the teachers further in the materials development process, but during Visit 2 in June 2017 the UoM team only managed to access the camp on one day. This was because the permit to visit the camp had been delayed due to the Ramadan holidays, when the relevant authorities were unavailable. This meant that the permit did not arrive until the very end of the team's visit, shrinking the meeting with the teachers to a single day.

Despite not being able to get to the camp, the SDTCCD team, including IUG's members, were able to continue to communicate via WhatsApp and to use a lesson plan drawn up by one of the Syrian teachers with feedback and suggestions from other colleagues. Since lesson planning and lesson management were identified as important areas for training and professional development, the sample lesson plan was produced by one of the Syrian language teachers following a WhatsApp discussion about storytelling. The teacher's lesson plan was complemented by teaching materials provided by colleagues at IUG. These were existing resources, and the SDTCCD team worked jointly to adapt them to suit the needs of the Syrian language teachers. Together with the lesson plan, the materials became one of the example lessons in the mobile course that was run on the Ustad Mobile app. Further language teaching materials tailored for the development of reading, listening and speaking skills in challenging situations were provided by the IUG team, who were able to make this contribution through ongoing communication via various online tools. The project representative from the UNRWA schools was able to make a video of a language class which was included in the mobile course, demonstrating how, although not able to exit Gaza, the Palestinian team members could still make a significant contribution to the project.

The Challenges

As may be gathered from the account of the SDTCCD Project made so far, this was a difficult project to run, for several reasons. It had been built on the basis that there would be access to experts from IUG who would be bilingual and who would also be able to offer expertise in working with refugees, thus aiding the Manchester team with their practical knowledge and insights. Because the IUG representative was unable to leave Gaza, interactions with the trainers, teachers and NGOs (run mostly by Arabic speakers on the ground) were quite difficult, as there were significant language and cultural issues which the IUG partner could have bridged. Using the internet for connectivity to solve some of the challenges faced through remote collaboration was also not available in the ways that we had anticipated. We had indeed been warned that this might prove difficult, but it would have been possible to achieve a lot more if the NGO working with the English teachers had allowed us access to the internet while in the informal school and, upon our return to the UK, had allowed us to use Skype to carry on our collaboration with the teachers. The UoM representative did maintain regular communication with colleagues at IUG and Manchester while staying in Jordan, but only after he had left the camp. The project would have been very different had both IUG and UoM representatives been able to be in Jordan at the same time. Despite this, the SDTCCD team were able to communicate online with the teachers in the camps after visits and to keep regular contact going for nine months. We did manage to work together to produce teacher development materials that can be accessed via the mobile app Ustad Mobile, and these materials are now being used by the 'Developing Language Teacher Quality and Resilience in Fragile Contexts through Inquiry-led Practice' Project in sub-Saharan Africa, funded through the Global Challenges Research Fund (GCRF) scheme of the UK Research and Innovation (UKRI) agency.

Conclusion

The project we have discussed here faced challenges arising from the bureaucratic barriers that are part of accessing any system that is trying to protect itself from outsiders and, at the same time, from the besieged state that is the reality for the colleagues at IUG. We attempted to overcome at least some of these barriers to ensure collaboration but, even though the Jordanian government issued visit permits, the political context in Gaza prevented the Palestinian team from meeting with colleagues and research participants in person. Despite this, IUG's researchers were able to work online with their British partners and with the Syrian teachers in the camp using the internet-based communication tools described throughout this chapter. Through online collaboration, IUG was able to exchange ideas and insights related to English language pedagogy in challenging circumstances and to the use of mobile technologies for learning. They were also able to provide linguistic support and English-Arabic translations on a number of occasions.

The study showed that teachers in the camp need support through the development of tailored practices for the specific context, such as making more use of differentiated learning. It also showed that mobile technologies could be effectively used to support language teachers, provided that there is a relaxation of the restrictions that prevent the teachers from accessing the internet at home, or that NGOs are allowed to give teachers access to the internet while they are in the informal school. Some of the teachers contributed to the creation of materials that were produced as a part of the project and, as mentioned above, we have continued working on the materials with other teacher groups.

The study has also shown that teaching and learning English is clearly being taken seriously in the camp as a vital means to pass and achieve a high score in the Tawjihi exam, thus enabling refugee learners to have access to Jordanian and other higher education institutions. Moreover, English proficiency can strengthen resilience and hope and create more opportunities for employment and a better life for communities in contexts of conflict and emergency, as is highlighted by several studies (e.g. Alhabahba *et al.*, 2016; Capstick & Delaney, 2017; Charitonos & Kukulska-Hulme, 2017).

A future project could build on the good relations that were established with the NGOs and the teachers in the course of the SDTCCD project to further develop the practices that were established. Ensuring that the teachers in the camps have access to a high-quality mobile-based internet connection and enabling them to take a more significant role in the development of the materials would be a very positive way forward. This would allow the cascading of knowledge and expertise to other teachers working in similar circumstances, ensuring that materials and approaches are tailored for the specific challenges they face.

Despite the impossibility of travelling imposed by the blockade, the IUG team were able to contribute to research instrument design and data analysis. They also made a significant contribution to the final materials that were made available through the Ustad Mobile app, a key output of the SDTCCD project. While we hope that in the future people in the Gaza Strip will be able to travel and be involved in projects worldwide in person, while the blockade lasts, reliable connectivity could also allow the IUG team to visit the camp virtually. This would ensure that they can play an even more significant role in a project of this type and in other projects elsewhere in the world for which their extensive expertise in dealing with prolonged situations of crisis can be invaluable.

Notes

(1) The United Nations Relief and Works Agency for Palestine Refugees in the Near East (UNRWA) is a relief and human development agency which in the Gaza Strip alone operates 274 schools (2018–2019), serving 278,991 students.
(2) See https://syria.britishcouncil.org/en/laser.
(3) The course that was set up and run by the British Council had a mixed community. It drew from four different NGOs. The two biggest groups were teachers in the informal schools who we focus on here, but there were also a significant number of trainers who were mostly attending the course to learn English. This was a pre-organized community and we were not in a position to make any changes; we had to take what was on offer.

References

Achilli, L. (2015) Syrian refugees in Jordan: A reality check. Migration Policy Centre Policy Brief 2015/02. See http://cadmus.eui.eu/handle/1814/34904 (accessed 8 January 2019).

Alexander, J., Boothby, N. and Wessells, M. (2010) Education and protection of children and youth affected by armed conflict: An essential link. See http://www.cpcnetwork.org/wp-content/uploads/2017/03/Alexander-Boothby-Wessells-Education-and-Protection-of-Children-and-Youth.pdf (accessed 19 July 2019).

Alhabahba, M.M., Pandian, A., Mahfoodh, O.H.A. and Gritter, K. (2016) English language education in Jordan: Some recent trends and challenges. *Cogent Education* 3 (1), 1–14.

Bachore, M.M. (2015) Language learning through mobile technologies: An opportunity for language learners and teachers. *Journal of Education and Practice* 6 (31), 50–53.

Brinkerhoff, J. (2009) *Digital Diasporas*. Cambridge: Cambridge University Press.

Bubbers, J. (2016) How language can enhance the resilience of Syrian refugees and host communities. *World Bank Blog Post*, 26 September. See http://blogs.worldbank.org/arabvoices/how-language-can-enhance-resilience-syrian-refugees (accessed 18 May 2019).

Bulos, N. (2014) At Zaatari refugee camp, Syrians build a makeshift city in the desert. *Los Angeles Times*, 1 March. See http://www.latimes.com/world/middleeast/la-fg-jordan-camp-20140301-story.html (accessed 24 March 2019).

Burde, D., Guven, O., Kelcey, J., Lahmann, H. and Al-Abbadi, K. (2015) *What Works to Promote Children's Educational Access, Quality of Learning, and Wellbeing in Crisis-affected Contexts*. Education Rigorous Literature Review. London: Department for International Development.

Capstick, T. and Delaney, M. (2017) *Language for Resilience: The Role of Language in Enhancing the Resilience of Syrian Refugees and Host Communities*. London: British Council. See https://www.britishcouncil.org/sites/default/files/language_for_resilience_-_cross-disciplinary_perspectives_0.pdf (accessed 19 July 2018).

Charitonos, K. (2018) Technology-enabled language learning for refugees and migrants. See http://www.open.ac.uk/ikd/blog/inclusive-innovation-and-development/technology-enabled-language-learning-refugees-and-migrants# (accessed 14 April 2019).

Charitonos, K. and Kukulska-Hulme, A. (2017) Community-based interventions for language learning among refugees and migrants. In *Refugees and HCI Workshop: The Role of HCI in Responding to the Refugee Crisis. Proceedings of the 8th International Conference on Communities and Technologies*, Troyes, France, 26–30 June.

Grandi, F. (2016) UNHCR press release. Syria conflict at 5 years: The biggest refugee and displacement crisis of our time demands a huge surge in solidarity. See http://www.unhcr.org/afr/news/press/2016/3/56e6e3249/syria-conflict-5-years-biggest-refugee-displacement-crisis-time-demands.html (accessed 16 June 2018).

Hannides, T., Bailey, N. and Kaoukji, D. (2016) Voices of refugees: Information and communication needs of refugees in Greece and Germany. *BBC Media Action*. See http://downloads.bbc.co.uk/mediaaction/pdf/research/voices-of-refugees-research-report.pdf (accessed 21 February 2019).

Harney, N. (2013) Precarity, affect and problem solving with mobile phones by asylum seekers: Refugees and migrants in Naples, Italy. *Journal of Refugee Studies* 26 (4), 541–557.

Human Rights Watch (2016) World report 2016. See https://www.hrw.org/world-report/2016 (accessed 19 July 2019).

JRPSC (2015) See https://www.undp.org/content/dam/jordan/docs/Publications/JRP+Final+Draft+2014.12.17.pdf (accessed 30 April 2020).

JRPSC (2016–2018) See https://reliefweb.int/sites/reliefweb.int/files/resources/JRP16_18_Document-final+draft.pdf (accessed 30 April 2020).

JRPSC (2018–2020) See https://lawsdocbox.com/Immigration/77915975-Jordan-response-plan-for-the-syria-crisis.html (accessed 11 December 2019).

Jungbluth, S. (2017) 'Smartphone refugees': Mobility, power regimes, and the impact of digital technologies. Master's thesis, University of Tampere.

Kukulska-Hulme, A., Norris, L. and Donohue, J. (2015) Mobile pedagogy for English language teaching: A guide for teachers. ELT Research Paper 14.07. London: British Council.

Lee, J. (2018) Syria's war: Inside Jordan's Zaatari refugee camp. *Al Jazeera*, 1 April. See https://www.aljazeera.com/indepth/inpictures/syria-war-jordan-zaatari-refugee-camp-180326115809170.html (accessed 12 December 2019).

Machel, G. (2001) *The Impact of War on Children: A Review of Progress since the 1996 United Nations Report on the Impact of Armed Conflict on Children*. Paris: UNESCO.

Motteram, G. (2017) Distance teacher education. In *The TESOL Encyclopedia of English Language Teaching*. TESOL and Wiley International.

Motteram, G., Forrester, G. and Bangxiang, L. (2006) Transforming Chinese teachers' thinking, learning and understanding via e-learning. *Journal of Education for Teaching* 32 (2), 197–212.

Motteram, G., Forrester, G., Goldrick, G. and McLachlan, A. (2007) Collaborating across boundaries: Managing the complexities of e-learning courseware production in a joint international project. In H. Spencer-Oatey (ed.) *e-Learning Initiatives in China: Sino-UK Perspectives on Policy, Pedagogy and Collaborative Design*. Hong Kong: Hong Kong University Press.

Thompson, E. (2009) Mobile phones, communities and social networks among foreign workers in Singapore. *Global Networks* 9 (3), 359–380.

Turner, L. (2015) Explaining the (non-)encampment of Syrian refugees: Security, class and the labour market in Lebanon and Jordan. *Mediterranean Politics* 20 (3), 386–404.

UNHCR (2016) Global trends: Forced displacement in 2016. See http://www.unhcr.org/globaltrends2016/ (accessed 19 December 2018).

UNHCR (2018) Syria emergency. See http://www.unhcr.org/syria-emergency.html (accessed 13 June 2018).

UNRWA (n.d.) Education in the Gaza Strip. See https://www.unrwa.org/activity/education-gaza-strip (accessed 26 October 2019).

Vernon, A., Deriche, K. and Eisenhauer, S. (2016) *Connecting Refugees: How Internet and Mobile Connectivity Can Improve Refugee Well-Being and Transform Humanitarian Action*. Geneva: UNHCR.

Wall, M., Campbell, M.O. and Janbek, D. (2015) Syrian refugees and information precarity. *New Media and Society* 19 (2), 240–254.

Xu, Y. and Maitland, C.F. (2015) Communicating abroad: A case study of Za'atari Syrian refugee camp. Report of the *Regional Conference of the International Telecommunications Society* (ITS), Los Angeles, CA, 25–28 October.

Zaatari Camp Management Council (2017) Michigan State University Model United Nations, Session XVIII: Background Guide. See https://www.msumun.org/uploads/7/8/8/3/78834658/zaatari_camp_.pdf (accessed 19 December 2018).

Part 2

Finding Motivation for Language Learning in a Situation of Forced Immobility

4 Motivational Strategies and Online Technologies: Are Palestinian EFL University Students in the Gaza Strip Empowered to be Bilingual?

Abedrabu Abu Alyan

In a globalized world characterized by multilingualism and multiculturalism, there is a growing interest in the English language, effective motivational strategies and online technologies. This chapter investigates the perception of Palestinian teachers and students of English as a foreign language (EFL) to explore and highlight successful motivational strategies, despite the significant barriers posed by the current political and socio-economic situation of the Gaza Strip. The population of the Strip, as detailed in the Introduction chapter of this edited collection, experiences a tight blockade, which results in immobility, frequent power outages and acute levels of unemployment among university graduates, together with other very challenging life conditions.

Motivation is one of the key determinants in effective foreign language (FL) teaching and learning (Hadfield & Dörnyei, 2013), especially in a context of pressure and pain, and developing skills to motivate students is pivotal for language teachers (Dörnyei, 2001), for they have the responsibility to facilitate their students' achievement. Further, promoting active engagement in classroom activities is particularly significant in FL contexts because face-to-face communication in the FL rarely occurs outside the classroom (Guilloteaux, 2013). In spite of the growing momentum motivation has been gaining, a substantial part of the scholarship in this area deals with younger students, so it is not very clear how applicable the findings may be to university level students (Kember, 2016). This study contributes to the body of knowledge in the field of EFL as it highlights teachers' and students' views on effective motivational strategies. It also explores the opportunities offered by online technologies as a possible motivating factor, in the fragile Gazan university context.

The Research Background

The context of siege enforces relentless socio-economic, affective, material and political constraints on the opportunities of the Palestinians to live the life they have a reason to value (Sen, 2009). Since 2007 the siege has had catastrophic effects on living conditions in the Gaza Strip. The tight blockade has left almost two million Palestinians stuck in extremely challenging living conditions.

Motivation is a key affective factor in strengthening the resilience and wellbeing of the Palestinians in the Gaza Strip. According to Marie *et al.* (2018), promoting resilience within oppressed and politically excluded communities can be sustained through revitalizing a culture that focuses on individual traits, positive attitudes and determination. Community resilience also requires developing strategies to survive in the context of prolonged adversity, collective punishment, trauma, social distress and unjust political oppression (Marie *et al.*, 2018).

A small-scale qualitative study was carried out specifically to develop original and up-to-date content for this chapter. Its overall purpose was to shed light on the issue of motivation and to raise awareness about the most effective motivational practices and use of online technologies by providing a 'menu' of potentially useful insights and suggestions for overcoming the limitations of the siege. This chapter discusses teachers' as well as students' views regarding motivational strategies and online technologies. The research questions that drove this study focused on motivational strategies in general, and therefore the use of online technologies as a tool that can serve to motivate EFL students emerged from the responses of the participants. The investigation was guided by the following research questions:

(1) What are the general views of EFL Palestinian university teachers on the most effective motivational strategies?
(2) What are the general views of EFL Palestinian university students on their teachers' motivational strategies?

We hope that existing theoretical work coupled with empirical insights can lead to practical recommendations for motivating students in the language classroom and engaging them more actively in various forms of autonomous learning. The next section discusses the available literature on motivation, highlighting different types and with a more specific focus on the EFL context.

Motivation

Throughout the past few decades, motivation has been the focus of attention as a key aspect of language learning and achievement (Brophy, 2010; Dörnyei, 2005; Gardner, 2001). The word motivation derives from the Latin verb *movere*, meaning *to move* (Dörnyei & Ushioda, 2011). Dörnyei (2005: 68) defines motivation as the 'effort, desire, and attitude towards learning'. There seems to be agreement on the notion that with lack of motivation, even individuals with high aptitude cannot achieve their long-term goals (Dörnyei & Csizér, 2005). There needs to be a focus on motivation, on movement and the effort that comes with it, to help students expand and persist in their effort to learn an FL (Dörnyei & Ushioda, 2011).

Foreign Language Learning Motivation

Some students attend EFL classes without the motivation required for success (Papi & Abdollahzadeh, 2012). Moreover, learning a second language (L2) is linked to a spectrum of social variables such as widespread attitudes towards the language, geopolitical considerations and prevailing cultural stereotypes (Papi & Abdollahzadeh, 2012). Therefore, developing multilingual and multicultural skills in the EFL classroom requires considerable effort and persistence (Gardner, 2001).

In the Gaza Strip, English is taught as an FL and the vast majority of learners have few opportunities to use the language communicatively and interculturally. By providing a conducive learning environment, teachers are able to motivate learners and encourage them to achieve their goals (Fareh, 2010; Kaker & Pathan, 2017). Teaching is a process that involves creating a thirst for learning, and teachers can influence learners' motivation in various ways. For example, they can influence learners' beliefs about their own abilities, their attitudes towards certain subjects, their intermediate and long-term goals, and their beliefs about success and failure (Dörnyei & Ushioda, 2011). The following section highlights different types of motivation in language classes.

Integrative motivation

According to Kramsch (1994), language is not a body of knowledge to be learned but a social practice and culture in which to participate. It is worth noting that integrative motivation reflects passion in learning another language because of a personal interest in the target culture and people. Gardner (1985) contends that integrative motivation seems to be a potential predictable factor for excelling in an L2. However, views that closely link language and culture have recently been challenged, as English has become a lingua franca for intercultural communication (Jenkins,

2016) and many learners study it for a variety of reasons, other than identifying with or having an interest in a particular community of speakers.

Instrumental motivation

Instrumental motivation refers to functional orientations in learning an FL, such as getting a well-paid job or passing a course exam. Because the majority of FL learners have few opportunities to closely interact with the FL speaking community, FL learning tends to be rather instrumentally motivated (Du & Jackson, 2018).

Intrinsic motivation

Self-determination theory (SDT; Deci & Ryan, 1985) distinguishes between intrinsic and extrinsic motivations. Intrinsic motivation refers to the personal interest, satisfaction and need for fulfilment when performing a task. It is associated with the interest and anticipated enjoyment of the language learning activity. Self-determination is an essential constituent to intrinsically motivated behavior (Deci & Ryan, 1985).

Extrinsic motivation

Extrinsic motivation, conversely, refers to performing a task in order to achieve a certain goal such as a job promotion or instrumental end. While SDT emphasizes a learner's autonomy and personal determination to learn, an extrinsically motivated learner requires external stimuli to drive achievement (Deci & Ryan, 1985).

English in the Palestinian Context

In the Palestinian context, as is the case in many Arab countries, English is a required school and/or university subject. However, it also plays a key role in university as a language of instruction, especially in scientific and technological fields. According to Dwaik and Shehadah (2010), motivation patterns among Palestinian students are extrinsic, i.e. students learn the language because it is a school/university requirement. However, the data discussed in this chapter appear to at least partly contradict this, and instead show that Palestinian students also have economic, political and cultural motivations to study English. Students in Gaza perceive English as a window to the outside world and a major means of intercultural communication in order to make others aware of the challenges faced by people in the Gaza Strip, in all their complexity. In a nutshell, Palestinian students are motivated to learn English due to the political, economic and cultural power it holds as a global language. Although it is widely believed that employing motivational strategies increases the positive attitudes of the students towards learning (e.g. Sugita & Takeuchi, 2010), there is little empirical evidence in the literature to support this claim. This chapter seeks to fill this gap by discussing teachers' and students' perceptions of effective motivational strategies and, in doing so, also shows the importance of online technologies in the Palestinian EFL university context.

Motivational Strategies

The main purpose of motivational strategies is to generate and ameliorate learner attitudes, to maintain ongoing positive approaches and to focus (Dörnyei & Ushioda, 2011). Research shows that motivational factors can 'override the aptitude effect' in language learning (Dörnyei, 2005: 65), redressing and reducing individual difficulties. In FL, motivational strategies are techniques used to promote and maintain the desires and attitudes of learners to learn. Dörnyei (2001: 28) defines motivational strategies as those '[...] influences that are consciously exerted to achieve some systematic and enduring effect'.

Dörnyei's (2001) motivational strategies framework is one of the earliest frameworks in this field, proposing 30 different motivational strategies, grouped into four major categories. The first category consists of components concerned with creating proper motivational conditions through practicing appropriate teacher behaviors and providing a conducive classroom atmosphere. The second category involves promoting the learner's appropriate language-related values and attitudes. The third category entails maintaining and protecting motivation by setting the goals of learners, enhancing self-confidence and autonomy and promoting cooperation and self-motivating strategies. The fourth category also entails promoting positive self-evaluation, motivational feedback and learner satisfaction (Chiew & Poh, 2015).

Williams and Burden (1997) also developed an L2 motivation model, which designates motivation as a multidimensional construct and acknowledges that motivation can be subject to contextual influences such as teachers, learning setting and educational system. Many researchers have probed motivational strategies in a range of EFL contexts (e.g. Alrabai, 2011; Cheng & Dörnyei, 2007; Dörnyei & Csizér, 1998; Guilloteaux & Dörnyei, 2008; Guilloteaux, 2013; Shakfa & Kabila, 2017). Although a number of studies have investigated motivational strategies in international and regional settings, there have been few research studies in the Palestinian EFL university context (e.g. Bianchi et al., 2017).

Previous Studies Investigating Motivational Strategies

Throughout the past decades, a number of studies have examined L2 motivational strategies in different socio-educational contexts such as

Hungary, Taiwan, South Korea, Turkey, Iran, Oman and Saudi Arabia. Dörnyei and Csizér (1998) conducted a study to examine the perception of teachers and use of motivational strategies in Hungarian schools. Teachers were asked to rank 51 motivational strategies based on their due importance and usefulness. The findings revealed 10 major macro-strategies called the 'ten commandments', which summarized the teachers' best motivational strategies in actual classroom practices. Teacher behavior, presenting tasks in an engaging way and building the confidence of students featured in the top five strategies in terms of significance and potential positive impact.

Cheng and Dörnyei (2007) replicated the above study in Taiwanese schools and universities. Their findings were rather similar to the Hungarian context, but in the Taiwanese socio-educational context teachers put recognizing the learners' efforts in second place in terms of importance. Another significant difference is that Taiwanese teachers ranked enhancing learners' autonomy as the least important motivational strategy. Further, Bernaus and Gardner (2008) investigated the use of 26 motivational strategies by teachers and students in the Spanish EFL context. Their findings showed similarities between the perceptions of teachers and learners of some strategies, although the responses of learners focused more frequently on attitudes and motivation.

Guilloteaux and Dörnyei (2008) probed the motivational strategies of teachers and learners' motivation in South Korea. The findings showed a positive correlation between the motivational practices of teachers and the behavior of students in the classroom. They revealed that language teachers could make a real difference in boosting the motivation of learners through putting into place effective strategies.

A range of studies have also explored the potential online technologies offer for EFL learning and teaching, particularly in motivating students and helping them acquire the skills they need to survive in a complex, highly technological knowledge-based world. For example, in order to investigate the impact of online technologies on the motivation of learners and linguistic achievement, Alsaleem (2013) carried out a study to explore the impact of using WhatsApp with female students majoring in languages and translation at Al-Imam Mohammad Ibn Saud Islamic University (Saudi Arabia). The project used the mobile application to keep English dialogue journals, aiming to develop speaking ability, writing, vocabulary and word choice. The study employed a quantitative, quasi-experimental methodology and showed how, after using WhatsApp applications, Saudi students showed improvements in writing skills, speaking ability, vocabulary acquisition and word choice.

Online Technologies and Motivation in an EFL Context

With the rapid evolution of communication technologies, language pedagogy and language use have changed, enabling new forms of discourse (Kern, 2006) and creating online opportunities for EFL teachers to develop the language skills of learners, intercultural communicative competence and intercultural awareness. As Graddol (2012: 18) states, 'technology lies at the heart of the globalization process, affecting work, education, and culture', and computer and digital technology now provide teachers and learners with rich and authentic textual and audio/video materials as well as Voice over Internet Protocol (VoIP) communication programs (e.g. Skype, Zoom), all of which can be very valuable in developing language skills (Bahrani, 2011). Moreover, Prensky (2001) coined the term 'digital natives' to refer to the generation of learners who grow up with technology integrated into their everyday lifestyle, who '[...] have spent their entire lives surrounded by and using computers, videogames, digital music players, video cams, cell phones, and all the other toys and tools of the digital age' (Prensky, 2001: 1). Increasingly, therefore, technology can enrich and expand the language learning experiences of young people who are familiar with online and digital tools and confident in their use.

Furthermore, technology can motivate learners, and even simple software programs can help to create a supportive learning atmosphere and to share knowledge with other online interactants (Mills, 2010). State-of-the-art technology in communications has made it possible for teachers and learners to have access to rich resources such as authentic input and communication opportunities with speakers of English from different parts of the globe. In addition, the use of digital libraries, dictionaries and thesauri have considerably facilitated vocabulary acquisition and led to breaking the learning barriers, as new domains in the global information age have been introduced (Alsulami, 2016).

According to Stockwell (2013), online technologies have the potential to boost EFL learners' motivation in and outside the classroom. Interestingly, learners with high motivation seek to increase their communication opportunities in the target language, so they join online communities and virtual environments (e.g. Second Life). Already in 2001, Ellinger *et al.* argued that the internet increases learners' autonomy and arouses motivation in the classroom. Further, authentic videos and films can help to motivate learners in EFL classes (Arcairo, 1993), and have been used in various formats for several decades. Websites such as YouTube or Vimeo now provide a wealth of video materials that can promote learners' autonomy and self-study (Watkins & Wilkins, 2011).

Besides the plethora of educational resources and the communicative opportunities they provide, online technologies have other uses in the Gaza Strip. For example, because of the ongoing blockade, aid cuts and growing unemployment rates, technologies offer new job opportunities, e.g. coding, freelancing, entrepreneurship or offering prototypes to companies and brands (e.g. Amazon, Facebook and Google), as well as other online services. Therefore, online technologies represent a gateway to the outside world, especially for the thousands of graduates who have nowhere to go (Imperiale et al., 2017; see also the chapter by Fassetta et al., this volume). Online tools can represent hope for these graduates to learn more skills and compete in the international work market offered by online work platforms such as Upwork, Freelancer and others.

The Study

In order to answer the research questions presented above, the study that informs this chapter used a qualitative research methodology, seeking to understand a particular phenomenon (i.e. motivation) within a naturalistic setting through the *voice* of participants (Kennedy & Edmonds, 2017). There were 12 participants (six lecturers and six students) from the department of English at the Islamic University of Gaza (IUG). The lecturers varied in terms of educational background, age, gender and teaching experience. The students were also from different levels and genders. Marshall and Rossman (1999) argue that decisions about sampling people are usually based on information-rich cases. Semi-structured interview (see Appendix 1) schedules were prepared and carried out with teachers and students. They were carried out in English, recorded, and transcribed for thematic analysis.

Findings and Interpretations

Views of teachers on effective motivational strategies

In analyzing the interview data of the EFL Palestinian teachers, several themes relating to motivation for language learning were identified, and they will be discussed in this section. The themes were: relaxing classroom atmosphere; developing a positive attitude towards the English language; setting goals of learners; promoting self-confidence, linguistic confidence and autonomy; offering chocolate and grades; personalizing teaching and sharing intercultural experiences; using competition and game-like activities; using teaching materials relevant to the Palestinian context; and online technologies to enhance education and bypass the siege.

(a) Relaxing classroom atmosphere

Teachers believe that creating a supportive, relaxing and pleasant classroom atmosphere can be motivating in an EFL classroom. For example, Sally (all names are pseudonyms) suggested: 'It's a pleasant atmosphere because I love telling jokes all the time. I'm very supportive especially with those who lack confidence.' In addition, Hind maintained: 'I like to shake hands with my students. I remember their names, and I ask them to talk about themselves. To make my students feel relaxed, I always like to arrange my classes especially in small groups and pairs.' Omar, a senior professor, made similar observations about classroom atmosphere: 'I start my class with a warming up activity and keep telling them jokes, creating an atmosphere of fun, making the class atmosphere as a real-life experience, without stress or tension.' In line with these findings is Good and Brophy's (1994) argument that a pleasant classroom atmosphere has positive effects on students' motivation, such as fostering their self-confidence, developing good rapport and making the learning experience stimulating and gratifying.

(b) Developing a positive attitude towards the English language

Teachers argued that one way of motivating learners is to reiterate the importance of English for students' academic and professional life. Omar pointed out that 'language development is important to their future. It's the key to their prosperity, it's the key to their progress, and it's the key to their success.' Further, Hind asserted that English is a privilege and a form of educational capital for those who speak it, also giving access to modern technologies: 'English gives you privilege, really. It's a global language and the capital it gives its speakers. It gives you access to all technologies, and it opens doors.'

However, Sally draws learners' attention to the importance of English in a different way: 'I assign my students to write "why English is important". As Palestinians, we need to bridge ourselves with the outside world. If you want your voice to be heard either as a Palestinian (a Muslim or Christian), or someone with a cause, you have to speak that language because everyone speaks it.' The sentiments of the teachers concur with the scholars. McKay (2002), for example, argues that proficiency in English is required to secure one's financial and professional success. English is needed to achieve higher education qualifications and has become a prerequisite for a successful career in most areas. Likewise, Dörnyei and Ushioda (2011) argue that the instrumental value of learning English could be boosted by reminding students of the role it plays in the world and its usefulness to them and their community. Moreover, according to Phipps and Gonzalez (2004), intercultural language teaching has the potential to develop intercultural wellbeing or a global citizen who embodies values of respect, humility, openness, critical thinking, tolerance and compassion.

(c) Setting learners' goals

To increase learners' motivation, teachers help them to set their short-term and long-term goals. Sally motivates her students by asking them to write about their goals. She explained: 'I ask them to tell me what they want to achieve, … I make sure to give them this activity where they have to write down two-year objectives and in five years, and to achieve the long-term goals you have to make sure that your short-term goals are related.'

Omar indicated that his way of teaching aspires students to set their goals: 'the way I teach aspires them to set their goals! Sometimes I tell a student, you're a good writer, a good translator, and a journalist, just keep working.' Likewise, Hind focuses on learners' long-term goals and strategic thinking. 'I focus on long-term goals', he stressed, echoing Kilmas (2011), who argues that helping students to set their learning goals can boost the level of their engagement, attention and attitudes. Teachers play a crucial role in helping students to set their learning goals, and this can have a positive impact on motivation.

(d) Promoting learners' self-confidence, linguistic confidence and autonomy

IUG teachers maintained that part of the teaching process is to help learners develop self-confidence, linguistic confidence and autonomy, something that students are seen to lack. Sally stated, 'Other problems include lack of confidence ... but they still feel ashamed of their grammatical mistakes they make or the lack of vocabulary ... lack of confidence'.

Hind also noted that she tries to increase the confidence of students by making them feel secure and relaxed in class: 'creating safe and secure atmosphere is one of the motivational strategies that I use specially with those who lack confidence speaking in public. Giving them confidence to speak is the first step, then I guide them to other sources to use in their free time'. To increase students' linguistic competence, Sally raises awareness about the difficulties people face in learning FLs: 'I show them YouTube videos of people from other cultures who try to learn Arabic. I tell them that it's a great thing that you speak English or even "poor" English.'

To develop students' self- and linguistic confidence, Omar encourages them to work in pairs and small groups in order to learn from their mistakes and help one another: 'I get them to read and read, talk and talk, listen and listen. I make them learn from each other in small groups. We engage in collaborative discussions, so learners learn from each other and learn from their mistakes.' Besides promoting self- and linguistic confidence, teachers also seek to increase the autonomy of learners. Sally promotes their autonomy by suggesting some materials and ideas to use: 'I usually provide them with a list of books they could start with; they usually start with big books and then stop after they read the first three pages. And I ask students to keep listening.'

However, Hind appeared to have a different perspective, and noted that 'students are not autonomous; they are dependent. It's a cultural thing; we depend on our teachers. Only few of them would come prepared, and the rest won't interact'. These findings echo Dörnyei and Ushioda (2011), who note that motivation, autonomy and learning accomplishment are closely related, and that they have a cyclical interaction in the EFL learning process.

(e) Offering treats and grades

Some teachers pointed out that students could be easily motivated by chocolate and grades. For example, Kareem noted, 'They like grades a lot, I usually give them bonus marks for creative work, and it works. Grades are the most rewarding thing for them, plus human feedback. ... I mean supportive feedback.' Mona also confirmed that grades and chocolate are very effective: 'grades and chocolate! Students care a lot about grades. Prizes and chocolate, these are symbolic, and they are not as rewarding as grades.' Interestingly, Sally also thinks that giving students gifts can be very motivating: 'another thing is books. If you offer them a book with a beautiful dedication. Wow! It's something precious. They want something they can touch, something that reminds them of their achievement.' In brief, some IUG teachers find that grades and gifts can be incredibly rewarding and motivational for students in EFL classes.

(f) Personalizing teaching and sharing intercultural experiences

According to teachers, personalizing teaching and the sharing of cultural experiences can be a powerful strategy for motivating students. Reem, a young professor, explained that being young and close to the students' age makes them open up to her and ask many questions. In the same way, Omar personalizes his teaching experience and says that sometimes 'I personalize myself as a hard worker, a very demanding teacher, but I don't keep talking about myself'.

Teachers revealed that sharing their cultural experiences is one of the most compelling motivational strategies. Reem, for instance, stated: 'learners need someone who was there; they become curious about that culture, and they trust the teacher more when they know that he got his degree from a native speaking country. It's part of motivating them and entertaining them and can contribute to the relaxing and friendly atmosphere.' Nonetheless, Hakim expressed caution about talking about the target culture in class because of the differences in religions: 'it's a difficult question because it is not only the culture that is difficult; it's religion as well. It creates this barrier. ... Students already know because English is an international language and English culture is international.' In brief, personalizing teaching and sharing intercultural experience with students is seen as motivating by the teachers.

(g) Using competition and game-like activities

The majority of students prefer to engage in competition and game-like activities. Omar noted: 'they enjoy activities that involve some creativity, when they have their fingerprints. They don't like parrot learning. They enjoy working together in pair or group work.' Further, Hind asserted that students like games and fun in class: 'they love games a lot, especially the interactive games.' IUG's EFL teachers advocated that games, class debates and discussions are effective motivational strategies. Likewise, Fromme (2003) maintains that games can lower anxiety and create a relaxing atmosphere, increase motivation and add to the variety of entertaining classroom activities.

(h) Using teaching materials relevant to the Palestinian context

From the teacher's vantage point, using teaching materials pertinent to the lives and interests of students can be a strong motivational strategy. For example, Sally asserted that she always likes to link her teaching with the Palestinian context: 'I try to associate with the Palestinian context all the time. When I was teaching poetry, we were talking about resistance poetry, we were talking about Mahmoud Darwish.'[1] Besides teaching material that is related to students' lives, Kareem thinks that teaching poetry is a way for self-development and empowerment to students: 'poetry is a way for promoting yourself and empowering your skills. We associate some literary works with the Palestinian context.'

The sentiments of the participants highlighted here align with similar observations by scholars. For example, Imperiale *et al.* (2017: 32) state:

> The English language pedagogy has the potential to nurture independent voices of individuals to 'talk back' or to 'write back', (re)appropriating, adapting and using the language in the way that seems most appropriate to the context in which people live ... This is what Canagarajah ... calls 'linguistic resistance'.

To sum up, one strategy to inspire learners' motivation in EFL classes can be through using relevant and interesting materials. Online technologies can be important motivational strategies, particularly in the fragile university context of the Gaza Strip. The next section specifically illustrates the teacher's points of view on online and mobile technologies as a means to increase students' motivation.

(i) Online technologies to enhance education and bypass the siege

Education does not stop at the end of the school day, for students have access to the resources and assignments of teachers via Facebook. Sally suggested that Facebook is very motivating for students, and it has been widely used for active communication and sharing knowledge: 'everyone is on Facebook, and it's available on cellphones, and it's easier for communication when they start a group where they post articles and share videos.' Rasheed also posted assignments and course articles via the Facebook platform. Godwin-Jones (2008) argues that online technology tools and platforms such as Facebook potentially enhance communication and interaction in language learning. Interestingly, Sally makes use of students' cellphones to bolster speaking classes. For Sally, it seems logical to align today's classroom with the way in which her students want to learn and are used to learning. Several teachers use PowerPoint to make presentations and post links of rich resources on university webpages so that students can use them independently. Moreover, other teachers record their classes and post them online. For example, Rasheed said, 'I recorded all my classes, and they are online in the university's YouTube section'.

Teachers at IUG use online technologies to find resources and attend virtual professional development seminars and conferences to get support from their colleagues, in order to bypass the limitations to movement and intercultural encounters imposed by the blockade of the Gaza Strip. Ameer said:

> Last year, I invited Professor R.S. Zaharna from the American University of Washington to talk to my MA students about an article she wrote on intercultural communication. It was a great experience; the students were very excited to talk to the author of the article.

In another example, the English club in the department invited Mr Mohammad Abu Asaker, the spokesperson of the UN High Commissioner for Refugees (UNHCR) to speak via Skype. Mr Asaker is a distinguished graduate of the English department at IUG, and the main goal of the video conference was to inspire other students to follow in his footsteps and to learn from his experience.

Teeler and Gray (2000) point out that using video-conferencing and cross-curricular projects through the internet can be a powerful motivating factor for classes that aim to develop speaking skills. Further, email projects and online collaborations help students build important skills such as linguistic competence, intercultural communication, critical thinking and cultural awareness (see also the chapters by Guariento and by Rolinska *et al.*, this volume). For instance, Ameer referred to a study he conducted in order to explore the outcomes of an intercultural communication email project between Palestinian English major students from IUG and graduate students from an American university. He told us:

> I wanted to explore how email with native speakers may develop students' intercultural communicative competence and language skills. Participants from both sides exchanged emails over a whole semester. They talked about different topics such as life experience, university life, foreign language experience, politics, food, marriage, values, etc. ... They had to write final reflective papers. The study concluded that both groups gained knowledge about their native cultures and foreign cultures. They described it as a positive experience and developed positive attitudes towards the *other*.

The above are real examples of how introducing online technologies can enhance the learning experience and create new academic opportunities (Fassetta *et al.*, 2017). They are further enriched by insights from Hammam, a senior professor, who articulated the significance of online technology, particularly in the Palestinian context in the Gaza Strip, due to the blockade, three destructive wars and the policy of isolating Gaza from the outside world:

> IUG would have not bypassed the limitations of the long siege imposed on the Gaza Strip for decades. Without technology, we would have been suffocated academically and research wise. Facts and statistics show the wide network that we have with the European universities. All the meetings are almost conducted via video conferences, Skype, WhatsApp, or email.

It is worth noting that Hammam and other teachers used Moodle to communicate with students and to post extra reading materials, assignments, videos and exams. In brief, online technology has become an integral part of the teaching-learning process in the university context of the Gaza Strip, because teachers want to enhance education, and students feel more motivated, excited and engaged in technology-based activities.

Views of students on teachers' motivational strategies

In analyzing the interview data of students in relation to motivational strategies, the following themes emerged: maintaining a comfortable class atmosphere and giving learners equal attention; setting students' goals; acknowledging teachers' influence; facilitating students' favorite activities; and developing language skills and making online friends.

(a) Maintaining a comfortable class atmosphere and giving learners equal attention

From the students' perspective, a potent motivational strategy is to provide a relaxing and supportive classroom atmosphere. Aseel explained: 'I think most of our teachers ... like ... try to make us feel comfortable. When they start a class, they tell us a story or a joke to ease our tension.' However, Ali complained about sudden quizzes and exams: 'some teachers are not supportive, and the thing I hate the most about these teachers is that they make us afraid of quizzes, exams, and grades. This makes class atmosphere very negative because students all the time are afraid; they are afraid of failure, of not getting high marks.'

(b) Setting goals of students

Unlike teachers, many students argue that teachers do not help them to set their goals directly, but sometimes this happens indirectly. Tasneem explained: 'It goes indirectly. When you see a teacher's performance in a class and like his passion for the subject, using all his powers to help you, you say, I'd like to be like that teacher in that domain or something. They inspire you to be something.' Likewise, Morad agreed with Tasneem in that 'teachers do not help students to set their goals, but if they believe that some students have abilities, they tell them, not all students, but when teachers tell them that, they become motivated and feel better'.

(c) Acknowledging teachers' influence

As reported by many students, teacher behaviors have a powerful influence on students in some ways. Morad, for instance, said: 'I guess that teachers help students to form their identity ... successful performance of the teachers will be reflected on the successful performance of the students.' Furthermore, Mona joined the English department because she was impressed by her school teacher: 'I joined the English department because of my teacher in the 10th grade. I loved the way she was teaching us.' Hattie (2002) notes that, in mainstream education, a teacher's personality is key to motivation. This is also true in relation to EFL learners' motivation, and all the participants asserted similar attitudes towards the role of teachers in increasing EFL students' motivation.

(d) Selecting the students' favorite activities

It seems that students enjoy discussion and group work activities involving topics related to their lives and interests. Hind noted: 'I like the discussions with our teachers. I like it when we take a play and change it into a Palestinian version.' Nour thinks that she feels more motivated when teachers explain why something is important to the lives of students, 'students need to understand why this is important to their life'. For example, students act some international plays in the English Department's annual show. For this show, students usually choose plays (e.g. Shakespeare's *Othello*) that portray struggle and perseverance against injustice, and contextualize the play by changing some of the references or giving the characters Palestinian names. Further, students themselves wrote other works and acted them on the stage, such as a play called *Feminism* in which women are striving for equality with men. To some extent, this finding resonates with Brophy (2010), who notes that teachers should find topics and activities that students really want to learn and enjoy doing, and then integrate them in the curriculum as much as possible.

(e) Developing language skills and making online friends

Online technology can give students great resources, new opportunities to collaborate virtually, and also a way to save money. Instead of the teacher being the only source of help in a classroom, students can access websites, online tutorials and more assistance. Online resources effectively engage students and build their skills. Zahra maintained, 'We actually ask professors if they have good online resources'. Mahmoud could not afford to take the IELTS course, so he enrolled in free online courses to develop his English through a structured program: 'Coursera is an educational platform for online courses. If you enroll, they give you assignment every week.'

Moreover, many participants have online friends from Anglophone countries. Wisam asserted: 'I have a friend from America. Luckily, he wants to learn Arabic. We meet three times a week. Mostly, we chat about cultural difference and politics. He is a big fan of Palestine.' Zahra is a member of a young writers' online project called *We are Not Numbers*, and members of this project are interested in collecting articles and features on different social, cultural, literary and educational topics and share these articles and ideas. Finally, Hala talked about her experience as part of a collaborative online project with a university from Montana, USA:

> Last year, we had an activity with students from another university, literature students from Montana ... We chatted and exchanged stories. We were assigned to write a story. ... We exchanged experiences. She got to know what Muslim means. I learned how they perceive women who wear a hijab.

In spite of the above-mentioned examples, all students expressed concern about the electricity rationing in the Gaza Strip, which has lasted for more than a decade and is part of the way in which life in the Strip is tightly controlled by the blockade. Some students do not have access to the internet at home, even though all students agreed with their teachers that online technologies are extremely motivating for them, especially Facebook group interactions. To sum up, technology is everywhere – intertwined in almost every part of our culture. It affects how we live, work, play and most importantly learn. Undoubtedly, online technologies empower Gaza's students to be creative, more connected and thus more motivated, although access to the internet can be challenging for some.

Conclusion

This chapter has provided an account of how motivation and active engagement in the FL Palestinian university context can be boosted by using effective motivational strategies and online technologies. The account was guided by a qualitative study to investigate teachers' as well as students' perceptions of effective motivational strategies. It was shown that effective motivational strategies include the following: creating a relaxing classroom atmosphere; reiterating the importance of the English language; and promoting students' self-confidence and linguistic confidence. Further, the study findings highlight the importance of integrating technology and online tools as a potent motivational strategy to bypass the limitations that the siege imposes on the Gaza Strip.

In the light of these research results, the following recommendations are offered as possible ways to empower learners' motivation in EFL classes. It is recommended to create a pleasant and relaxing classroom atmosphere and give learners positive feedback through supportive reinforcement. To promote students' motivation, teachers are also recommended to help them set their short-term and long-term goals. Due to the significance of promoting learners' positive attitudes towards the English language, it is recommended to reiterate the role of English as a global language and lingua franca and major medium for intercultural communication and to emphasize its importance for learners' lives and community. Teachers should also be aware of the fact that their behaviors in class can influence students, for they can be motivating or demotivating. Further, in order to engage students actively in class activities, teachers may use competition and game-like activities, especially using topics related to the Palestinian context and learners' lives, age and interests.

Learner's autonomy, self-confidence, and linguistic confidence can be highly boosted through continuous reinforcement and nourishing self-study and independent research activities.

Use of the internet, social media and modern technology can be extremely useful for students to practice the language within and outside the classroom. Moreover, it is recommended that teachers give equal attention to all students and use a variety of engaging activities such as debates, discussions, role-plays and pair and group work. Policy makers and teacher trainers are invited to integrate effective motivational strategies and online technologies in pre-service and in-service teacher training/education programs tailored to the specific context of the Gaza Strip. Finally, for future research, the study suggests exploring the role of online technology in motivating Palestinian EFL learners, such as formal online tools used by teachers and independent informal technologies used by learners.

Appendix 1

Teachers' interview questions

(1) What are some of the problems that you face in your teaching?
(2) What are some of the activities that your students enjoy the most?
(3) Do you personalize your experience in teaching? What do you do?
(4) Do you help your students to set their goals or keep reminding them of their goals?
(5) Do you reiterate the role of English and its potential usefulness in our modern world?
(6) What are some of the extrinsic rewards (grades, prizes, etc.) that your students like the most?
(7) What are some of the motivational strategies that you use to engage students in your classroom activities?
(8) What do you do to provide learners with a supportive and relaxing learning atmosphere?
(9) What do you do to make your students enjoy class tasks or activities?
(10) Do you think that your teaching materials are relevant to students' lives?
(11) What do you think is the most demotivating factor/s for students?
(12) What do you do to maintain and protect your students' motivation?

(13) How can teachers cope with demotivated students?
(14) What should teachers do to engage all students in classroom activities?
(15) What is the most interesting/appealing activity to your students?
(16) Do you think that teachers have an influence on their students? How?
(17) Do you share your learning or cultural experience with your students?
(18) How can you describe the learning atmosphere in your class? Pleasant/supportive/relaxing?
(19) How do you present a task in your class to make it more interesting?
(20) How would you describe your relationship with your students?
(21) What do you do to increase your learners' linguistic confidence?
(22) What do you do to promote learners' autonomy/linguistic confidence?
(23) Do you familiarize your students with the target culture?
(24) What should teachers do to empower students' motivation? Name the most important motivational strategies that you use.

Students' interview questions

(1) What are the activities that you like the most in your class (teachers' presentation, explanation, preparation, pair work, group work, role-play)?
(2) Do you think that your teachers are enthusiastic or motivated when they come to class?
(3) Do teachers provide students with a supportive and relaxing classroom atmosphere? What do they do?
(4) Do you think that teachers give equal attention to all students?
(5) Do you think that teachers are fair?
(6) Do teachers use different strategies to stimulate students in class? Can you mention some?
(7) Are the courses relevant to your life? Do they interest you?
(8) Do teachers help learners to set their goals and achieve them?
(9) What is the most interesting and enjoyable course in your program? Why do you think so?
(10) To what extent does that program/major match your expectations?
(11) How do you compare your motivation before and after enrolling in this program? What is the reason for this change?
(12) Do you think that teachers have an influence of their students? How?
(13) How do you describe your relationship with your teachers?
(14) What should teachers do to empower (maintain/protect) students' motivation?
(15) Do teachers promote students' self-confidence? What do they do?
(16) Do teachers promote/support learners' self-confidence/linguistic confidence/autonomy?

Note

(1) Mahmoud Darwish (1941–2008) was a Palestinian poet and author. His works gave a voice to the struggles of Palestinian people, and he is widely recognized as Palestine's national poet (see https://www.britannica.com/biography/Mahmoud-Darwish).

References

Alrabai, F. (2011) Motivational instruction in practice: Do EFL instructors at King Khalid University motivate their students to learn English as a foreign language? *Arab World Journal* 2 (4), 257–285.

Alsaleem, B. (2013) The effect of 'WhatsApp' electronic dialogue journaling on improving writing vocabulary word choice and voice of EFL undergraduate Saudi Students. *Arab World English Journal* 4 (3), 213–225.

Alsulami, S. (2016) The effects of technology on learning English as a foreign language among female EFL students at Effatt College: An exploratory study. *Studies in Literature and Language* 12 (4), 1–16.

Arcario, P. (1993) Criteria for selecting video materials. In S. Stempleski and P. Arcario (eds) *Video in Second Language Teaching: Using, Selecting, and Producing Video for the Classroom* (pp. 109–122). Alexandria, VA: TESOL Inc., 109–122.

Bahrani, T. (2011) Speaking fluency: Technology in EFL context or social interaction in ESL context? *Studies in Literature and Language* 2 (2), 162–168.

Bernaus, M. and Gardner, C. (2008) Teacher motivation strategies, student perceptions, student motivation, and English achievement. *The Modern Language Journal* 92 (3), 387–401.

Bianchi, R., Hussein, A. and Razeq, A. (2017) The English language teaching situation in Palestine. In R. Kirkpatrick (ed.) *English Language Education Policy in the Middle East and North Africa* (pp. 147–170). Cham: Springer.

Brophy, J. (2010) *Motivating Students to Learn*. New York: Routledge.

Cheng, F. and Dörnyei, Z. (2007) The use of motivational strategies in language instruction: The case of EFL teaching in Taiwan. *Innovation in Language Learning and Teaching* 1 (1), 153–174.

Chiew, N. and Poh, N. (2015) A review of intrinsic and extrinsic motivations of ESL learners. *International Journal of Languages, Literature and Linguistics* 1 (2), 98–105.

Deci, D. and Ryan, M. (1985) *Intrinsic Motivation and Self-determination in Human Behavior*. New York: Plenum Press.

Dörnyei, Z. (2001) *Motivational Strategies in the Language Classroom*. Cambridge: Cambridge University Press.

Dörnyei, Z. (2005) *The Psychology of Language Learners*. Hillsdale, NJ: Lawrence Erlbaum.

Dörnyei, Z. and Csizér, K. (1998) Ten commandments for motivating language learners: Results of an empirical study. *Language Teaching Research* 2 (3), 203–229.

Dörnyei, Z. and Csizér, K. (2005) The internal structure of language learning motivation and its relationship with language choice and learning effort. *The Modern Language Journal* 99 (1), 19–36.

Dörnyei, Z. and Ushioda, E. (2011) *Teaching and Researching Motivation* (2nd edn). Harlow: Longman.

Du, X. and Jackson, J. (2018) From EFL to EMI: The evolving of English learning motivation of Mainland Chinese students in a Hong Kong university. *System* 76, 158–169.

Dwaik, R. and Shehadah, A. (2010) Motivation types among EFL college students: Insights from the Palestinian context. *An-Najah University Journal of Research (Humanities)* 24 (1), 334–360.

Ellinger, B.S., Sandler, D., Chayen, D., Goldfrad, K. and Yarosky, J. (2001) Weaving the web into EAP reading program. *English Teaching Forum* 39 (2), 22–25.

Fareh, S. (2010) Challenges of teaching English in the Arab world: Why can't EFL programs deliver as expected? *Procedia Social and Behavioral Sciences* 2, 3600–3604.

Fassetta, G., Imperiale, M.G., Attia, M. and Al-Masri, N. (2017) Online teacher training in a context of forced immobility: The case of Gaza, Palestine. *European Education* 49 (2–3), 133–150.

Fromme, J. (2003) Computer games as a part of children's culture. *Game Studies* 3 (1). See http://gamestudies.org/0301/fromme (accessed 1 July 2018).

Gardner, C. (1985) *Social Psychology and Second Language Learning: The Role of Attitudes and Motivation*. London: Edward Arnold.

Gardner, C. (2001) Integrative motivation and second language acquisition. In Z. Dörnyei and R. Schmidt (eds) *Motivational and Second Language Learning* (pp. 1–20). Honolulu, HI: University of Hawaii Press.

Godwin-Jones, R. (2008) Mobile computing technologies: Lighter, faster, smarter. *Language Learning Technologies* 12 (3), 3–9.

Good, T.L. and Brophy, J.E. (1994) *Looking in Classrooms* (6th edn). New York: HarperCollins.

Graddol, D. (2012) The impact of macro socioeconomic trends on the future of the English language. Doctoral thesis, Stockholm University. See http://www.diva-portal.org/smash/record.jsf?pid=diva2%3A490357&dswid=6496 (accessed 19 December 2019).

Guilloteaux, J. (2013) Motivational strategies for the language classroom: Perceptions of Korean secondary schools English teachers. *System* 41 (3), 3–14.

Guilloteaux, J. and Dörnyei, Z. (2008) Motivating language learners: A classroom-oriented investigation of the effects of motivational strategies on student motivation. *TESOL Quarterly* 42 (1), 55–77.

Hadfield, J. and Dörnyei, Z. (2013) *Motivating Learning*. Harlow: Longman.

Hattie, A. (2002) What are the attributes of excellent teachers? In New Zealand Council for Education (eds) *Teachers Make a Difference: What is the Research Evidence?* (pp. 3–26). Wellington: New Zealand Council for Education Research.

Imperiale, M., Fassetta, G., Phipps, A. and Al-Masri, N. (2017) Pedagogies of hope and resistance in the context of the Gaza Strip, Palestine. In E.J. Erling (ed.) *English across the Fracture Lines* (pp. 31–38). London: British Council.

Jenkins, J. (2016) Accommodating (to) ELF in the international university. *Journal of Pragmatics* 43 (4), 926–936.

Kaker, S. and Pathan, Z. (2017) Exploring the motivational strategies practiced by Pakistani EFL teachers to motivate students in learning English language. *International Journal of English Linguistics* 7 (2), 117–123.

Kember, D. (2016) *Understanding the Nature of Motivation and Motivating Students through Teaching and Learning in Higher Education*. New York: Springer.

Kennedy, T. and Edmonds, W. (2017) *An Applied Guide to Research Design* (2nd edn). Los Angeles, CA: Sage.

Kern, R. (2006) Perspectives on technology in learning and teaching languages. *TESOL Quarterly* 40 (1), 183–210.

Kilmas, A. (2011) *Enhancing EFL Learners' Motivation by a Goal Setting Procedure*. Wratislaviensia: CNS.

Kramsch, C. (1994) *Context and Culture in Language Teaching*. Oxford: Oxford University Press.

Marie, M., Hannigan, B. and Jones, A. (2018) Social ecology of resilience and Sumud of Palestinians. *Health* 22 (1), 20–35.

Marshall, C. and Rossman, G. (1999) *Designing Qualitative Research* (3rd edn). London: Sage.

McKay, S.L. (2002) *Teaching English as an International Language*. Oxford: Oxford University Press.

Mills, K.A. (2010) A review of the 'digital turn' in the new literacy studies. *Review of Educational Research* 80 (2), 246–271.
Papi, M. and Abdollahzadeh, E. (2012) Teacher motivation practice, student motivation, and possible L2 selves: An examination in the Iranian EFL context. *Language Learning* 62 (2), 571–594.
Phipps, A. and Gonzalez, M. (2004) *Modern Languages: Learning and Teaching in an Intercultural Field*. London: Sage.
Prensky, M. (2001) Digital natives, digital immigrants. *On the Horizon* 9 (5), 1–6.
Sen, A. (2009) *The Idea of Justice*. London: Penguin.
Shakfa, D. and Kabila, M. (2017) The role of motivation in enhancing the Palestinian students' English language learning. *Journal of Islamic Studies in Indonesia and Southeast Asia* 2 (1), 1–16.
Stockwell, G. (2013) Technology and motivation in English-language teaching and learning. In E. Ushioda (ed.) *International Perspective on Motivation* (pp. 156–175). New York: Palgrave Macmillan.
Sugita, M. and Takeuchi, O. (2010) What can teachers do to motivate their students? A classroom research on motivational strategy use in the Japanese EFL context. *Innovation in Language Learning and Teaching* 4 (1), 21–35.
Teeler, D. and Gray, P. (2000) *How to Use the Internet in ELT*. Harlow: Longman.
Watkins, J. and Wilkins, M. (2011) Using YouTube in the EFL classroom. *Language Education in Asia* 2 (1), 113–119.
Williams, M. and Burden, L. (1997) *Psychology for Language Teachers*. Cambridge: Cambridge University Press.

5 'Really Talking' to Gaza: From Active to Transformative Learning in Distributed Environments and under Highly Pressured Conditions

Anna Rolinska, Bill Guariento, Ghadeer Abouda and Ongkarn Nakprada[1]

The need for transformation in the Gaza Strip is enormous, and obvious. Economic isolation, particularly since the blockade initiated by Israel and Egypt in 2007, has brought truly existential economic challenges. On top of this, the Strip's inhabitants have had to confront regular military attacks leading to thousands of civilian deaths. A corollary of these intense physical hardships has been emotional and psychological impacts, born not just of poverty and the violence endured, but also of the near-impossibility of egress from Gaza (see Phipps *et al.*, Introduction chapter, this volume).

Such physical and psychological impacts would be expected to militate against successful involvement in international collaborative projects. Mezirow (2000: 15) states explicitly that 'hungry, homeless, desperate, threatened, sick or frightened adults are less likely to be able to participate effectively in discourse'. This seems almost to have been written with the everyday suffering within Gaza in mind; yet, as we shall see in this chapter, the opposite holds true. Despite severe limitations on movement out of and into Gaza, engineering students from the Islamic University of Gaza (IUG) have proven eminently able to 'participate effectively in discourse', skilfully using online spaces for this purpose. What is more, this collaboration across borders, cultures and languages proved to be of mutual benefit, both to themselves and to peers overseas.

Since 2015, each summer, engineering students from IUG have partnered online with graduates in similar disciplines on the Science,

Engineering and Technology (SET) strand of the pre-sessional course at the University of Glasgow (UofG). Together, they have investigated a series of engineering-related challenges from the Gaza Strip which the IUG students identify as the most urgent or interesting. This 'English for Academic Study Telecollaboration (EAST) Project' was devised to simulate an experiential learning environment in which the students can engage in their disciplinary discourses, practices and processes and thus develop their identity as engineers. The preliminary analysis of the beliefs, attitudes and behaviours displayed by the students in the project, and presented in this chapter, highlights the importance of active learning in higher education, particularly in sociopolitico-economically challenged contexts, and its transformative potential.

This chapter outlines the original 2015 pilot EAST Project (for details of the three iterations of the EAST Project that have been held since then, see the chapter by Guariento, this volume), focusing on the active learning precepts that underlie its pedagogy. Using the post-course student survey, this chapter looks specifically at students' progress made in terms of communication, team working and problem solving, skills representative of the 3D Global Engineering Competencies proposed by Patil and Codner (2007). It then moves on to examine in detail two case studies (one each from Gaza and Glasgow), providing exemplars of the potentially transformative outcomes that emerged from the active learning precepts of the course. The data are analysed in close relation to multiple contextual challenges which the participants had to tackle on a regular basis.

Active Learning

Conceptually, active learning is an umbrella term that 'involves students in doing things and thinking about the things they are doing' (Bonwell & Eison, 1991: 2). This broad but widely accepted definition links active learning to learning activities, instructional strategies, teaching methods and pedagogical approaches that are intended to activate or develop the students' thinking in the learning process. Examples of these include, but are not limited to: group discussions, case studies, collaborative learning, problem-based learning and inquiry-based learning. The principles supporting the flipped classroom approach, in which students undertake preparatory reading and research activities at home, allowing class time to become an opportunity for them to actually externalize these competencies, are also grounded in theoretical understandings of active learning (e.g. Meyers & Jones, 1993; Silberman, 1996).

What these teaching approaches have in common is that they allow the students to 'negotiate, construct, and reconstruct new meanings from the contributions of others, in a genuine process of shared knowledge construction' (Mayordomo & Onrubia, 2015: 96). Apart from exchanging 'hard' or 'core' knowledge, such initiatives also facilitate the development of various soft skills and attributes, which are sought after in students and graduates by their lecturers and prospective employers. In its Graduate Attributes Matrix,[2] UofG promises to produce students who are 'experienced in working in groups and teams of varying sizes and in a variety of roles', and able to 'conduct themselves professionally and contribute positively when working in a team'. This closely reflects employers' needs. For example, in a survey conducted among Australian employers, oral communication, written communication, capacity to learn new skills, capacity for cooperation and teamwork and interpersonal skills with colleagues and clients were rated as the most important skills for engineering graduates (Nair *et al.*, 2009). The opportunities for active learning have of course been greatly enhanced by the potential offered by digital platforms, and present-day learning and working environments will expect participants to work online, and with others, as stipulated by the Digital Capabilities Framework[3] created by the Joint Information Systems Committee.[4]

As English for academic purposes (EAP) lecturers working in a British higher education institution, our role is to ensure that overseas students develop the necessary language and study skills to comfortably function on their future degree programmes. But we also see ourselves as 'teachers of meaning' (Kramsch, 2014: 309), and we strive, through devising active learning interventions, to help our students to socialize into their prospective disciplinary communities and start to develop their disciplinary and professional identity. Introducing the telecollaboration with Gaza was our attempt to directly actualize that need as it provided what in our view was an authentic, real-world contextualization of the course content, and a safe environment in which the students could engage with the idea of taking on the responsibility for their own linguistic choices when initiating and responding to their interlocutors' choices (Kramsch, 2014: 305).

The EAST Project

The first iteration of the EAST Project was a relatively small-scale online collaboration pilot run in July/August 2015. Twenty Palestinian students and 37 Glasgow-based overseas students (80% of whom were from China, Saudi Arabia or Brazil), divided into small groups, collaborated on authentic and highly contextualized SET-related scenarios from the Gaza Strip. The IUG students proposed scenarios to be investigated, and then acted as critical friends, providing content-oriented support throughout the five-week project.

Traditional teaching methods remain strongly teacher-led around the world, and for many of the participating students, whether in Glasgow or Gaza, this course represented a first systematic exposure to active learning precepts. The IUG participants were trained in an important aspect of active learning via a purpose-built intensive online preparatory course in providing constructive feedback,[5] prior to teaming up with their partners in Glasgow. Based on the guidance from their peer mentors in Gaza, the students in Glasgow analysed and evaluated possible solutions to the challenges within each scenario. As the course developed, communication and collaboration depended on a range of digital platforms, ranging from WiziQ for synchronous group events, via Facebook and Skype used for ongoing communication, to Google Docs which served as a space for collaborative writing. This variety was designed to overcome the regular power outages in Gaza, and any accessibility issues, as well as to enable rapidity of interaction. The collaboration culminated when the students in Glasgow delivered presentations to the audience in Gaza via a videoconference link. Audience members in both Gaza and Glasgow were able to ask the presenters questions. On the final day of the project, students at IUG joined with their digital friends in Glasgow in an online party, and some IUG students showed videos they had made in illustration of the issues they had been working on (for further information, see https://east telecollaboration.wordpress.com).

Course Survey Results

The course had a significant immediate impact on the students, in both Glasgow and Gaza. In an end-of-project survey, with an 81% rate of completion, the students from both universities commented on a range of positive outcomes of the participation, such as development of digital literacies, extensive language practice, enhancement of content knowledge, engagement with real-world issues and opportunities to work within international teams.

In this section, we focus on the three areas most relevant to active learning: the development of *communication*, *team-working* and *problem-solving* skills, in each case illustrating quantitative findings with relevant comments from the students. We will then build on these findings via two case studies, and evaluate them in terms of possible transformative effects.

Communication skills

The majority of the students perceived the course as beneficial for the development of their communication skills (Table 5.1). The open comments reveal that there were different reasons for such assessment. Since both IUG and UofG students had normally worked in monolingual groups, which can make using a foreign language slightly awkward, they appeared to appreciate being put in a situation in which communication in English was the only possible means of conveying meaning (students'

Table 5.1 To what extent was the project useful in developing your communication skills?

	All participants (%)	UofG participants (%)	IUG participants (%)
Very useful	56.5	55.6	57.9
Quite useful	37.0	44.4	26.3
A little useful	6.5	0	15.8
Not useful	0	0	0

comments from the survey's open questions are reported unedited for spelling and/or grammar).

> Our group was formed by 3 students of different nationalities. So we needed to speak just in English and be as clear as possible. (UofG student)

Specific references to the affective issues related to communication were made, too:

> I think I have courage now to try speaking English without spend a lot of time to order the words in my mind or be afraid of grammars faults. (IUG student)

The active learning-related value of working to deadline, within a structured project, was also noted:

> Presenting a work of a subject I barely knew five weeks before, to people I did not know, with different backgrounds and cultural characteristics requires twice more preparation than to present a known subject to my peers. (UofG student)

> Keeping in touch with people that I newly know them, and when they ask me help it is really important that how I feel that I should help them, even if I was so tired and just arrived from work or even have to work on something else. (IUG student)

For some, the need for regular communication brought concomitant (and perhaps at first challenging) issues of appropriacy, resonating with Kramsch's notion of the importance that the student is aware that 'a choice has been made' (Kramsch, 2014: 305), which in online environments may mean focusing on comprehensibility and accepting that it may 'trump accuracy and appropriateness' (Kramsch, 2014: 300):

> At first, I didn't know how to communicate with foreigners online and I needed to check whether it was an appropriate phrase before talking to them. But I don't worry about that now, because I don't think it's so difficult. (UofG student)

Finally, opportunities for the development of subject-specific language proved of significance too:

> We have been pushed to move on the topic by expressing what you think and improved our spoken English in the process. (UofG student)

Table 5.2 To what extent was the project useful in developing your team-working skills?

	All participants (%)	UofG participants (%)	IUG participants (%)
Very useful	54.3	55.6	52.6
Quite useful	39.1	37.0	42.1
A little useful	6.5	7.4	5.3
Not useful	0	0	0

All the comments point clearly to the students developing communicative competency within their disciplinary and professional communities.

Team-working skills

A crucial element of active learning is the ability to work alongside others. Specifically, regarding engineers, Schaeffer *et al.* (2012: 385) state that 'learning is inherently social, which makes student interaction an important part of education', hence the engineering educator will ideally include activities that promote dialogue and teamwork, and that recognize the value of both product *and* process. As Table 5.2 shows, the students perceived the EAST Project as being of considerable value in this respect.

The students' open comments allow us to unpack a little of what they actually learnt about processes related to team work, for instance the significance of active listening, knowledge construction and task management:

> The solution was the main part to show that skill. Each of us would persuade others that her or his solution could be helpful for current situation in Gaza. communication, argument and clarification were all the positive results of co-working. (UofG student)

> It allowed me to share my thoughts with others and work on the distribution of work between us more ... (IUG student)

Problem-solving skills

Choices in the world beyond academia are not in the main binary and involve interaction with challenges that present many facets. If a course can combine measurable outcomes while allowing the students the liberty to express themselves and to take risks, it will be likely to foster the active learning skills that the student will encounter in his/her post-university career among the complex and untidy problems of the workplace.

The engineering-related situations provided by the Gazan students demanded an active learning approach, as the most obvious responses proposed by the Glasgow-based students were inappropriate in the majority of cases, given the constraints of life in Gaza; for example, to solve the problem of waste disposal, UofG students would suggest building a waste treatment plant, which is an unfeasible solution due to lack of building materials in the Gaza Strip, resulting from the longstanding and ongoing blockade of the Strip. As Daly *et al*. (2014: 418) put it, 'to encourage students to embrace ambiguity, avoid premature closure, and increase reflection may greatly improve their creative skills'. As the students were, in many cases, working across SET-related specializations (i.e. outside their specific fields of expertise), the need for negotiation and problem solving was, if anything, enhanced, as demonstrated by the statistics from Table 5.3 and by the open comments below:

> I like how they give different solutions and then start to compare and contrast between the possible solutions. This was great. (IUG student)

> I always have these problem i never get to solve problems well ... but in these project when we had some problem everyone has his own way to deal with it i really took benefits in this i learned how to think first then take actions. (IUG student)

These comments suggest the potential offered by a socio-constructivist framework (Ligorio *et al*., 2011) for the students, who may be better able in their post-EAST careers to work with future colleagues in an authentic negotiation, construction and reconstruction of knowledge and new meanings, making use of the active learning nature of their involvement in problem solving gained during the EAST Project.

We believe that the statistics and comments above suggest that the course was seen as having met the three key indicators of active learning by a majority of the participants, and that the Gazan students' contribution was absolutely central to the success of the EAST Project, allowing them to work effectively as mentors for Glasgow-based students who came to the project with little or no basic knowledge of the Palestinian context. They were able to clarify queries from Glasgow with patience, and participated with resilience and dedication to overcome challenges regarding internet connections, power outages and their own outside commitments.

While the conclusions that we were able to draw from the survey may be generalizable, they also lack specificity, focusing on an overall

Table 5.3 To what extent was the project useful in developing your problem-solving skills?

	All participants (%)	UofG participants (%)	IUG participants (%)
Very useful	56.5	66.7	42.1
Quite useful	34.8	29.6	42.1
A little useful	8.7	33.3	15.8
Not useful	0	0	0

evaluation of the project rather than offering a detailed picture of how the students actually operate in learning environments that are open, volatile and distributed. We were interested to know what the project really involved on the part of the students and, even more importantly, whether the undoubted challenges of the course might have provoked longer term and more deep-seated *transformative* benefits among any of the participants. The next section provides a short literature review of transformational learning before we describe the methods used to gain a deeper insight into the students' learning during EAST.

Transformative Learning

Transformative learning is an area of study first outlined in the 1980s and its development since then has followed work largely initiated by Jack Mezirow. He posited learning as a process of 'using a prior interpretation to construe a new or revised interpretation of the meaning of one's experience in order to guide future action' (Mezirow, 1996: 162), and suggested that beliefs and worldviews can change as a result of what he termed 'disorienting dilemmas', or experiences at odds with a person's current beliefs about the world. As a result of such a dilemma, a person may be brought to recalibrate these beliefs in order to reconcile the new experience with the worldview already extant, i.e. be forced to transform what he termed 'problematic frames of reference'. These frames of reference 'provide us with a sense of stability, coherence, community, and identity. Consequently, they are often emotionally charged and strongly defended' (Mezirow, 2000: 18). However, precisely because they carry so much significance, a *successfully challenged* frame of reference can lead to the subject's becoming 'more inclusive, discriminating, reflective, open, and emotionally able to change' (Mezirow, 2003: 58). We felt that the challenges inherent in a timebound, intensive and highly collaborative project such as EAST would provide participants with potential 'disorienting dilemmas' and offer the chance to interact with peers who may have been undergoing a similar process of development.

Although Mezirow is one of the founders of the field of transformative learning, suggestions for ways to build on and modify his original precepts have subsequently been provided by other researchers, and three are of particular relevance to the EAST Project. Firstly, Clark and Wilson (1991: 76) suggest that Mezirow was failing to 'maintain the essential link between the meaning of experience and the *context in which it arises and by which it is interpreted*'. The italics are ours, as they highlight the type of context that we thought was of paramount importance to the concept of EAST. While, along with Mezirow, we appreciated the individual circumstances of every participating student, we also believed, following Clark (1991), cited in Taylor (2000), that a wider context in which the learning experience was situated has to be considered and this includes acknowledgement of the socioeconomic and political circumstances, both in reference to the engineering problems that the students were to research and to the participants themselves. A relevant educational experience should not be limited to the classroom but should look to the surrounding areas and people as parts of the learning environment. Through working with Gaza, an example of a conflicted context in which due to greater unlikelihood of satisfying basic human needs there is supposedly less ability to participate effectively in discourse (Mezirow, 2000: 5), we wanted to re-evaluate the importance of contextualized learning not only for building communities of practice where knowledge is constructed and shared – allowing both the group and the individual to grow (Wenger, 1998) – but also for building relationships that would foster 'questioning discussions, shar[ing] information openly and achiev[ing] mutual and consensual understanding' (Taylor, 2007: 179).

Beyond the possibility that he was neglecting the importance of context, others have suggested that Mezirow's original theory of transformative learning also underemphasized the potential for *social-emancipatory* transformation. Kegan (1995: 34), for instance, talks of the need to transform our epistemologies, 'liberating ourselves from that in which we were embedded, making what was subject into object so that we can "have it" rather than "be had" by it – this is the most powerful way I know to conceptualize the growth of the mind'. This foregrounding of people as subjects, needing and able to constantly reflect on and aim for social transformation, thus allows the oppressed to demythicize reality and to develop what Freire (1970) termed 'conscientization', or a critical consciousness. It is a form of pedagogy that necessitates democratic engagement, utilizing Freire's ideas of *dialogic* education rather than a 'banking' model in which students are just receiving and repeating ready-digested information. When designing the project, we hoped that through bringing Glasgow-based students (the majority of whom originate from positions of relative societal privilege) face-to-face with authentic challenges that confront students and societies in the Global South we would create conditions described by Belenky and colleagues (1986: 143) as 'really talking', which emphasize the need to listen actively, reciprocate, suspend judgement and empathize in order to understand the situation. What we wanted to build into the project is 'a capacity at the position of constructed knowledge to attend to another person and to feel related to that person in spite of what may be enormous difference' (Belenky *et al.*, 1986: 143). We thought foregrounding empathy was crucial to developing the connected procedures for knowing.

Thirdly, in his original iteration of transformative learning, Mezirow (2000: 22) suggested that, following the disorienting dilemma, transformations often require clarifications involving a phase of meaning that involves 'self-conception and self-examination', but scholars have subsequently built on and suggested revisions to this precept, too. Dix (2016: 143), for example, suggests that 'transformation may occur even if it involves little *self*-awareness but is instead wholly or mostly *problem-focussed*' (italics in original). Focus on the problematic situation might be 'just as emotionally intense, disorienting, critically exploratory, and meta cognitively critical of previous ways of thinking and just as strongly motivating, as would a challenge to one's self-conception and self-evaluation' (Dix, 2016: 143). We felt that the centrality of the problem (as outlined by Dix) to the potential for transformative learning married well with a third key organizational principle of EAST. The project is based around a *Situation-Problem-Response-Evaluation* (SPRE) structure, a common report pattern identified in studies of discourse analysis (see Winter, 1976, in Hoey, 1986). In the case of the EAST Project, the students from Glasgow are provided with a *situation* in Gaza, inherent within which lies an engineering *problem*. By working with their Gazan peers, the Glasgow students undertake library and internet-based research to determine their *responses*, which they then write up and present orally, alongside their Gazan peers: the *evaluation* stage. This SPRE structure, combined with a collaborative and process-oriented approach, requires dialogue, compromise and group action. Critical questions are necessary, as is the need to look beyond sources offered by a structured curriculum. Whatever pooled information that is therefore found needs to be used, collectively, to solve the initial problem. At the same time, we imagined the time- and space-bound constraints of the project could also create opportunities for disoriented dilemmas in relation to the ways in which the students made communication and constructed knowledge.

In short, we hoped that the real-life contextualization, the key Global South focus, and the centrality of the problem-situation within the project, would make it particularly suited to an exploration of transformative learning. The students would work together, negotiating meaning with their peers in Glasgow and in Gaza, and by so doing develop deeper understanding. By encouraging learners to take opportunities for critical reflection, and by following up on their experiences subsequent to the course, we hoped to find out whether and to what extent the learners involved in the case studies would have been able to act on the recalibration of their 'frames of reference'. In specifically language-related terms, we hoped that the inherent 'emotional charge' (mentioned above) could help the students become 'multilingual individuals, sensitive to linguistic, cultural, and above all, semiotic diversity, and willing to engage with difference, that is, to grapple with differences in social, cultural, political, and religious worldviews' (Kramsch, 2014: 305), a much needed postmodernist update on the modernist pedagogy that is oriented towards the development of accuracy, fluency and complexity (Kramsch, 2014: 305).

The Case Study Method

Our desire was to use the Glasgow-Gaza EAST Project to make pedagogy more stimulating, leading to engaged, active, critical students, willing to take initiative and responsibility for their own learning. Since the survey results seemed to be in line with our hopes of developing a more authentic learning environment, we were curious to find out more about the transformative potential of EAST, and whether there was any effect beyond the project duration and into the students' subsequent study or work. We wanted to understand if it had impacted on their ability to manage communication effectively and, hopefully, also more broadly on the issue of language *use* (i.e. the need to communicate authentically and with empathy, rather than just mastering the forms of the language).

To uncover the nature of behaviours, actions, attitudes, beliefs and values, we used ethnomethodology as the methodological basis of our investigation. This meant the students engaging in the 'study of work' (Psathas, 1995: 139–155) themselves, whereby 'work' refers to the EAST Project and how the students accomplished it within the parameters and constraints of the project. In other words, and using Garfinkel's definition of ethnomethodology, we asked our students to reflect on 'the things that persons in particular situations do, the methods they use, to create the patterned orderliness of social life' (Garfinkel, 2002: 4). This seemed to resonate with the active learning framework too (see Bonwell & Eison, 1991).

To recruit student co-researchers, we announced a call for voluntary participation. We were aware that the students who would positively respond to our request were likely to be curious, reflective and self-directed by nature, introducing bias. We decided, though, that a benefit of gaining deeper insights into students' engagement in the project outweighs the risk of skewing the interpretation and so justifies the adoption of this intensity type of purposive sampling (Coe, 2012).

The response rate was low, perhaps due to the fact that the students were already back studying and therefore busy, and there was a self-selection inherent in the process, with more mature and reflective participants likely to offer their time and involvement. We chose one female participant from Gaza to work with us – Ghadeer – and, for the sake of balance of representation of genders, educational and cultural backgrounds, we approached a male Thai participant from Glasgow – Ongkarn.

To account for the time that passed between the end of the project and the reflection as well as to give the students some structure to guide them in their reflecting process, we used the UofG Graduate Attributes Matrix, referenced before. The students were asked whether the EAST Project had brought them any opportunities for development of any of the attributes and, if so, in what way. We were particularly interested in any critical incidents or 'disorienting dilemmas' that might have arisen during the project, i.e. moments when students faced a situation or a problem that was a real challenge. In the process of overcoming this problem, the students would be likely to learn something about the subject they are studying, perhaps also something about the wider educational context in which they are studying as well as the political and socio-economic context of their partners, their whole approach to constructing knowledge of the subject and of themselves and others. Such transformative moments could have occurred either during the project itself or some time afterwards, as long as they could be linked in some way to the project participation.

To facilitate the 'study of work', we opted for Kolb's action-reflection model: initial or new experience, reflection and observation, development of a new concept, and experimentation. To deepen the reflections, we encouraged the students to consider 'the larger context, the meaning, and the implications of an experience or action' (Branch & Paranjape, 2002: 1185). Ghadeer and Ongkarn had an opportunity to familiarize themselves with the framework through a presentation and conversation with us. Then they were given time to reflect on their experience, to select an appropriate focus, and to write their reflections on which we commented, trying to tease out details, motivations and implications. They had an opportunity to respond to our questions and suggestions and it was their choice whether they would act on our 'feedback' and how they would do that. As noted earlier, throughout this dialogic process, we, as authors and researchers in this study, were mindful of our own positionality as two university lecturers and the power dynamics within the relationship between us and the participating students. Similarly, in seeking to answer our research questions about the value of active learning and its potential for transformative learning, we strove to be conscious at all times of how our position as insiders embedded within the story of the project may have coloured our interpretations (Lather, 1991).

Case Studies[6]

Case study 1. Submitted by Ghadeer

Ghadeer investigated Optical Recognition Technology with a group of three UofG students in summer 2015.

After the first get-to-know-each-other conference with my UofG colleagues, we held two meetings to discuss the problem with the optical recognition software in more detail. I outlined the points that I thought were very important to address during the research work. We discussed and explained them quite thoroughly, or at least I thought we did. The UofG students seemed to be engaging with the problem during the discussions. Therefore, I concluded that nothing else was needed and we could start writing the report. A week later one of my Glasgow friends sent me a Facebook message requesting an additional meeting to discuss the idea further. He also claimed that they needed answers to a few questions and ideas. I thought the answers had been given and discussed from different perspectives in the earlier meetings so their need to go through them again puzzled me. Immediately, many conflicting thoughts came to my mind. What else would be needed? Did not we explain everything to each other? Something must have gone amiss though since they were asking for more clarification. Did that mean I lacked the skills needed for teaching and guidance? I also suddenly became worried that they would not do well in the report because of me lacking an ability to give clear explanations. I suddenly felt very uncomfortable about my performance and I blamed myself for inadequate contribution. I had chosen to join EAST Project to contribute something useful and share my knowledge with others. For me, teaching was one of the important tasks during the project. I felt responsible for my team and their performance.

Despite those feelings of self-blame, guilt and weakened confidence, I decided to handle the situation in a professional way. After all, that was supposed to be my role in the project. I was the one who had proposed the problem and I should explain it clearly and in a more scientific way, even if it meant another ten meetings. Therefore, I sent a message to my UofG partners stating my availability which depended on the electricity supply in Gaza.

We arranged to meet in two days. I tried to prepare myself for the meeting and to predict the points that would need more elaboration. Generally, the computational methods from our scenario seemed to cause most difficulty, particularly for those members who did not specialize in computer science, and so I predicted they would probably have to be discussed again. In the previous meetings we had just held a discussion so I decided to follow a different approach by using other exploratory methods. Namely, I sketched a diagram of the system architecture and specified the main functionality of each step and component. I also developed a list of reading resources and tutorials that I thought would be helpful in explaining the problem in more depth.

At the meeting, I showed the sketch to my team and used it to revise the main research themes. My team seemed more engaged with the ideas and decided they were ready to start writing the report. They sent it to me to ensure they had covered all ideas. The report was impressive. They explained each point effectively. They referenced important resources. They handled the problem from different perspectives and they did it better than I had expected. They pointed out the importance of the problem considering the Gazan context and proposed excellent solutions. For instance, they noted that the optical character recognition technique provides the basis for important software products that serve blind people and help them read books and articles by transforming the text to audio so they can listen to the content. In Gaza, the number of blind people is on the increase because many have suffered from the low quality medical services in local hospitals, the lack of healthcare equipment and facilities, in addition to the difficulties of traveling to pursue treatment outside Gaza.

Moreover, the students delivered a great presentation during the seminar day, the most amazing presentation of all the EAST groups! They received many positive comments from the audience and from the Palestinian Ambassador who happened to be visiting Glasgow at the time. They were able to respond to every question and convince everybody of their expertise even though they had been completely new to the topic a few weeks earlier.

This incident was important because the EAST Project was supposed to be completed in a limited time and they had to write their report and their presentation in addition to their regular coursework. That is why I invested all my available time to help them and tried to be supportive rather than create an additional obstacle. Without me realizing and reflecting on the initial misunderstanding, we might have needed more time and they would have probably failed to meet the submission deadlines. I was prepared to do that even though it put a lot of pressure on my personality. I realized that the leader should use more engaging methods when interacting and collaborating with her team. She should follow up on the team input as early as possible and be sensitive to their specific needs. Moreover, she should pay attention to the variations in study backgrounds of her team members. For instance, I did not take into account that each member of my group had a different specialism. Not everyone studied computer science and if I had realized that earlier, it would have made a big difference. To sum up, the leaders should be aware of their team's strengths and weaknesses. In addition, the leader should adopt diverse communication media to facilitate team collaboration. Although we used Skype calls for communicating during the EAST Project, I should also have used some written and visual materials to facilitate comprehension in every possible way, and allow the students to have a useful reference point at the times when I was unable to go online due to electricity shortages. I also understood there was no problem with the team as they were very active throughout our collaboration, but in the learning context I believe the learner should be convinced of the importance of information in order to look for it and properly engage with it.

Moreover, although our EAST group did not follow any predetermined or hierarchical structure, the teamwork was achieved in a seamless, coherent manner. I was in charge of posing the research questions, ensuring the ideas' coverage and evaluating the team's achievements and reflections, whereas each of the Glasgow colleagues had to analyse, elaborate and write on a specific research question. I naturally took on a role of a manager too, helping my teammates to identify tasks and stay on track. The implicit role of managing necessitated the duty towards the team. The team leader in a research project should determine what and when the team should take the next step during research work. Initially, I thought that my team was ready for the report writing phase, but I was wrong. I should have ensured they understood the topic, the problem domain and the research questions first. I should have let them speak and share their ideas. The successful team leader in a research project should know the research path and establish a big picture of the problem and, throughout the meetings, she must ensure all the members are on the same page. And that was what I succeeded in doing in the end.

Overall, this incident had a positive impact on me, developing a set of skills needed to be a successful and effective researcher, which is my future career. In future, I will teach a new curriculum to new students, and I am hoping to put what I have learnt through this incident in action. I am going to try to enrich the lectures with the collaborative learning methods to increase students' participation. I will ask the students to form groups and hold regular meetings so that they can speak for themselves and reflect on their progress on each piece of coursework.

Case study 2. Submitted by Ongkarn

Ongkarn examined lack of addresses in Gaza city with two fellow UofG students and two IUG students in summer 2017.

Before the EAST Project, I barely knew anything about Gaza. I just knew that Gaza is a city located in the Middle East and always engaged in conflicts. During the project, I and my UofG teammates were assigned a scenario of the lack of addresses in Gaza. Our Gazan partners were computer engineering students. We communicated via Facebook and Skype. We contacted our Gazan peers and asked them about the current situation in regard to the problem. However, their initial explanation was not clear enough to help us understand the challenge. Therefore, our team brainstormed and made a list of more detailed questions which we sent to Gaza. Our peers' answers provided a more detailed explanation of the background situation, the problem itself and possible suggestions of how to approach it. This helped us understand better what the 'lack of addresses in the Gaza Strip' actually meant. However, we still felt we were held back by the lack of a basic understanding of the Gazan circumstances and so struggled to develop a clear and comprehensive picture of the assigned problem. Therefore, based on the information we had received from our peers, I decided to create a diagram that would gather and organize all the information we had in a visual way (Figure 5.1).

The diagram takes the form of a mindmap with each branch being a summary of our peers' answers to our initial questions, marked with numbers for easier reference. For example, node number 1 gathers information in reply to the question why the lack of addresses is a problem. The delivery service is provided by a private company called 'Mersal'. Since there is no effective way of delivering packages and parcels, what Mersal does is notify the recipient that there is a parcel waiting for them in the courier office and they have to collect it for themselves. Node number 8, on the other hand, deals with the government role in alleviating the problem. While the

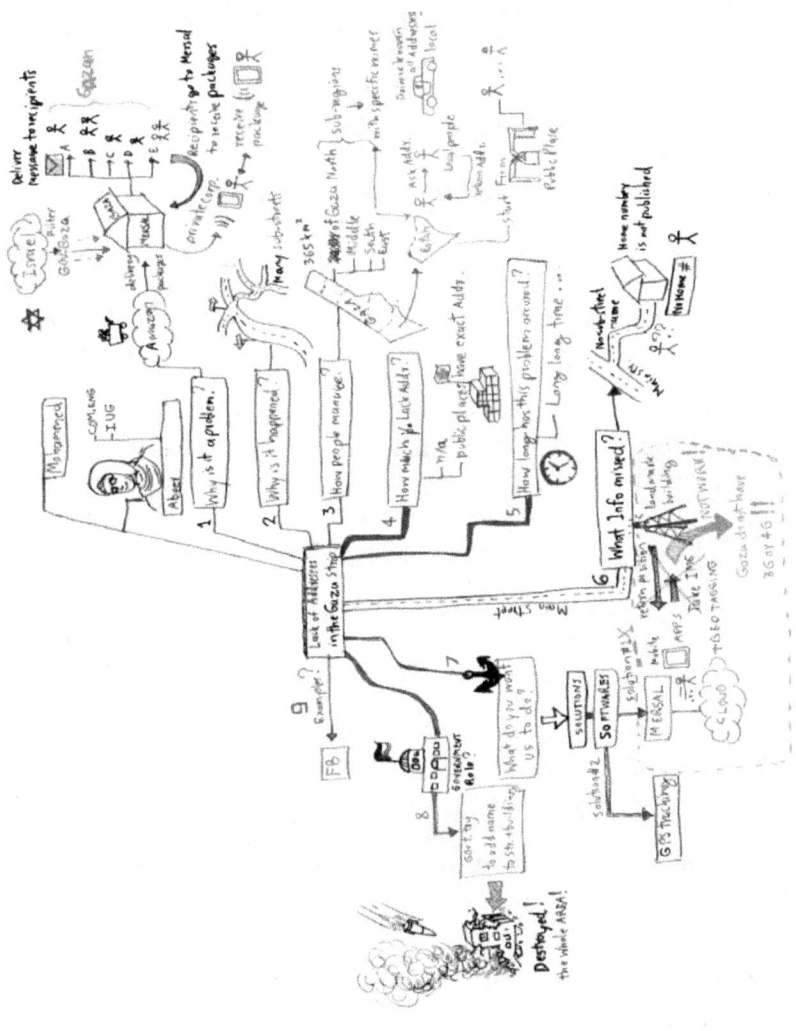

Figure 5.1 A visual mindmap gathering and organizing the information about the Gazan scenario

government does acknowledge that the problem exists, establishing a modern address system even in parts of the city is very challenging. Due to the ongoing conflict with Israel, whole blocks of buildings (can) get destroyed in attacks, and if they do, the addresses (would) disappear too.

Using this visual method helped our team consolidate and fine-tune our understanding of the situation in Gaza and how the different aspects were linked with each other. Then, each team member tried to explore possible options to address this problem. After a period of study, we had several possible methods which we evaluated together in order to filter out which were least likely to succeed. In this way we identified three solutions which in our opinion were the most useful. We presented them to our peers in Gaza via a Skype link. Our partners indicated that some of the proposed methods may not work in Gaza due to the lack of supporting infrastructure required for our solutions to work, for example 3G connectivity. This was an illuminating moment and probably the most valuable lesson during the project. While dealing with engineering problems in low-resource development contexts, practical and economic aspects have to be carefully considered. From that moment onward, such constraints remained at the forefront of my mind whenever I worked on any project.

Participating in the EAST Project equipped me with other skills too as it offered 'lessons' that would be difficult to find elsewhere. First and foremost, I gained experience in working as a team, with peers from different cultures, and also across physical borders, which meant working in technology-mediated environments. Additionally, my partners in Gaza, despite the hardship they were continuously exposed to, seemed unfazed by their circumstances, which provided me with a great model of resilience and determination. The practice this gave me in cross-cultural communication and online collaboration proved very useful during my subsequent MSc study at the UofG School of Computing Science. As part of my post-graduate study I had to complete a number of group assignments which required me to work with randomly assigned peers from different cultural and ethnic backgrounds, e.g. Scottish, Swedish, Polish or Taiwanese. Thanks to the collaborative experience during the EAST Project I found it easier to get accustomed to their different English accents and working styles and so I could collaborate more successfully.

Discussion

Ghadeer's journey seems to embody the transformative learning process as outlined by Mezirow, who talks about 'using a prior interpretation to construe a new or revised interpretation of the meaning of one's experience in order to guide future action' (Mezirow, 1996: 162). When Mezirow describes beliefs and worldviews that can change as a result of what he terms 'disorienting dilemmas', or experiences at odds with a person's current beliefs about the world, it seems to capture what Ghadeer experienced during EAST. But what is worth emphasizing is Ghadeer's sense of responsibility and the split identity of the engineer and the teacher. These were both strong identities, although perhaps the added sense of ownership provided by the latter role meant that the 'frame of reference' was successfully challenged and, as a result, Ghadeer became 'more inclusive, discriminating, reflective, open, and emotionally able to change' (Mezirow, 2003: 58). An interesting question is whether such a successful challenge can occur without any external interference or internal inclinations/tendencies: To what extent was Ghadeer's transformative experience driven by the 'hand-holding' done by us (and we had a particular agenda too) and by the availability of the structured guidance, and to what extent did her personality traits and personal circumstances contribute? She seems to have invested a lot into the project, seeing it as one of the ways/windows to engage in the discourse with the world outside Gaza. She is a strong student in terms of self-direction, driven also by her teaching inclination, and is, perhaps, reflective by nature. One can speculate that she would have realized that the varied methods of presenting complex data are likely to work better than an instructive approach based on one medium. Her teaching identity seems to have been well formed at the time so perhaps she was already sensitized to any opportunity to develop in this respect and was (perhaps subconsciously) looking for opportunities to develop her teaching craft. Also of interest are her emotional intelligence and empathy, so crucial in the process of constructing the knowledge and building a relationship with the group, and perhaps also the emotional resilience (or '*sumud*') particular to Palestinian students (see also the chapter by Guariento, this volume).

Ongkarn's trajectory is slightly different. When faced with a problem of understanding the situation, he resorted to mindmaps, his default when thinking and processing information. He did not seem to problematize in any way the value of using visualization tools in the process of co-constructing knowledge. In his reflection he reports on using them in a matter-of-fact manner, seemingly unaware of their benefit to the collective understanding of the situation in Gaza. As course organizers, however, we could see that the mindmaps were visible within the essays produced by Ongkarn's team members, providing evidence of the effectiveness of the visuals as learning tools for the whole group. Ongkarn's autonomy meant that the guidance given to him was minimal – in a way this is strange, as the linguistically stronger student (Ghadeer) was given more guidance than the less strong one. His experience seems to fit more into the revised version by Dix (2016) rather than Mezirow's (1996) early description, the former loosening the link between transformation and self-awareness and suggesting that transformation may be problem-focused. Despite his clear shock at the level of destruction in Gaza, Ongkarn appears to have approached the problem of miscommunication less emotionally than Ghadeer, at least on paper, and instead of painstakingly deliberating on possible solutions he seems to have put on his problem-solving hat and approached the issue pragmatically; that is at least an image that transpires from the reflection. This could have been possible for him as somebody outside the context of Gaza, unaffected by it in any immediate way. Such distancing for Ghadeer, being placed in the heart of the conflicting context, probably required more energy and time in order to let her liberate herself from grasp of her own circumstances and personal perspective. Of course, additional explanations for this could include gender and other sociocultural background factors.

While it is interesting to use Dix's broader definition of transformative learning, a worry is that the educator may take it for granted that if the right conditions are created (active learning, SPRE), then transformative learning will happen unaided. Is this the case? For us, the key question is: To what extent can a student undergo transformation without being explicitly guided to reflect on the process, and to what extent is this related to being able to articulate clearly that they have undergone some sort of transformation? A related issue follows on from this: How much of the transformation goes unnoticed and unreflected on, and can any student regardless of their personality experience such transformation? A further question is whether less reflective or self-directed students can be led to transformation, and whether parity and equality can be ensured if the starting positions for individual students are different (for whatever reasons).

Conclusion

In his introduction to issues surrounding transformative learning, Kagan (1995) posits two greatest yearnings in human experience: to be included, and to have a sense of agency. Human beings are essentially relational or, as Mezirow (2000: 27) puts it, 'our identity is formed in webs of affiliation within a shared life world'. Clearly there is a value in 'being included', and the comments and case studies here suggest that this 'web of affiliation' can be provided, *faut de mieux*, by online collaboration.

The EAST Project is flawed, in that it offers limited agency to the Gazan participants,[7] but we would argue that it is a model that does offer significant levels of inclusion; namely, it does create an environment where Belenky *et al.*'s (1986: 143) 'really talking' can take place. We feel that Ghadeer's and Ongkarn's frames of reference have been recalibrated to some extent through the process of intercultural understanding, echoing Freadman's promise that 'one's own voice may, as in music, harmonize in any cultural environment only on condition of a well-attuned ear for the stories of other' (Freadman, 2014: 374). The project created conditions for the revised version of transformative learning that foregrounds contextual factors. The evidence of active listening, mutual consensus and empathy in both case studies is clear, as well as is the gain in knowledge of the circumstances the other is situated in, and this can probably be traced back to the wider context for the project. Since that context cannot be learnt about from a textbook, the only method of acquiring and verifying the knowledge is through dynamic communication, a strength of the project and an incentive for transformative learning.

Overall, we feel that the case studies examined here suggest that, despite asymmetries in benefits, EAST has been of considerable value in terms of providing culturally authentic opportunities to communicate not only for those in Glasgow looking forward to their future studies in Scotland but also those in a conflicted area that are said to find it challenging to participate in discourse. The project work creates a safe place for both groups of students to work collaboratively, to debate, disagree, compromise and resolve problems, all of which allow the students to experiment with language and select the practices most appropriate at the time. EAST lacks the pressures of the real world but, crucially, working with and within contextual constraints can enable participants working on engineering challenges to figure themselves out, perhaps transformatively and compassionately, through a language that is not native to either group: who they are, what they do, and (we hope) what they stand for.

Notes

(1) The chapter was written collaboratively by four authors. Two were lecturers and course organizers at the University of Glasgow. Two at the time were participants in the project and provided the case studies. In the course of this chapter we will refer to the lecturers/course organizers as 'we', and to the case study providers directly by name, respectively, Ghadeer (from the Gaza Strip) and Ongkarn (from Thailand but studying in Glasgow).
(2) See https://www.gla.ac.uk/media/media_183776_en.pdf (accessed 13 February 2019).
(3) See https://www.jisc.ac.uk/rd/projects/building-digital-capability (accessed 13 February 2019).
(4) A government initiative whose remit is to enhance the digital capabilities of UK research institutions.
(5) See https://goo.gl/ifxdh7 (accessed 13 February 2019).
(6) The case studies have been edited, for conciseness of expression.
(7) For a more detailed discussion of the power imbalances that make it difficult for the Glasgow and Gazan partners to participate in EAST as true equals, see the chapter by Guariento, this volume.

References

Belenky, M., Clinchy, B., Goldberger, N. and Trule, J. (1986) *Women's Ways of Knowing*. New York: Basic Books.
Bonwell, C.C. and Eison, J.A. (1991) *Active Learning: Creating Excitement in the Classroom*. Washington, DC: Association for the Study of Higher Education, George Washington University.
Branch, W.T. Jr. and Paranjape, A. (2002) Feedback and reflection: Teaching methods for clinical settings. *Academic Medicine* 77 (12/1), 1185–1188.
Clark, M.C. and Wilson A.L. (1991) Context and rationality in Mezirow's theory of transformational learning. *Adult Education Quarterly* 41 (2), 75–91.
Coe, R. (2012) Conducting your research. In J. Arthur, M. Waring, R. Coe and L.V. Hedges (eds) *Research Methods & Methodologies in Education* (pp. 41–52). London: Sage.

Daly, S.R., Mosyjowski, E.A. and Seifert, C.M. (2014) Teaching creativity in engineering courses. *Journal of Engineering Education* 103 (3), 417–449.

Dix, M. (2016) The cognitive spectrum of transformative learning. *Journal of Transformative Learning* 14 (2), 139–162.

Freadman, A. (2014) Fragmented memory in a global age: The place of storytelling in modern languages curricula. *The Modern Language Journal* 98 (1), 373–385.

Freire, P. (1970) Cultural action and conscientization. *Harvard Educational Review* 40 (3), 452–477.

Garfinkel, H. (2002) *Ethnomethodology's Program*. New York: Rowman & Littlefield.

Hoey, M. (1986) Overlapping patterns of discourse organisation and their implications for clause relational analysis of problem-solution texts. In C. Cooper and S. Greenbaum (eds) *Studying Writing: Linguistic Approaches* (pp. 187–214). London: Sage.

Kegan, R. (1995) *In Over our Heads: The Mental Demands of Modern Life*. Cambridge, MA: Harvard University Press.

Kramsch, C. (2014) Teaching foreign languages in an era of globalization: Introduction. *The Modern Language Journal* 98 (1), 296–311.

Lather, P. (1991) *Getting Smart: Feminist Research and Pedagogy with/in the Postmodern*. New York: Routledge.

Ligorio, M.B., Loperfido, F.F., Sansone, N. and Spadaro, P.F. (2011) Blending educational models to design blended activities. In F. Pozzi and D. Persico (eds) *Techniques for Fostering Collaboration in Online Learning Communities: Theoretical and Practical Perspectives* (pp. 64–81). Hershey, PA: IGI Global.

Mayordomo, R.M. and Onrubia, J. (2015) Work coordination and collaborative knowledge construction in a small group collaborative virtual task. *Internet and Higher Education* 25 (1), 96–104.

Meyers, C. and Jones, T.B. (1993) *Promoting Active Learning: Strategies for the College Classroom*. San Francisco, CA: Jossey-Bass.

Mezirow, J. (1996) Contemporary paradigms of learning. *Adult Education Quarterly* 46, 158–172.

Mezirow, J. (2000) Learning to think like an adult: Core concepts of transformation theory. In J. Mezirow and associates (eds) *Learning as Transformation: Critical Perspectives on a Theory in Progress* (pp. 3–33). San Francisco, CA: Jossey-Bass.

Mezirow, J. (2003) Transformative learning as discourse. *Journal of Transformative Education* 1 (1), 58–63.

Nair, C.S., Patil, A. and Mertova, P. (2009) Re-engineering graduate skills – a case study. *European Journal of Engineering Education* 34 (2), 131–139.

Patil, A. and Codner, G. (2007) Accreditation of engineering education: Review, observations and proposal for global accreditation. *European Journal of Engineering Education* 32 (6), 639–651.

Psathas, G. (1995) 'Talk and social structure', and 'Studies of work'. *Human Studies* 18, 139–155.

Schaeffer, D., Panchal, J.H., Thames, J.L., Haroon, S. and Mistree, F. (2012) Educating engineers for the near tomorrow. *International Journal of Engineering Education* 28 (2), 381–396.

Silberman, M.L. (1996) *Active Learning: 101 Strategies to Teach Any Subject*. Upper Saddle River, NJ: Prentice Hall.

Taylor, E. (2007) An update of transformative learning theory: A critical review of the empirical research (1999–2005). *International Journal of Lifelong Education* 26 (2), 173–191.

Taylor, E. (2000) Fostering Mezirow's transformative learning theory in the adult education classroom: A critical review. *Canadian Journal for the Study of Adult Education* 14 (2), 1–28.

Wenger, E. (1998) *Communities of Practice: Learning, Meaning and Identity*. Cambridge: Cambridge University Press.

Part 3

Palestine and the Arabic Language

6 Gaza Teaches Arabic Online: Opportunities, Challenges and Ways Forward

Giovanna Fassetta, Nazmi Al-Masri, Mariam Attia and Alison Phipps

For centuries, Arabic has been taught to speakers of other languages and, in more recent years, it has emerged as one of the world's dominant languages (Graddol, 2006). Over time, the drive towards the study of Arabic has shifted from historical purposes (i.e. the study of ancient Semitic cultures) to an increasing interest in the contemporary Arab world (Versteegh, 2013). A growing number of learners are interested in learning contemporary Arabic, both its literary form (i.e. Modern Standard Arabic) and its many colloquial variations, as a gateway to the very large and complex community of Arabic speakers, and as a key to a wide range of cultures and literary traditions. Arabic is in the top five modern foreign languages identified as essential for the UK 'to become a truly global nation' (Tinsley & Board, 2017). As Ernst (2013: 197) notes: '[…] from its ancient origins, Arabic has become a language of major significance, one of the six official languages of the United Nations, an enduring cultural property in the global heritage of civilization.'

Recent rapid developments in information and communication technology (ICT), such as software for real-time audio and video communication and social networking websites, have allowed people from different backgrounds to engage across borders by interacting through online applications. In order to exploit the combined benefits of the global importance of Arabic on the one hand, and of the opportunities afforded by ICT on the other, in 2016 the Islamic University of Gaza (IUG) initiated an online programme for Teaching Arabic to Speakers of Other Languages (TASOL) based at the IUG Arabic Center. This necessitated training the teachers to use online tools in a creative and flexible way, and to adapt their teaching practices to suit the specific requirements of face-to-screen interactions.

To meet this need for training, a collaborative project was designed and developed as part of the *Researching Multilingually at the Borders of Language, the Body, Law and the State* (hereafter RM Borders) Project, funded by the UK's Arts and Humanities Research Council (AHRC) between 2014 and 2017. The RM Borders Project, based at the University of Glasgow (UofG) in the UK, comprised five case studies, including the collaborative TASOL training discussed in this chapter. The TASOL case study saw the co-design, co-development and delivery of a training course for a group of eight Arabic language teachers based at IUG. The course was specifically tailored to prepare the teachers to work remotely and deliver Arabic language courses from the Gaza Strip using online tools.

One of the foundational activities of the RM Borders Project was to document and analyse the need for a TASOL programme in a context such as that of the Gaza Strip. The TASOL research element aimed to explore what happens to language pedagogies when they are adapted to work online in a context of 52-year occupation and 12-year siege. Alongside this, the project also aimed to lay the grounds for TASOL courses to be offered online from the Gaza Strip to potential learners worldwide, and as a means to expand opportunities for intercultural exchanges (Tawil-Souri & Matar, 2016).

Scope and Objectives of this Chapter

The aim of this chapter is to illustrate how online Arabic language teaching can represent a solution (albeit partial and temporary) to the isolation and unemployment experienced by university graduates in the Gaza Strip, Palestine. As a consequence of a blockade[1] imposed by Israel and Egypt which has now lasted for over a decade, people living in the Strip struggle to earn a living and are also – apart from rare and haphazard exceptions – unable to move elsewhere to work or study. The combination of the hardship the blockade imposes, the large-scale death and destruction caused by recent wars[2] and the virtual isolation and strict limitations to self-determination has had severe physical and mental implications for many of the people living in the Gaza Strip. The internet represents, for large parts of the population of the Strip, a far from ideal yet very important way to engage with the rest of the world.

The chapter demonstrates how combining the demand for Arabic language teaching with the opportunities offered by online communication tools may represent a way for tens of thousands of unemployed Palestinian youth to improve their economic conditions through online employment. It also discusses what is needed in order to expand the results of the training project to a scale that may ensure capacity building and sustainability.

In this chapter, we first illustrate the linguistic and social context of the Gaza Strip in terms of their specific relevance to the RM Borders TASOL programme. We then consider Arabic language teaching from a historical and contemporary perspective; we also discuss the role that can be played by communication technologies in online language teaching and learning. Following this, we briefly illustrate the TASOL collaboration between IUG and UofG in the context of the RM Borders Project, and what this collaboration managed to achieve within the parameters of an action research study and within the limited timeframe and resources available. Finally, we discuss what is still needed in order for the seeds planted in the course of the RM Borders Project to take root and grow to ensure a sustainable TASOL programme that can contribute to improve the lives of young graduates in the Gaza Strip and to offer high-quality, professional language courses to learners worldwide.

At the same time, this chapter also represents a claim for the teaching of languages to be recast as a humanities project, one that goes beyond technicist references to skills and competences. It intends to be a plea for the need for language teaching to reach into history, politics, economics and intercultural relations and, in so doing, it offers a concrete example of how languages may indeed act to bridge divides.

Opportunities

Arabic language: A Gazan resource that cannot be restricted

The fate of Arabic in Israel is a clear, recent example of the way in which languages can become sites for the symbolic power that derives from having official recognition as being 'legitimate' (Bourdieu, 1991). In July 2018, Arabic was removed as one of the official languages of the State of Israel,[3] a symbolic move that resulted in protests and in public Arabic language lessons which were attended by thousands of people. Moreover, Arabic sometimes suffers from xenophobic representation as a 'natural vehicle' for extremist ideas. 'Though Islam is not itself a language', writes sociolinguist Deborah Cameron (2012: 242), 'the negative qualities ascribed to it are often projected onto the languages used by Muslims, and especially onto Arabic, the language of the Qur'an'. This has, in a few cases, even resulted in people denouncing fellow travellers reading or writing in Arabic on flights (e.g. Khaleeli, 2016) and similar incidents.

Despite some anxieties around the Arabic language, it is an important language and is increasingly studied for a variety of reasons. Several authors (e.g. Ernst, 2013; Graddol, 2006; Versteegh, 2013) have discussed the reasons behind an increase in the demand for foreign language learning generally, and for Arabic specifically. Reviewing motivations for learning the Arabic language, Ahmed (2011) posits that these vary from one community to another, but they generally encompass economic, media, military or cultural interests. These four motives are additional to earlier and more established ones, such as reading the Holy Qur'an, Islamic studies, and Arab countries' culture, art and literature. Ahmed's review demonstrates the extent to which the rationale for teaching and learning Arabic has broadened over the years. Similarly, Al-Busheikhi (2002) highlights four key purposes for learning Arabic: (1) religious purposes – to be able to read the Holy Qur'an, the Hadith (the Sayings of the Prophet) and other religious texts; (2) professional purposes – to use Arabic in communication, orally and in writing, in specific profession-related fields such as management, commerce, diplomacy, tourism or other professions; (3) scientific purposes – to use Arabic for scholarly research and communication; and (4) cultural purposes – to know more about the Islamic Arab civilization in terms of its culture, history, arts and tourism.

Covering a variety of key thematic areas and different motivational spheres, the studies discussed above illustrate the extent to which Arabic is an international language that people aspire to learn for a wide range of purposes, including political, economic, military, diplomatic, touristic, religious, scientific, linguistic, cultural, social, artistic and literary purposes. The teaching of Arabic, however, necessitates the availability of Arabic language teaching specialists, who have full understanding of the key factors that facilitate learning, and who are educated and trained in such a way as to reflect the rapidly changing contexts for the teaching and learning of this particular language. In the next section, we discuss the ways in which online and mobile technologies can create job opportunities for trained teachers in the Gaza Strip, and at the same time raise their intercultural awareness and allow academic engagement with academic institutions beyond the Strip.

Availability of online teaching and learning

While there is a substantial focus on online and mobile teaching/learning tools and strategies to address educational needs in situations of emergency (e.g. Dankova & Giner, 2011; Ferrer *et al.*, 2013), little scholarship is available on the use of online tools to increase employment opportunities for people living in an enduring situation of crisis, as is the case in the Gaza Strip. Gaza is trying to make use of any available collaborations and of recent technologies to deliver online Arabic courses in order to create job prospects for university graduates. The flexibility remote working offers is particularly important for female teachers – who represent the majority of those working at the IUG Arabic Center – who can combine work and care duties and also avoid having to travel to the Center in the evenings.

Opportunities for online and mobile teaching/learning rest on the availability of reliable internet connections, of suitable hardware and software and of appropriate knowledge and skills, all of which are not necessarily bounded by geographical location. Higher education institutions (HEIs) in the Gaza Strip, such as IUG, have invested quite substantially in developing and maintaining reliable internet access. Connectivity in Gaza is not without its problems, especially since the internet provider is an Israeli company and thus outside Palestinian control (Tawil-Souri & Aouragh, 2014), but the internet has, so far, been an extremely important resource for Palestinians in the Gaza Strip. As a consequence, 'virtual mobility' (Aouragh, 2011a, 2011b) is increasingly becoming a way to circumvent forced physical immobility in the Strip. While no technological fix can 'transcend economic gaps' in the Strip (Aouragh, 2011b: 52), the internet can at least help to reduce isolation for Gaza's population, and provide them with an opportunity to engage in social and educational exchanges at the international level.

Electricity supply in the Gaza Strip is usually only available for four hours a day, but considerable financial and logistic efforts have been made by services, academic institutions and also individuals to ensure that generators keep the connection active and reliable for as many hours as possible. The internet maintains a link between Palestinians in the Gaza Strip, those living in the West Bank, and the Palestinian diaspora. It is also a tool for information, education, activism and campaigning, and a way for communicating and establishing personal relationships with individuals and groups worldwide. In this context, it is perhaps not surprising that reports '[...] show a systematic increase in household computer ownership from 26.4 percent in 2004 to 49.2 percent in 2009, and an increase in home internet access from 9.2 percent in 2004 to 28.5 percent in 2009 and to 57.7 percent in 2012' (Tawil-Souri & Aouragh, 2014: 199). As these figures are several years old, we can speculate that access has improved even further in more recent years, in particular through the use of mobile technologies.

With a (relatively) reliable internet connection, online opportunities for work become an option which can, however partially, redress the lack of employment for young graduates in the Gaza Strip (Fassetta et al., 2017). While, of course, not all jobs translate to an online environment, education worldwide increasingly depends on blended learning and virtual classrooms (Boyd, 2016), and online educational software and programmes tailored to situations of emergency and crisis are receiving increasing attention.[4] As Holmes and Gardner (2006) note, a major advantage of online educational spaces is the flexibility to teach international learners any time, anywhere, thereby bypassing spatial and temporal limitations. Promoting the use of flexible online teaching in Palestine is, therefore, 'an important key to combating unemployment, sharing knowledge, [and] overcoming restrictions on movement' imposed by the blockade (Pacetti, 2008: 2).

As well as tools to engage in maintaining connections to people outside the Gaza Strip, the internet also offers a range of educational platforms (e.g. Moodle, WizIQ, Massive Open Online Courses) that facilitate access to – and the sharing of – information, knowledge and understanding. Language teaching and learning is one area where the internet can offer opportunities otherwise unavailable and, with these, new employment prospects for online language courses open up. In the next section we illustrate the online training course that was at the heart of the RM Borders TASOL case study, which aimed to bring together global interest in Arabic language learning with increasingly reliable and accessible online teaching tools to prepare teachers in the Gaza Strip to work remotely.

Collaboration across borders

A 2016 RecoNow-TEMPUS report lists 49 tertiary education institutions in Palestine. These include universities, university colleges (offering both academic and technical or professional programmes), polytechnics and community colleges. More than 221,000 students were enrolled in these institutions at the time when the report was compiled, and the enrolment rate for the age group 18–24 years was more than 25.8%, a relatively high percentage by international standards in general, but particularly in comparison to other Middle Eastern countries (RecoNow, 2016).

The focus of Palestinian universities and colleges in the West Bank and the Gaza Strip is not just on gaining educational qualifications, but also on: increasing employability; improving standards of living; contributing to the development of the local community; preserving national identity and culture; and building academic and cultural bridges with the outside world. As Pacetti (2008: 2) notes: 'Education in Palestine has become a community investment in human resources whose benefits are not only economic, but also cultural and social.' In other words, for young Palestinians, education is the only 'rope of hope' to get a job, to be socially mobile, and to achieve a degree of independence.

As several other chapters in this volume point out (e.g. Abou Dagga, this volume), the Islamic University of Gaza's Strategic Plan for the 2015–2019 period emphasizes the importance of initiating teaching and training programmes and courses using online technologies and in partnership with local, regional and international institutions, in order to expand employment opportunities for its graduates. Much of the development of IUG's strategic plan draws on deep understanding and innovative strategies to overcome the numerous challenges facing HEIs in Gaza and to improve the future prospects of Gaza's graduates.

The Life-long Learning in Palestine (LLIP) TEMPUS Project (funded by the EU between 2012 and 2014) explored the potential for learning throughout the lifespan and across the vocational and academic divide in the Gaza Strip. It identified a critical need both for capacity building through lifelong learning in Palestine and for Arabic language teaching, in particular teaching delivered from the Gaza Strip (Hammond, 2012). Until 2016, however, only four universities in the West Bank offered limited and irregular TASOL courses for international students, and no university in the Gaza Strip had any TASOL provision. Furthermore, no university in the West Bank or Gaza offered any online TASOL programme centred on intercultural, interfaith and holistic principles. These considerations shaped the TASOL case study of the RM Borders Project, grounding the training of teachers of Arabic online.

The practical outcome planned for the TASOL case study was to demonstrate that an innovative, quality TASOL programme in Gaza, tailored for online delivery, would likely attract learners from around the world and lead to further international partnerships, regionally and globally. These partnerships are of immense importance to those experiencing a situation of siege, as they help to break, at least in part, the academic and intellectual isolation imposed by the blockade, thereby enabling scholars in the Gaza Strip to maintain academic, linguistic and intercultural relations with colleagues worldwide. Moreover, the TASOL case study aimed to show that a TASOL programme could help to create employment opportunities through the provision of a variety of academic and non-academic services for international learners, offering Arabic language courses online, and with the hope of further expanding this to face-to-face courses at IUG at such a time as the blockade may be lifted. This would be a modest employability objective considering the high rates of unemployment among graduates in Gaza and, in particular, in the field of teacher training and education sciences – where unemployment reaches 81.9% (Palestinian Central Bureau of Statistics, 2018) – but an important and ambitious goal nevertheless.

In light of the above considerations, and within the wider context of the AHRC RM Borders Project, the TASOL case study connected international researchers in intercultural language education based at UofG with language teachers at IUG. The Gazan teachers were, for the most part, trained EFL teachers wishing to expand their repertoire by adding online Arabic teaching to their skills. The objective was to ensure the provision of a high-quality and academically rigorous training programme to be delivered online in collaboration with UofG. Offering quality academic programmes and promoting the use of technology in teaching and learning have long been a top priority for IUG, and the TASOL programme was the first of its kind in Gaza, and in Palestine more widely.

The RM Borders TASOL training course started in May 2016 and lasted for 10 weeks. As anticipated earlier, eight IUG graduates were trained by a team of four international researchers and foreign language instructors who designed, developed and delivered a 60-hour bespoke course. Aiming to redress the lack in Palestine of TASOL trained teachers – in particular of teachers with expertise in online delivery (which will be discussed in more detail below) – the training was designed in very close collaboration with the teachers in the Gaza Strip. The training course was designed building on the teachers' knowledge, skills and expertise, and following a consultation to assess their needs and requirements. It was structured around five main modules of ten hours each, focusing on context, technology, pedagogy, language and creative methodologies, with the addition of a final reflection and forward planning module. Each module comprised six hours of asynchronous work for preparation, background reading and critical revisiting of materials and notes, as well as four hours of synchronous 'face-to-screen' meetings held via Skype. The course was developed as a piece of action research (Watts, 1985) based on a participatory, Freirean approach, which strived to start from – and build on – the trainees' existing knowledge, expertise and skills, and to avoid uncritical, decontextualized educational transfer (Perry & Tor, 2008).

As well as focusing on theory and strategies for language teaching, the course aimed to engage specifically with language teaching in an online environment, including on ways to minimize the challenges and maximize the opportunities offered by online tools. The course also included short practice lessons with volunteer learners, which were observed by the trainers and discussed with the trainee teachers both individually and collectively. As the training course was delivered via Skype, joint reflections by trainers and trainees at the end of meetings were held as an ongoing form of evaluation of the course and as a way to redress any shortcomings. This was informed by the collaborative spirit in which the course was structured and by the action research ethos that underpinned it (Fassetta et al., 2017).

Following the conclusion of the TASOL training course, all eight teachers received a certification to attest the successful completion of the course and later joined the Arabic Language Center at IUG. As part of the case study, moreover, a budget was allocated for the development of a website that would function as a portal for prospective students, offering an overview of the Arabic Center's courses and a way to enrol and pay for them. Additionally, to promote the course, a special launch offer consisting of a six-week free Arabic language course was widely advertised on social media. A total of 25 learners enrolled in the first run of the course; ten of these were Malaysian students studying at IUG, while 15 were online students from a range of different countries, including the USA, Italy, the UK, Turkey and Sweden.

Challenges and Ways Forward

Feedback on the experience of learning Arabic online was collected from the 15 online learners, and it was extremely positive. The Arabic teachers' dedication and commitment were highlighted as one of the strengths of the course, as well as their competent and thoughtful lesson planning and back-up strategies to bypass technical challenges. However, difficulties were also noted in relation to the quality of the internet connection, which was at times unreliable, and to delays due to power cuts which meant that lessons did not always start at the agreed time. More importantly, the lack of a curriculum fully grounded in Palestinian culture was identified as a weakness of the course, despite the fact that the teachers at the Arabic Center did their utmost to adapt existing materials developed in other Arabic speaking countries and materials for TESOL.

The need for qualified teachers

Although Gaza possesses the human, technical and institutional resources necessary for developing TASOL programmes tailored for online delivery, it also lacks enough qualified TASOL teachers, a shortage that several other Arab countries also lament (Alhawary, 2013, cited in Al-Hilali, 2014; Bashaar, 2011). The main cause for this problem is a lack of accredited TASOL teacher education programmes. As Ingold and Wang (2010: 12) emphasize, certification is 'a core aspect of the world language teacher supply system that must be reviewed and revised in light of new demands for a wider array of languages, program types, and delivery models'. However, no Palestinian university (and only a few Arab States universities) offer internationally recognized TASOL qualifications, such as Master's degrees, diplomas or certificates. While the RM Borders TASOL training course did result in a certification, this could only be a proof of attendance, as the course could not be accredited by either UofG or IUG, since it was not formally assessed nor part of the official programme of study at either university.

Redressing this challenge – and building capacity for the Arabic Center to function as a hub of excellence for online language teaching – requires the creation of a cohort of trainers with expertise, experience and know-how that are officially accredited, and who can train new language teachers as required. The first step in this direction was made with the TASOL case study, but a substantial investment in human resources and technical infrastructure for online teaching/learning is now needed. The extremely challenging situation created by the blockade for all sectors of society, including higher education, means that further training and expansion of the Arabic Center to ensure sustainability has to rely on 'academic solidarity' (Phipps & Barnett, 2007). The support of international institutions willing to share knowledge and expertise and to consider Palestinian institutions as potential partners with which to build further opportunities remains vital for the Arabic language programme to gain enough momentum to become sustainable.

The need for appropriate educational material

Another challenge the language programme faces is the serious shortage of innovative, engaging material that suits international learners who wish to learn Arabic for general and specific purposes (Alhawary, 2013, cited in Al-Hilali, 2014). In addition, there is a lack of pedagogical knowledge of ways to effectively incorporate educational technologies into

Arabic language teaching which is, as discussed above, crucial to the context of the Gaza Strip. As online courses such as Massive Open Online Courses (MOOCs) become increasingly the norm – at least in economically developed countries' institutions (Longstaff, 2014) – and as mobile learning gains more popularity as a way to deliver education in situations of emergencies and crisis,[4] opportunities for the design and development of an Arabic language course tailored for online delivery are within reach. Collaboration between academic institutions in the Gaza Strip and global partners with the necessary expertise is needed in order to ensure capacity building and to attract learners. The co-development of materials with language experts in the Gaza Strip is essential to guarantee that future language courses can be used in conjunction with accessible online tools, and that they are based on innovative and effective pedagogies fully grounded in Palestinian culture. The pedagogies we envisage draw from social justice theory, such as the capabilities approach (CA) pioneered by Sen (2009) and further articulated by Nussbaum (2000, 2011). The strength of the CA for language learning to be delivered from the Gaza Strip lies in the emphasis it puts on education (and this can include language education), not just as a means for economic development but also – and crucially, for this specific context – as a way to foster '[…] democratic citizenship, and understanding and solidarity under conditions of cultural difference and diversity' (Walker, 2003: 170).

The need for a strong technological infrastructure

Last, but certainly not least, online language delivery needs the support of technological infrastructures that are reliable, widely accessible and easily maintained and updated. This implies substantial costs that IUG, like all other institutions in the Gaza Strip and other parts of Palestine, cannot readily afford. Palestinian public universities, including IUG, suffer from severe and increasing financial deficits ranging between '20% and 50%' as reported by the Independent Commission for Human Rights (2017: 25). This deficit is mainly caused by the inability of students' families to the pay tuition fees, as almost 80% of Palestinians in Gaza depend on international humanitarian assistance for survival (UNWRA, 2015). To redress this shortcoming, IUG has taken several tough measures over the last few years. For example, over the past four years, IUG employees have been receiving, on average, 60% of their salaries, in addition to a further reduction to these same salaries of 10%. Of course, this is not sustainable nor, in the long run, good for Gaza's economy. Until the blockade is lifted, therefore, the only other possible route to developing a much needed technological infrastructure is through project partnerships with other HEIs or through donations from charitable organizations. Far from being the best possible solution, these remain the only viable options for Palestinian universities under the current circumstances.

Despite the inevitable challenges, the RM Borders TASOL programme has offered a first step towards initiating online Arabic language provision from the Gaza Strip. It has resulted in paid work for all the trained teachers, in further collaborations between IUG and UofG, and in some cases even in new, personal friendships. All of this cannot be underestimated, and it represents a foundation on which a lot more can be built. However, the RM Borders TASOL case study represents only a first step, and challenges as well as opportunities lie ahead.

Conclusion and Recommendations

> We do what prisoners do,
> And what the jobless do:
> We cultivate hope.
>
> (From the poem, 'Under siege' by Mahmoud Darwish, 1942–2008)[5]

Suggesting ways in which the 'Palestinian question' can be solved is, of course, well beyond the scope of this chapter, although ultimately the only way to ease the situation of pain and pressure endured by the people of the Gaza Strip is for the blockade to end. In the current circumstances, the people of the Gaza Strip are denied the opportunity to live the lives they have reason to value (Sen, 2009), and to enjoy the essential freedoms of safety and self-determination that represent the foundations of social justice (Nussbaum, 2011). As Feldman (2016: 101) writes: '[…] Gazans are immobilized in every sense: cut off from other members of their community, isolated from the "international community", deprived of economic opportunities, basic goods, and access to advanced medical care. Imposed immobility is itself a form of violence against people, and it cruelly magnifies the violence of military assault.' The Gaza Strip has now been isolated almost entirely for over 10 years. Recurrent bombings have killed large numbers of civilians and destroyed infrastructures. Life in the Gaza Strip is hard.

Despite these challenges, however, Gazans endeavour to defy the limitations that are imposed on them and to change their circumstances, resisting the isolation and impotence the blockade forces on them. The internet is an important tool in this struggle, allowing people in the Gaza Strip to maintain contact with the world, to know others and to let others know them, despite the almost impassable boundaries within which they are confined. Importantly, online tools for communication open up opportunities for online employment, sharing with others the language and culture of the Strip.

In this chapter, we discussed the increasing demand for Arabic language learning and the opening up of opportunities allowed by online tools and the ways in which these two elements can combine to offer employment for teachers in the Gaza Strip. We illustrated the TASOL training programme that was part of the RM Borders Project and its outcomes, demonstrating the importance of collaborative work and partnerships developed through networks of academic and international solidarity. While this showed ways in which online opportunities can help to meet, albeit on a small scale, the employment needs of Gazan graduates, we also highlighted what is yet to be achieved before online Arabic language teaching from the Gaza Strip can become an effective source of income for Palestinian language teachers.

To ensure a sustainable, certified TASOL programme for the Gaza Strip that builds on the knowledge and experience gathered in the course of the RM Borders Project and of the existing skills developed by Palestinian academics and teachers, we offer a set of recommendations: first, supporting the development of TASOL teachers in Gaza through the design of regular training courses in partnership with experts from partner universities; secondly, the design of appropriate learning materials that not only reflect the diverse motives for learning Arabic, but are also thoroughly grounded in Palestinian culture, and aim to develop human connections across borders; thirdly, adopting educational technologies as ways to overcome restrictions on human mobility and to support both TASOL and teacher education programmes; and fourthly, forging partnerships to facilitate the development of an accredited teacher education programme in TASOL to be delivered virtually, on campus or through blended learning.

Many would agree that the situation in the Gaza Strip is one of the clearest manifestations of injustice in modern times. As a form of peaceful resistance, the TASOL programme supports efforts to restore self-determination and dignity to a population that has had these rights curtailed for far too long.

Notes

(1) Israel and Egypt control virtually all movement of people and goods to/from the Gaza Strip, by land, air and water. We refer to this situation with the term 'blockade' throughout the paper. However, we will also use the term 'state of siege' to refer to the circumstances experienced by people in the Gaza Strip, in line with the definition of the Online Collins Dictionary: 'A state of siege is a situation in which a government or other authority puts restrictions on the movement of people into or out of a country, town, or building' (see https://www.collinsdictionary.com/dictionary/english/state-of-siege).
(2) 2008/2009 Operation Cast Led; 2012 Operation Pillar of Defence; 2014 Operation Protective Edge.
(3) See https://www.haaretz.com/by-degrading-arabic-israel-has-degraded-arabs-1.629 2827 (accessed 18 September 2018).
(4) Since 2011 UNESCO has hosted a yearly 'Mobile Learning Week', during which international experts from the public, private and third sector share insights on the use of online and mobile learning technologies to deliver education for all. The 2017 edition of the event, organized in collaboration with UNHCR, focused on online and mobile education 'in situations of emergencies and crisis' (see http://www.unesco.org/new/en/mlw).

(5) Mahmoud Darwish (1941–2008) was a Palestinian poet and author. His works gave a voice to the struggles of Palestinian people, and he is widely recognized as Palestine's national poet (see https://www.britannica.com/biography/Mahmoud-Darwish).

References

Ahmed, R.A. (2011) *Nithaam tafaa'uli lita'leem al 'arabiyya li ghayr al- naatiqeen biha [An Interactive Approach to Teaching Arabic to Speakers of Other Languages]*. Vol. 1. Majma': Mijallat Jami'at Al Madina Al-'Aalamiyya. See http://ojs.mediu.edu.my/index.php/majmaa/article/view/29 (accessed 25 April 2016).

Al-Busheikhi, E. (2002) Ta'leem al-lugha al-'arabiyya lil-naatiqeen bighayriha min man-thuur watheefi [A functional approach to teaching Arabic to speakers of other languages]. In *Proceedings of Al-lugha al-'arabiyya ila ayn [Arabic Language: Where To] Conference*, Rabat, Morocco, 2002. Rabat: Islamic Educational, Scientific and Cultural Organization (ISESCO). See https://www.isesco.org.ma/ar/publications/ (accessed 19 July 2019).

Al-Hilali, Z. (2014) Towards enhancing the status quo of Arabic as a foreign language (AFL). In *Proceedings of the Fifth Annual Gulf Comparative Education Society Symposium: Locating the National in the International*, 8–10 April (pp. 86–94). Dubai: Gulf Comparative Education Society (GCES) Publications. See http://gces.ae/wp-content/uploads/2016/09/Fifth-Annual-GCES-Symposium-Conference-Proceedings.pdf (accessed 3 June 2018).

Aouragh, M. (2011a) Confined offline, traversing online Palestinian mobility through the prism of the internet. *Mobilities* 6 (3), 375–397.

Aouragh, M. (2011b) *Palestine Online: Transnationalism, the Internet and the Construction of Identity*. London: Tauris Academic Studies.

Bashaar, S. (2011) *Nahwa manhaj tatbeeqi lita'leem al-lugha al-arabiyya li-ghaiyr al-naatiqeen biha [Towards a Functional Methodology for Teaching Arabic to Speakers of Other Languages]*. Al-yaum al-diraasi hawla al-manaahij. Tizi Ouzu, Algeria: Tizi Ouzu University.

Bourdieu, P. (1991) *Language and Symbolic Power*. Cambridge: Polity Press.

Boyd, D. (2016) What would Paulo Freire think of Blackboard™: Critical pedagogy in an age of online learning. *International Journal of Critical Pedagogy* 7 (1), 165–186.

Cameron, D. (2012) *Verbal Hygiene*. Abingdon: Routledge.

Dankova, P. and Giner, C. (2011) Technology in aid of learning for isolated refugees. *Forced Migration Review* 38, 11–12.

Enrst, C.W. (2013) *It's Not Just Academic! Essays on Sufism and Islamic Studies*. London: Sage.

Fassetta, G., Imperiale, M.G., Frimberger, K., Attia, M. and Al-Masri, N. (2017) Online teacher training in a context of forced immobility: The case of Gaza, Palestine. *European Education* 49 (2–3), 133–150.

Feldman, I. (2016) Gaza: Isolation. In H. Tawil-Souri and D. Matar (eds) *Gaza as Metaphor* (pp. 95–101). London: Hurst.

Ferrer, M.H, Hodges, J. and Bonnardel, N. (2013) *The MoLE Project: An International Experiment about Mobile Learning Environment*. In *Proceedings of ECCE '13, the 31st European Conference on Cognitive Ergonomics*, Toulouse, France, 26–28 August.

Graddol, D. (2006) *English Next: Why Global English May Mean the End of English as a Foreign Language*. London: British Council.

Hammond, K. (2012) Lifelong learning in Palestine. *Holy Land Studies* 11 (1), 79–85.

Holmes, B. and Gardner, J. (2006) *E-learning: Concepts and Practice*. London: Sage.

Ingold, C.W. and Wang, S.C. (2010) *The Teachers We Need: Transforming World Language Education in the United States*. College Park, MD: National Foreign Language Center at the University of Maryland.

Khaleeli, H. (2016) The perils of 'flying while Muslim'. *The Guardian*, 8 August. See https://www.theguardian.com/world/2016/aug/08/the-perils-of-flying-while-muslim (accessed 7 May 2019).

Longstaff, E. (2014) The prehistory of MOOCs: Inclusive and exclusive access in the cyclical evolution of higher education. *Journal of Organisational Transformation & Social Change* 11 (3), 164–184.

Nussbaum, M. (2000) *Women and Human Development: The Capabilities Approach*. Cambridge, MA: Cambridge University Press.

Nussbaum, M. (2011) *Creating Capabilities: The Human Development Approach*. Cambridge, MA: Harvard University Press.

Pacetti, E. (2008) Improving the quality of education in Palestine through e-learning and ICT: The bottom-up approach for a sustainable pedagogy. In *Proceedings of the Conference Knowledge Construction in E-learning Context: CSCL, ODL, ICT and SNA in Education*, 1–2 September, Cesena, Italy. See http://ceur-ws.org/Vol-398/ (accessed 8 June 2018).

Palestinian Central Bureau of Statistics (2018) A Special Press Release For The Students Who Sit For The General Secondary School Certification Examinations 'Tawjihi'. See http://www.pcbs.gov.ps/post.aspx?lang=en&ItemID=3513# (accessed 30 April 2020).

Perry, L.B. and Tor, G. (2008) Understanding educational transfer: Theoretical perspectives and conceptual frameworks. *Prospects* 38, 509–526.

Phipps, A. and Barnett, R. (2007) Academic hospitality. *Arts and Humanities in Higher Education* 6 (3), 237–254.

RecoNow-TEMUPS (2016) The higher education system in Palestine. National report. See http://www.reconow.eu/files/fileusers/5140_National-Report-Palestine-RecoNOW.pdf (accessed 8 June 2018).

Sen, A. (2009) *The Idea of Justice*. London: Penguin.

Tawil-Souri, H. and Aouragh, M. (2014) Intifada 3.0? Cyber colonialism and Palestinian resistance. *Arab Studies Journal* 22 (1), 102–133.

Tawil-Souri, H. and Matar, D. (2016) (eds) *Gaza as Metaphor*. London: Hurst.

The Independent Commission for Human Rights (2017) *Alhaqu fi Alta'leem wa alazma almalia fi aljami'at alfilastinia al'ama [The right to education and the financial crisis in Palestinian public universities]*. Report 89. See https://ichr.ps/ar/1/8.

Tinsley, T. and Board, K. (2017) *Languages for the Future: The Foreign Languages the United Kingdom Needs to Become a Truly Global Nation*. London: British Council.

UNRWA (UN Relief and Work Agency) (2015) Gaza situation report 94. See https://www.unrwa.org/newsroom/emergency-reports/gaza-situation-report-94 (accessed 6 June 2018).

Versteegh, K. (2013) History of Arabic language teaching. In K. Wahba, Z. Taha and L. England (eds) *Handbook for Arabic Language Teaching Professionals in the 21st Century* (pp. 3–12). New York: Routledge.

Walker, M. (2003) Framing social justice in education: What does the 'capabilities' approach offer? *British Journal of Educational Studies* 51 (2), 168–187.

Watts, H. (1985) When teachers are researchers, teaching improves. *Journal of Staff Development* 6 (2), 118–127.

7 (In)articulability of Pain and Trauma: Idioms of Distress in the Gaza Strip

Maria Grazia Imperiale

This chapter explores ways in which distress is expressed in the Gaza Strip. The study on which the chapter is based was developed as part of an Art and Humanities Research Council (AHRC) – Global Challenge Research Fund (GCRF) project entitled *Idioms of Distress, Resilience and Wellbeing: Enhancing Understanding about Mental Health in Multilingual Contexts* (henceforth: *Idioms of Distress, Resilience and Wellbeing*), led by the P.I. Professor Alison Phipps at the University of Glasgow. The project was an interdisciplinary and international research study which included partners in the UK (University of Glasgow, University of Liverpool, University of Manchester), in Uganda (Makerere University), in Ghana (University of Ghana) and in the Gaza Strip (Islamic University of Gaza), with contributions also from a UK-based Zimbabwean poet and academic.

The Idioms of Distress, Resilience and Wellbeing Project aimed to enhance understanding about ways of expressing distress and wellbeing in the non-UK countries involved. It made use of art-based methodologies (e.g. storytelling methodologies) in order to elicit idioms of distress, resilience and wellbeing used in the different contexts, working multilingually and through linguistic ethnographies. One of the main outputs of the project was a dance performance produced in Ghana, with the young dancers of the Noyam African Dance Institute. Guided by some of the project team members, the young people devised a dance performance which comprised an inter-semiotic translation and artistic representation of the linguistic idioms of distress, resilience and wellbeing gathered in Ghana, Zimbabwe, Uganda and Gaza. The aim was to promote intercultural understanding of different ways of expressing distress and, by producing a digital and artistic representation of linguistic data, it also aimed to develop training materials on mental health and intercultural communication to be used in human development activities.

In this chapter I focus on the Gaza case study that was part of the project outlined above, as this case study entails considerable contextual differences – in terms of research context, methodologies, findings and ways of working – when compared to the other research settings. I analyze what in global mental health are called 'idioms of distress' (Nichter, 1981), that is, culturally constituted ways to express distress that are associated with values, norms and health concerns. 'Idioms of distress' have not received attention in applied linguistics and in language education, as will be shown in the literature review below, whereas they have been extensively explored in the field of global mental health, developing intercultural understandings of mental wellbeing and context-sensitive psychosocial support and interventions.

Due to the siege and closure of borders that makes getting in and out of the Gaza Strip extremely challenging, this international collaboration was conducted online. Rather than using storytelling methodologies, as done in the other contexts, the research team opted to collect *secondary* data on idioms of distress, resilience and wellbeing by scrutinizing media coverage of the 2014 military operation launched by the Israeli army against the Gaza Strip. This choice was dictated by ethical considerations, further discussed later in this chapter. The idioms collected were translated from Arabic into English, and were then analyzed thematically, working multilingually and interculturally. In order to understand the idioms used and the meanings they carry, the translation adopted a context-based approach, considering not only the idiom but also the context in which the idiom is used.

In this chapter, I present a preliminary analysis of two of the categories into which the idioms were classified. These focus on the contrast between the unspeakability of trauma and pain, vis-à-vis the use of vivid body metaphors, which describe in detail war scenes. As the analysis of the secondary data will show, if on the one hand trauma and pain might be 'language destroying' (Scarry, 1985), on the other hand, vivid bodily metaphors were used in order to denounce the injustice and the sufferings caused by the war.

This chapter is organized as follows. I introduce literature in global mental health and in applied linguistics on 'idioms of distress, resilience and wellbeing'. I then describe the methodology and the remote ways of working that were adopted in the Gaza case study. Finally, I analyze and discuss the idioms collected and conclude with some recommendations for future work.

Idioms of Distress, Resilience and Wellbeing: A Review of the Literature

In global mental health

'Idioms of distress' are culturally and contextually grounded expressions through which people articulate and frame their experiences of mental distress, of pain and pressure. The concept has been developed and used in global mental health, in order to provide appropriate psychological interventions and assessment of distress. Especially in times of mobility of populations affected by natural and man-made disasters, the concept of 'idioms of distress' can aid the work of practitioners engaging with people who suffer from mental distress, trauma, post-traumatic stress disorders and other issues (Nichter, 1981, 2010).

The literature in global mental health is vast. The concept was originally developed by Mark Nichter. In his initial work, Nichter (1981) focused on the analysis of alternative modes for expressing distress used by women in South India: he was interested in the reasons why particular groups embrace different ways of expressing distress, focusing on pragmatics and the micropolitics of expressing distress. He argued that being attentive to the ways in which distress was communicated – i.e. to the idioms of distress, especially to metaphors – helped him build emphatic connections with the individuals suffering from mental distress. His studies were framed by an understanding of the dynamic social contexts that affect ways in which collective stress and anxiety are expressed, as well as of individuals' manifestations and expressions.

Nichter (2010), furthermore, understood that some idioms are 'commonplace', whereas others are 'culturally unique'. For example, references to cleanliness and order are considered common ways of expressing distress, as they are universal processes in the expression of a psychological condition identifiable with obsessive compulsive disorder. However, for Brahman women in India, cleanliness is associated with purity and individuals' identity, hence it carries deep localized cultural meanings. Nichter therefore highlighted the importance of identifying culturally unique idioms in order to develop localized and context-sensitive interventions. He also noted that, despite being culturally resonant ways of expression, idioms of distress are not static and may be even be contradictory. He argued for an approach attentive to the semantics, pragmatics and micropolitics of communication which avoids static representations and rather allows for contradictory and negotiable presentations to emerge.

In his latest definition of 'idioms of distress', he states:

> Idioms of distress are socially and culturally resonant means of experiencing and expressing distress in local worlds. They are evocative and index past traumatic memories as well as present stressors, such as anger, powerlessness, social marginalization and insecurity, and possible future sources of anxiety, loss and angst. Idioms of distress communicate experiential states that lie on a trajectory from the mildly stressful to depths of suffering that render individuals and groups incapable of functioning as productive members of society. In some cases, idioms of distress are culturally and interpersonally effective ways of expressing and coping with distress, and in other cases, they are indicative of psychopathological states that undermine individual and collective states of well-being. (Nichter, 2010: 405)

Nichter (2010) posited that the importance of idioms of distress consists not only in enhancing understandings about mental distress, but also in perceiving them as constructs and alternative modes of expressions of coping mechanisms. Embedded in the concept of idioms of distress, therefore, are also those of resilience and wellbeing.

Furthermore, it is important to note that idioms of distress are not independent of the sociopolitical context in which they are produced. For example, in a case study analyzing individual expression of distress in Guinea Bissau, de Jong and Reis (2010) argued that idioms of distress need to be considered and understood within the sociopolitical contexts, and not just in terms of psychological processes: the expression of distress, in their study, is associated with symbols that carry cultural resonance within a social movement to communicate traumatic stress and sufferings caused by war.

Within the Idioms of Distress, Resilience and Wellbeing research project I reviewed the literature on Arabic idioms of distress and, in particular, on Palestinian expressions of trauma. Rothenberg (2004) conducted an anthropological study in which she described the Westernized medicalization of mental health, vis-à-vis local beliefs in jinns (spirits) and traditional healers' treatments in the Gaza Strip and the West Bank. In her book, she discusses the language of spirit possession, which may be interpreted in terms of idioms of distress.

More relevant to our work, because of its focus on language, were a study on the word *hamm* (Nasir *et al.*, 2018) and a study on the idiom 'feeling broken/destroyed' in the Palestinian contexts (Barber *et al.*, 2016). The former focused on the definition, causes and consequences of *hamm*, which is a multilayered Arabic word used to express suffering. Participants defined it as a feeling of sadness, stress, anxiety or discomfort, often caused by social, economic and political factors: gender issues and family obligations were reported to be among the main causes, as well as the Israeli military occupation which causes family separation, difficult living conditions and mental distress for the Palestinian population. The latter study identified and developed a quantitative measure of the construct of mental suffering expressed by the idiom 'feeling broken or destroyed' in the Palestinian context. The study involved a mixed-methods research methodology: through interviews, participants articulated in Arabic characterizations of suffering, using words such as being broken, exhausted, tired, crushed, destroyed and shaken up (Barber *et al.*, 2016: 7). In the survey, the researchers asked participants how many times they were feeling broken/destroyed/emotionally exhausted and worried about the future.

The authors found that 'feeling broken or destroyed' was commonly experienced, although these were also constructs signifying depression and trauma-related stress. The study highlighted that these sentiments directly reflect the political history of the protracted conflict that

Palestinians experience. The authors decided to label the feelings as the participants did, i.e. using the original language, since they:

> found no existing construct that could adequately serve as an overarching concept for the sentiments that were articulated in the narratives and that we subsequently coded, quantified, and tested. (Barber *et al.*, 2016: 13)

Retaining original language helped foreground the role of context in defining this particular form of mental suffering since, as reported by participants, it was the economic, sociopolitical and everyday difficult living conditions that impacted on individuals' mental wellbeing.

In a recent report, a similar approach addressing the mental health of displaced Syrian people was used by Hassan *et al.* (2015) to develop a list of idioms of distress used by the Syrian population, giving translations of Arabic and Kurdish idioms into English. The report aimed to provide information on the sociocultural background of Syrians in addition to cultural aspects related to mental health and psychosocial wellbeing. As a result of the ongoing violence and the difficult circumstances in which displaced Syrians live, psychological and social distress is manifested in social behavior, and in emotional and cognitive problems.

In applied linguistics and intercultural studies

In intercultural studies and applied linguistics, several projects investigated the expressions of emotions in different languages.[1] However, to the best of my knowledge, the concept of 'idioms of distress' – as defined above – received no attention in these fields. In order to shed light on studies on 'idioms of distress' in applied linguistics and intercultural studies, I reviewed and examined leading journals in the respective fields (e.g. *Applied Linguistics, International Journal of Applied Linguistics, Language and Intercultural Communication Journal*), after a systematic literature search in the main databases in Translation Studies and Education brought no relevant results. The results of the systematic literature review show that there is a considerable gap both in theoretical understanding of the concept and in empirical research in the areas of intercultural studies, applied linguistics and linguistic anthropology. The systematic literature review revealed that there are *no* relevant studies in those fields.

However, in my doctoral research (Imperiale, 2018) which focused on English language education in the Gaza Strip, I discussed the idea of 'languaging wellbeing' and 'languaging distress', understood as capabilities that students and language teachers in the Gaza Strip are keen to develop through language education. I use the term 'capability' instead of skill, as I drew upon the capabilities approach as developed by Martha Nussbaum (1997, 2000) and Amartya Sen (1999). The capabilities approach is a normative framework for evaluating wellbeing, which is defined as the freedom to pursue the life that individuals value and have reason to value.

The findings of my doctoral research showed that the participants, who were pre-service English teachers, valued the development of a teaching approach that considers language education for wellbeing. In the Gaza Strip, this meant to address and resist, through language, the difficult living conditions and the injustice of the occupation. English language education helps construct individuals' wellbeing as it helps to develop voice and agency. Rather than focusing only on 'expressing' distress and wellbeing, participants in the doctoral study showed that in language and relationality new realities can be constructed: I therefore called this 'languaging distress/wellbeing'.

Languaging is the faculty of making meaning using one's own language(s) – including the ones in which the person is less competent. Languaging is an embodied way of being and a way of knowing in order to become a critical social being (Phipps & Gonzalez, 2004). In the post-war context of the Gaza Strip, the participants of my doctoral study nurtured their capability of 'languaging distress', and also of 'languaging wellbeing'. Languaging in this context is not a synonym for 'externalizing' emotions as in psychologized approaches, but it rather encompasses the construction of emotions through social interaction. The capability of 'languaging distress' highlights how these participants, in language, worked through their distress, which was caused mainly by frequent military operations and the siege. The process of 'languaging wellbeing' highlights how they not only expressed distress, but also insisted on smiling and laughing in the face of despair, shaping their mental wellbeing in interaction (Imperiale, 2018).

Methodology and Remote Ways of Working

The AHRC-GCRF Idioms of Distress, Resilience and Wellbeing Project adopted storytelling methodologies and linguistic ethnographies in Ghana, Zimbabwe and Uganda. However, with regard to the context of the Gaza Strip, borders were virtually impassable (see Phipps *et al.*, this volume), and pressure and pain as experienced by potential participants in Gaza were different from the other research settings. The research team working in the Gaza context was composed of the Co-Investigator (Co-I) on the project, Dr Nazmi Al Masri, and two Master's students: Safaa Abu Rahma and Yaser Alsattari. They were based at the Islamic University of Gaza (IUG), while I worked as the project's researcher, based at the University of Glasgow (UofG). We adopted a different approach from the other case studies, which best responded to the context needs, which included working online, across imposed borders and barriers, and which involved the collection of secondary data.

Our online ways of working built upon online methodologies developed in previous research projects in which some members of the team were also involved (Fassetta *et al.*, 2017; Imperiale, 2018). We established weekly Skype meetings for which accurate minutes were written up and then shared among the research team via email. For more immediate communication we used Facebook Messenger and WhatsApp. As also discussed in our previous studies (Fassetta *et al.*, 2017; Imperiale, 2018), the difficulties of working online were numerous. First of all, the internet connection at IUG and at UofG was not always reliable and, as a consequence, several meetings lasted longer than expected, since time was spent on trying – patiently and persistently – to get reconnected. In addition, frequent power-cuts in Gaza meant that the Master's students were restricted mostly to the times when they could be physically present at IUG, where generators ensure the smooth running of electricity and the internet.

Another constraint that we had to face was that the Master's students did not have access to the same resources as the Co-I and I did, since we had, respectively, a guest account and a staff account for the UofG library. The database at IUG's library, which the Master's students used, offers access to a limited number of journals and monographs compared to the one at UofG. This was a major challenge for the research team, especially at the stage of conducting the literature review. As I had access to a larger number of journals, I focused on the desk-review whereas the Master's students, with appropriate supervision, focused on the data collection.

As part of our online ways of working, we ensured that our communication was *open, frank* and *straightforward* at all times, both during our Skype meetings and in our email exchanges. Being aware of the possible communicative misunderstandings that may arise when working in an intercultural team *and* at a distance, this was an important feature of the online dimension of our research, and we deliberately agreed on having a transparent, clear and open way of communicating. Even though at times all the members of the team risked sounding too direct, we decided that it was the best way to maximize our learning and therefore our research encounter. Fortunately – and in all likelihood due to the relationship of trust that the P.I., Co-I and myself had already established over several years of working together on a range of projects – there were no significant tensions, as each and every team member recognized the importance of adopting transparent and respectful ways of communicating.

An example of our approach to collaboration occurred when the team decided to collect secondary data rather than using (digital) storytelling or other art-based methodologies as employed by the other case studies of the project. While having a conversation on ethics and ethical ways of approaching potential participants to be involved in storytelling, one of the two Master's students clearly stated that it would have been better *not* to use those methodologies in this particular case study, since we 'would not want to make people who had lived the traumatic experience of war, relive it by re-telling their experiences *just* for a research project, would we?!' (minutes of a Skype meeting). In addition, none of us working on the

Gaza case study was a trained psychologist or held a degree in global mental health. As a matter of researchers' deontological code of ethics, based on the principle of duty of care for potential participants, there was immediate agreement on ensuring that we would not run the risk that anyone might be hurt or negatively affected by the research nor be made to relive difficult and traumatic memories. Tuhiwai-Smith (2012) expresses her disdain for the word 'research' as something that is associated with the careers of academics who build their fame on the pain of others. The reflections of the Master's student quoted above, who is a Palestinian living in Gaza and therefore shares the same difficult knowledge and traumatic experiences of potential participants, echoed Tuhiwai-Smith's concerns about the exploitation of pain and helped to ensure that the research project was conducted to the highest ethical standards. The ways in which these concerns were expressed – very frankly and honestly – demonstrates the transparency that we adopted in our communication, while the fact that the Master's student felt able to express these concerns in this way shows how a truly collaborative relationship was achieved among all the team members.

The two IUG Master's students achieved consent to access and then scrutinized the archives of *Al Jazeera Arabic*, *Maan TV* (a local media agency in Gaza), and of the websites *Palestine Today* and *The Palestine Information Center*. They focused on audio- and video-recorded interviews and on written recounts collected during the war in the summer of 2014.

Even though we predominantly used English as a lingua franca for our meetings, the idioms collected were in Standard Arabic and in colloquial Palestinian Arabic. They were then translated into English by the Master's students. The analysis was conducted on the English translation, cross-referencing the original. Since I have an intermediate knowledge of standard Arabic and of Palestinian Arabic, I was able to follow the interviews and to use the transcripts both in Arabic and in their English translation. In the initial phase of the study, a list of 191 idioms was compiled. Some of them were repeated throughout the data, whereas others were excluded since they were not found to be idioms of distress, following Nichter's definition.

I subsequently developed a preliminary analysis of the idioms and of the interviews collected. While I started to analyze the *list* of idioms collected, I soon realized that using this format would have led to misleading interpretations and misunderstanding – as will be shown in the following section. I therefore opted for analyzing the idioms *in context*, looking at the whole interviews and written recounts from which these were taken.

In the following section I present idioms related to the unspeakability of traumatic experiences, vis-à-vis the vivid descriptions of images of wars that emerged in interviews. I show how constructs such as 'We were destroyed' and 'I couldn't breathe' were not only used metaphorically, but rather indicated a real, physical condition due to bombardments and military attacks.

Discussion of Findings

The unspeakability of trauma

In situations of intense pain and pressure, of mental distress and of trauma, it is often posited that language fails and the self needs to find a new coherent way to express the experience and its related feelings and emotions. In *The Body in Pain,* Elaine Scarry (1985) reflects on the unspeakable dimension of trauma and pain, suggesting that intense pain requires others to translate it into words and speech:

> Intense pain is also language-destroying: as the content of one's world disintegrates, so that which would express and project the self is robbed of its source and its subject. Words, self and voice are lost, or nearly lost, through the intense pain. (Scarry, 1985: 35)

Pain and trauma, therefore, are often unspeakable. In the video-interviews we collected and examined as part of our secondary data analysis, we found that, on several occasions, the interviewee hesitates to speak, and openly declares that there is nothing that can be said, making, instead, frequent use of proverbs invoking Allah and expressing thankfulness to Allah and the prophet Mohammed. It is difficult in those cases to assess the level of distress.

For example, in a video-interview conducted by Maan TV, a man shows the interviewer the interior of his house, which was destroyed during the military operations in 2014. A group of young men who were in the house at the time were killed by Israeli soldiers, and one of them was stabbed to death. The interviewee shows the knife that was used to stab one of his friends, still covered in blood. He also shows seven bullets to the camera. During the interview the man repeatedly says the following sentences, without describing what happened:

حسبى الله و انت نعم الوكيل إيش بدنا نقول أكتر من هيك	²Sufficient for us is Allah is he is the best disposer of affairs, what can I say more For us Allah
حسبى الله و نعم الوكيل فيهم	Sufficient for us is Allah is he is the best disposer of affairs
اشى لا يتصوره العقل	It is something beyond imagination
مش عارفين ايش نحكي	We don't know what to say
إحنا أقوى من هيك إن شا الله	We are stronger than such trial InshAllah

All these idioms refer to the difficulty of articulating pain and suffering in the face of adversity, of death and destruction. They suggest that the man who was being interviewed avoided describing the traumatic experience he lived, since language is failing, and he may find restoration only in Allah.

During the interview, the man interviewed most of the time looked away from the camera. His eyes rather looked at the floor or towards his left. He shook his hand, bringing it on the side of his forehead, and he then pulled his arm down, his eyes averted. He shook his head, lifted his eyebrows in a frown showing disagreement. His non-verbal communication appears to show that he is feeling negative emotions, and he is speechless. His body gestures and the duration of his looking away during the interaction might indicate that he was suffering. It was only when showing the seven bullets that he looked straight into the camera and at the interviewer. While pointing at the bullets, looking straight into the camera, he said:

| مش عارفين ايش نحكي | ³We don't know what to say |

At this point, another person – also present at the interview – took over, describing in detail how the Israeli soldiers entered the room and how the fight started, causing the death of four Palestinians. As Phipps (2014) suggests, when language fails we might need other individuals to translate our pain into words: the interviewee in this video clip relies on others to tell his story, and on the showing of the bullets in order to silently tell what he had been through. The interviewer, bearing witness to what happened, has a responsibility towards the interviewee, that is, to translate personal and invisible pain into a visible documentary which testifies to traumatic knowledge and experiences.

We gathered many idioms of this kind, which I categorized under the theme of 'unspeakability of trauma'. What is evident in these examples is, in addition to the inability to speak, a frequent use of religious invocations.

الواحد إيش يوصفلك	⁴How can I describe it for you
القول مش حينفع/ لا اله الا الله محمد رسول الله و بس	Words are sterile/there is no God but Allah and Mohammed is His messenger and that is sufficient
اكثر من هيك ايش بدي اوصف ايش بدي اقول	What can I say describe or say more
مش حقدر اوصفلك	I will not be able to describe to you

This confirms the findings of Hassan *et al.* (2015) who, similarly, noted that Syrian displaced people made frequent use of references to Allah and the prophet Mohammed, making it more difficult to assess the actual level of anxiety and distress vis-à-vis the manifestation of their religious beliefs. Hassan *et al.* (2015) associated these sentences with the expression of despair and a sense of helplessness and hopelessness.

The idioms 'We are broken/destroyed' and 'I could not breathe', and vivid descriptions of war scenes

In contrast with the idioms related to the unspeakability of pain and trauma discussed above, we found a high frequency of idioms such as 'we are broken and destroyed' and 'I could not breathe'. In previous studies these idioms are usually classified as metaphorical manifestations of despair, distress and post-traumatic stress disorders (see Barber *et al.*, 2016). However, in our case study, we also found that these idioms were used to describe actual war scenes.

In the interviews we analyzed, we found that the following idioms were often repeated:

ادمرنا دمار شامل	⁵We are completely destroyed
اتحطمنا ميتين احنا مش عايشين	We are broken, we are dead not alive

We also considered the synonyms used, such as, for example, broken, crushed (محطمة muḥaṭṭima), shaken up (مهزوزة mahzūza), destroyed, (مدمرة mudammira). In addition, several idioms included references to difficulties in breathing, for example:

وكنت أتنفس بصعوبة بالغة جدا	I was hardly breathing

Overall, idioms that mention breathing difficulties are not uncommon as these are widely used metaphorical expressions of distress. However, by analyzing the idioms in context, we found that, in some cases, these were not metaphorical representations. To illustrate this, I report below an account taken from The Palestinian Information Centre website, which reproduces the story of two families whose houses were bombed, and who had family members killed in the explosion, while other family members were found still alive under the rubble:

ويقول نائل: 'حضرت آلية أخرى لرفع الركام وبقينا نبحث حتى طلع الصبح فعثرنا على هايل 29 سنة وأطفاله أشلاء وبقايا من أشلاء زوجته فارتفعت حصيلة الشهداء لخمسة و4 مصابين .. رحمهم الله'. [...]	⁶Nael says: 'Another crane came to lift the rubble as we remained searching till the sunrise. Later, we found Hael, 29 years old, and ***his children in pieces***, we found also remaining of his wife's body. The martyrs' number raised to become 5, as causalities became 4, Allah rest the lot of them. [...].'
'أبو عماد' الذي لا يزال يتلقى العلاج في أحد مستشفيات قطاع غزة يؤكد أن معية الله كانت أكثر ما يبعث في نفوسهم الطمأنينة، ويزيدهم يقيناً بأن النصر حليفهم وأنه قريب ويقول: 'لم يكن لدينا شك ما أعده كتائب القسام بعد توكلها على الله يمكنها من الانتصار في هذه المعركة، وهو ما كان بفضل الله'.	Abu Emad, who still receives treatment at one of the Strip's hospitals, confirming that feeling that Allah is always with them was the thing that mostly brought tranquility to them, and made them more certain that they will win. He says: 'We had no doubt that what our fighters had prepared, after relying on Allah, will lead us to win this battle and that is what occurred by Allah's grace.'
ويقول:' لم أصدق حينها أنني لا أستطيع أن أكون معهم أخفف عنهم وأزيل عنهم الخطر وأبعد عنهم ألم الحرمان من مسكنهم وبيتهم الجميل، لكن عزاءنا أن الله عز وجل يكتب لنا أجر المرابطين الصابرين، وبيتنا هو بيت الخلود في جنات ونهر في مقعد صدق عند مليك مقتدر '. [...]	He says: 'I couldn't believe that I can't be with them to alleviate their pain after they have lost their beautiful house, but our solace is that Allah would reward us for our struggle and endurance. Our home is in eternity amid gardens and rivers "In an Assembly of Truth, in the Presence of a Sovereign Omnipotent" [...].'

تتابع: 'من رحمة الله بي أن كان هنالك فراغ صغير كقبضة اليد أمام أنفي وفمي فقط بينما كان باقي وجهي وكامل جسدي مضغوطاً بالرمل والطين والحجارة حتى تنمّلت أطرافي وأنا على جانبي الأيمن، وكنت أتنفس بصعوبة بالغة جداً ولم أتوقف عن التشهد والاستغفار والقول 'يا الله !'.	She continued: 'Part of Allah's mercy to me that there has been a space in the size of a hand grip before my nose and mouth as the rest of my face and body was pressed by sand, mud and stones until I started ***feeling numbness in my limbs*** while I was laying at my right side. ***I was hardly breathing*** and never stopped saying "Al Tashahud", "Al Esteghphar" and "Ya Allah".'
تزيد: 'كان الضغط رهيباً على جسدي والأرض ساخنة جداً بفعل الموجة الانفجارية للصاروخ، لم أفقد وعيي مطلقاً وظللت أستغيث بالله 'يا الله' حتى بدأت أسمع أصواتاً بعيدة، فبادرني أمل في الله بأن أخرج مما أنا فيه، كانت أصوات طواقم الدفاع المدني وهم يحاولون البحث عنّي'.	She added: '***I was feeling so much pressure on my body*** and the ground was so hot due to the explosion. I didn't lose my consciousness and stayed repeating "Ya Allah" until I started hearing distant voices. A hope in Allah has come to me that I will be saved. The voices were for civil defense.'
وتضيف: 'حفظ الله أبنائي حين بقيت بناتي عند الدرج ولم تُصب إلا إيمان إصابة طفيفة، وحمزة بحمد الله كان قد خرج من المكان في لمح البصر -دون وعي- لحظة سقوط الصاروخ وسلّمه الله'.	She added: 'Allah saved my children for me when they stayed at the stairwell except for my daughter, Eman, who has been slight injured. For Hamza, thank Allah, he went out of the house quickly and unconsciously when the missile hit the house; Allah kept him safe.'
لكنها بلسان الواثقين قالت: 'إن ابنها الذي طالما حلمت بضمه إلى صدرها ذهب إلى ربه شهيدا يشكو إليه ظلم الظالمين وتخاذل المتخاذلين', وبابتسامة حزينة تقول: هو الآن عصفور في الجنة، وسيكون شفيعا لي يوم القيامة .	She said confidently that her baby that she has dreamed of embracing, went to Allah as a martyr where he will complain about the obsession of oppressors and the inaction of Arabs who gave up on them. With a sad smile she says: 'He is now a sparrow in the paradise, and he will be my intercessor on the day of Judgment.'

In the narrative above, idioms evidenced in bold italics – such as 'being in pieces', 'hardly breathing', 'feeling pressure', 'feeling numbness' – were *not* metaphorical descriptions used to convey mental distress, but were rather used as part of detailed, physical descriptions of the consequences of war and bombardments. It is also noticeable throughout the extracts that there is a frequent use of religious proverbs and invocations, which attest the faith in Allah in times of disgrace and despair. In contrast to the interview presented above, where the interviewee relied on others to tell the story of what happened, in these extracts language is abundant and vivid scenes accompany the narrative.

We found many other examples of narratives similar to the ones reported above, describing bodies of children in pieces, shattered and fragmented bodies, destroyed infrastructures and broken lives. 'Feeling broken and destroyed', hence, acquires a different meaning in contrast with similar, metaphorical expressions we encountered in the literature review. It is important to note that, had we approached those idioms of distress in terms of a translatable *list* of expressions, our interpretation would have been misleading, since the causes of distress and despair would not have emerged, as they did here, from the context. In addition, several idioms might have lost the 'culturally unique' nuance that they carry, that is, the specific protracted context of war and military operations experienced in the Gaza Strip.

Conclusion and Recommendations

In this chapter I presented a preliminary analysis of the findings of the Idioms of Distress, Resilience, and Wellbeing research project, focusing on the case study that involved the Gaza Strip. The case study focused on the analysis of the 'idioms of distress' that appeared on media news agencies during the 2014 war that destroyed the Gaza Strip. The preliminary findings suggest that, in some cases, traumatic experiences were untranslatable in linguistic terms as words failed. In other cases, vivid descriptions of war scenes were told to the interviewer, and several idioms of distress were used. A considerable number of idioms referred to 'being broken', 'being destroyed' and the difficulties of breathing: these are idioms commonly used metaphorically in other languages and contexts. However, in our research setting, they also emerge as culturally and locally connoted, since they referred to particular war scenes, and were *not* metaphorical expressions but rather physical conditions. The project made use of secondary data and of online ways of working since the borders of the Gaza Strip are virtually impassable. Even though working at a distance, the team ensured that, through regular meetings and open and frank ways of communicating, interactions were maximized in order to produce a high-quality, ethical piece of research.

As a result of this research project, the following recommendations emerged, concerning the different stages of the research:

(1) As the literature review has shown, there is a considerable gap in the knowledge about 'idioms of distress' in the fields of intercultural studies and applied linguistics. It is suggested that further studies, addressing issues related to a context-based approach to translation and to intercultural understanding of idioms of distress, should be developed. Such studies will be of interest for practitioners and for language teachers working with refugees who may have suffered similar experiences to the ones described in this chapter.
(2) Ethical considerations about research purposefulness and research methodologies need to be critically evaluated during the design phase of each research project. Whereas storytelling methodologies and linguistic ethnographies were adopted in other case studies of the same research project, these were found inappropriate for the specific context of the Gaza Strip. Working in partnership with local scholars ensured that the research was ethically grounded and conducted, even though this differed from the initial plan. We therefore stress the need for data collection methods to be carefully evaluated and all potential

repercussions considered when a research project addresses painful memories and traumatic experiences.
(3) A context-based approach to the translation of idioms of distress, which considers the narratives and not only the list of idioms, may strengthen understanding and interpretation of the meanings carried by the idioms. As the literature review has shown, in most of the studies that have been reviewed, a multilingual *list* of idioms was provided. It may be interesting to further develop a qualitative analysis of the narratives in which idioms of distress are used in order to ensure that they are appropriately contextualized.
(4) Further research which adopts different analytical lenses and methodologies such as conversational analysis and critical discourse analysis could address the same topic and open further avenues for interesting discussions.
(5) Finally, in relation to interdisciplinary research projects, we argue that – despite the challenges they may pose – it is a worthwhile endeavor to develop common ways of working which respond to ethical considerations as well as disciplinary requirements. In addition, a critical dialogue between the different fields of applied linguistics, intercultural communication and global mental health seems to be much needed, especially at a time when increasing numbers of people are displaced, and may produce knowledge that further develops the respective fields.

Acknowledgements

The author is grateful to the AHRC-GCRF grant that funded this research project, to the P.I. Professor Alison Phipps and to the Co-I Dr Nazmi Al-Masri. Sincere and profound gratitude goes to the Master's students Yasser Alsattari and Safaa Abu Rahma, who collected the data discussed in this paper, translated the original Arabic into English and enriched several conversations with their precious insights. I am also indebted to the peer reviewers who strengthened this book chapter with their comments and suggestions.

Notes

(1) See the extensive work developed by the linguist Aneta Pavlenko.
(2) Translation from Arabic into English by Yaser Alsattari.
(3) Translation from Arabic into English by Yaser Alsattari.
(4) Translation from Arabic into English by Yaser Alsattari.
(5) Translation from Arabic into English by Yaser Alsattari.
(6) Translation from Arabic into English by Safaa Abu Rahma.

References

Barber, B.K., McNeely, C.A., El Sarraj, E., Daher, M., Giacaman, R. and Arafat, C. (2016) Mental suffering in protracted political conflict: Feeling broken or destroyed. *PLoS ONE* 11 (5).

de Jong, J.T. and Reis, R. (2010) Kiyang-yang, a West-African postwar idiom of distress. *Culture, Medicine and Psychiatry* 34 (2), 301–321.

Fassetta, G., Imperiale, M.G., Frimberger, K., Attia, M. and Al-Masri, N. (2017) Online teacher training in a context of forced immobility: The case of the Gaza Strip. *European Education* 49 (2–3), 133–150.

Hassan, G., Kirmayer, L.J., Mekki-Berrada, A., *et al.* (2015) *Culture, Context and the Mental Health and Psychosocial Wellbeing of Syrians: A Review for Mental Health and Psychosocial Support Staff Working with Syrians Affected by Armed Conflict.* Geneva: UNHCR.

Imperiale, M.G. (2018) Developing language education in the Gaza Strip: pedagogies of capability and resistance. Unpublished PhD thesis, University of Glasgow.

Nasir, A.A., Salah, R., Ahmad, A.A., *et al.* (2018) Definition, causes and consequences of Hamm (idiom of distress in Arabic) in the Palestinian context: A qualitative study. *The Lancet* 391, S1.

Nichter, M. (1981) Idioms of distress: Alternatives in the expression of psychosocial distress: A case study from South India. *Cultural Medicine Psychiatry* 5 (4), 379–408.

Nichter, M. (2010) Idioms of distress revisited. *Cultural Medicine Psychiatry* 34 (2), 401–416.

Nussbaum, M. (1997) *Cultivating Humanity*. Cambridge, MA: Harvard University Press.

Nussbaum, M. (2000) *Women and Human Development: The Capabilities Approach*. Cambridge: Cambridge University Press.

Phipps A. (2014) 'They are bombing now': 'Intercultural dialogue' in times of conflict. *Language and Intercultural Communication* 14 (1), 108–124.

Phipps, A. and Gonzalez, M. (2004) *Modern Languages*. London: Sage.

Rothenberg, C.E. (2004) *Spirits of Palestine: Gender, Society, and the Stories of the Jinn*. Minneapolis, MN: Lexington Books.

Scarry, E. (1985) *The Body in Pain: The Making and Unmaking of the World*. Oxford: Oxford University Press.

Sen, A. (1999) *Development as Freedom*. Oxford: Oxford University Press.

Tuhiwai-Smith, L. (2012) *Decolonizing Methodologies* (2nd edn). Dunedin: University of Otago Press.

Part 4
Making Connections

8 The Experience of the Islamic University of Gaza in Cross-border Academic Collaboration: T-MEDA Project as a Case Study

Ahmed S. Muhaisen

The Gaza Strip has been under blockade, due to complicated political and security issues, for more than 12 years. All aspects of life have been negatively affected by the restrictions imposed on the freedom of mobility of people and goods, which are in place with few exceptions or lifted only for urgent humanitarian reasons. Opportunities for face-to-face academic collaborations between local institutions in the Gaza Strip and their counterparts in the rest of the world, particularly in Europe, have been negatively affected by the blockade (Fassetta *et al.*, 2017; see also Phipps *et al.*, this volume).

The Islamic University of Gaza (IUG), a leading academic institution in the Gaza Strip, realized the risk of isolation – and of the consequent fossilization of knowledge and skills – early on, and accordingly developed an innovative plan to overcome the constraints imposed by the blockade. As will be discussed later in this chapter, this included using technology-based communication facilities and promoting the English language as an effective medium of communication to circumvent the limitations of movement from/to the Strip. The results have been a considerable improvement in IUG's international academic network and, connecting more specifically to the focus of this chapter, involvement in many EU-funded programmes.

This chapter outlines IUG's experience, and specifically its faculties of Engineering and Nursing and Law, in participating successfully in a multidisciplinary project called 'T-MEDA', funded by the EU's Tempus programme (2013–2016). The project's main objective was to develop a new framework – based on the Bologna Process – for the development of academic programmes in the targeted regions. For this purpose, institutions from 17 different countries, speaking eight different languages, participated in the T-MEDA Project. The environment was naturally multilingual but, to facilitate communication between teams, English was the main language used for contacts, presentations, instructions and discussions. Using English as a lingua franca for communication among the T-MEDA team helped with exchanging knowledge and experiences and with understanding the cultural diversity of the participants from various backgrounds. Although the IUG's team was unable to participate in person in any of the organized meetings because of the travel restrictions imposed by the blockade, it managed to take part actively by making use of online tools. As a result, IUG widened its academic network, shared its experience and expertise, developed its academic programmes and signed a bilateral agreement for future collaboration with the Spanish institution leading the T-MEDA Project.

The chapter starts by discussing the importance of higher education for national development and the particular role that international collaborations have in a context of protracted crisis and isolation. It highlights the efforts made to ensure that the English language and online technologies at IUG are as widely available as possible to allow a broad range of international collaboration to be established despite the blockade. The chapter goes on to describe the T-MEDA Project as an example of how English and technology were mobilized for an international collaboration between IUG and the international academic community.

Higher Education and National Development

Higher education plays a significant role in the development of countries and in nation-building (Anderson, 2006; Gellner, 2006). It invests in human capital, which contributes – together with other factors including the development of civil society organizations and public participation in governance – to the success of national plans to achieve freedom, economic growth and sustainable development (Mugizi, 2018). Higher education is important to social and economic development and is considered a way to improve the quality of life. Ndaruhutsehigher and Thompson (2016) note that higher education is linked to environmental awareness and sustainability, post-conflict resolution, poverty alleviation, upholding human rights, addressing health care issues, and cultural preservation or change. According to Cloete *et al.* (2017: 1), higher education has four functions: 'producing values and social legitimation, selecting the elite, training of the labour force, and producing new knowledge'. These functions, the authors argue, are essential in order to develop societies and to lead a change towards growth of performance, prosperity and competitiveness. Cloete *et al.* (2017) note that there is wide agreement about the positive impact of higher education on the development of societies, through the education of qualified graduates, the production of knowledge, the creation of understanding about the challenges facing societies, and the identification of ways to handle these challenges.

Providing higher education in the occupied territories has been essential to ensuring access to higher education for young Palestinians (Baramki, 1996). While young people used to travel abroad (mainly to Egypt) to study at university level, this was an opportunity not available to most young people in Gaza, because of the limited financial resources of Palestinian families and also due to the restrictions on mobility to/from the Gaza Strip, both during the direct Israeli occupation – which ended in 2005 – and then during the blockade.

Although the creation and consolidation of higher education institutions has been a challenging and complex process, Palestinian determination has resulted in a significant step towards having their own higher education system and institutions to serve the local communities and alleviate the challenges. Gaza's universities have been striving to offer a high standard of academic and research services. However, because of the blockade and its devastating results on all aspects of life in Gaza (see also Fassetta et al., this volume; Phipps et al., this volume), this has been very difficult to achieve.

The Importance of International Collaboration

International collaboration between academic institutions has grown in recent decades, to facilitate the flow of knowledge, the sharing of ideas and the promotion of common understanding between partners (Amaratunga et al., 2018). As Zagonel, et al. (2018) notes, universities rely on international collaboration to better serve their students, staff and societies.

Engaging in international collaborative relations with universities worldwide is seen by universities in the Gaza Strip as a way to circumvent the blockade and further the development process (Fassetta et al., 2017; Imperiale et al., 2017). The results of a workshop on the internationalization of Gaza universities, organized at IUG in February 2018 and attended by representatives of local academic institutions (IUG Internationalization News, 2018), show that most Palestinian universities have become aware of the importance of developing their academic and research relations with overseas international institutions. As a consequence, many higher education institutions in the Gaza Strip are developing plans for internationalization and for strengthening their presence within the international academic community. One of the most important steps towards achieving this is to develop collaborative cross-border academic and research relations based on joint projects that meet mutual interests. As a result of the workshop mentioned above, the following objectives for international collaborations were identified and shared by Gaza academic institutions, including IUG:

- Overcoming the blockade on Gaza's academic institutions.
- Exchanging knowledge and experience.
- Developing academic and research systems and services at local universities.
- Exchanging staff and students.
- Providing a partial source of income.
- Increasing the opportunities for local graduates to find jobs.
- Enhancing the international reputation of local institutions.
- Increasing the opportunities to network and join international unions and organizations.

IUG's Plan to Overcome the Blockade

IUG strives to provide the best possible academic services to the people of Gaza, and to be one of the leading institutions in the region. To this end, it has developed plans to provide a well-equipped academic and research environment, highly qualified staff, up-to-date academic curricula and strong collaborative relations with regional and international institutions. The outcome has been without doubt a positive one, as in just four decades it has physically developed from primitive tents with few staff and no international relations to very well-established permanent buildings with hundreds of staff and an extensive international network. This is widely considered as a success story for a local university, particularly given the very tight restrictions of the Israeli occupation (El-Namrouti, 2013).

Despite its many achievements, IUG has been struggling to overcome the blockade imposed on the Gaza Strip since 2007. As noted earlier, the blockade has impacted negatively on Gazan society, including its education sector. IUG mobilized early to remedy this, developing a plan to respond to such an unusual situation. This was of considerable importance to stop the regression in the exchange of knowledge and experiences and consequently a deskilling of local staff, as well as to improve IUG's regional and international position, which was also suffering. The main pillar of the plan was to encourage cross-border collaborations, making use of the English language and available technological means to communicate and engage with the outside world.

English language and technology as an effective medium of communication

The English language is widely used as a medium of communication by IUG's staff to open new horizons of collaboration and create bridges with international partners, since English is commonly used as an official language and for delivering academic services in many institutions worldwide (British Council, 2013). The English language is used at IUG not only for academic purposes, but also to articulate the hardships and unjust circumstances that Gazan universities have been experiencing for many years. It has also been an effective way to spread IUG's message of hope and aspiration for a better future in Gaza to a wider international audience (Imperiale *et al.*, 2017; Rolinska *et al.*, this volume).

As a result of the choice to give English a prominent role in the life of IUG's academic community, English has become the main language of international contact, such as emails, official letters, agreements, proposals and distance meetings with native and non-native English speakers. IUG's website is available in both Arabic and English, as is the majority of the material it offers (e.g. news, information, programme details). To ensure effective implementation, all external relations staff, who are in charge of conducting such communications, are carefully selected, prioritizing those with excellent proficiency in English. Academics and researchers with knowledge of the English language are also encouraged to establish new relations and partnerships with their counterparts in external universities. In addition, students are strongly encouraged to develop their English language skills, and supported in doing that, in order to interact more easily with international students abroad. IUG has facilitated this through engaging students in various international projects that include using the English language as a medium to work with international peers. For example, IUG has collaborated with the University of Glasgow (UofG) to implement the *English for Academic Studies Telecollaboration* (EAST) Project, concerned with exchanging knowledge between international students at UofG and IUG students studying Science, Engineering and Technology (SET) (see IUG EAST News, 2018; see also the chapters by Guariento and by Rolinska *et al.*, this volume). In addition, IUG has been engaged in a similar experience with students at the Zurich University of Applied Science (Switzerland), connecting virtually about 30 students from the Environmental Engineering department at IUG with their peers at Zurich University. The aim of this project was to discuss environmental problems in Gaza and to propose some solutions based on joint research, using the English language as a medium for communication (IUG Zurich News, 2016).

It should be emphasized that, for Gaza's students, the English language is not only the language of academic study, but also a language of increased opportunities to find jobs, obtain scholarships to study abroad for higher education, and to work towards continuous development in their fields. The collective efforts of the external relations office, academic staff and students using the English language, in many different activities, have contributed significantly to ameliorating the devastating effects of the blockade on IUG.

Alongside increasing overall English language use and proficiency, technological means have also been used by IUG to facilitate cross-border communication and collaboration. Using technology in communication has become a necessity in everyday life, not only for individuals but also for business and official contacts. It has revolutionized the way people communicate with one another, greatly facilitating international connections. Many institutions worldwide have embraced technology in communications to improve their public profile, to contact broader groups of potential users and to deliver their services (Paas, 2008). For the Gaza Strip, however, online tools for communication and for real-time exchange of information and materials have an even greater importance.

IUG engages with various technological means for communication, including emails, texting, mobile applications, video-conferencing tools and social media platforms. These means have been employed to keep continuous contact with people and institutions outside the Gaza strip. Their advantages have made them attractive and workable alternative solutions for personal or direct contacts. Although they cannot be an real alternative to the freedom to travel that is enjoyed by most academics worldwide (Fassetta *et al.*, 2017), they are free or cheap, easily available and a generally fast means to communicate.

Face-to-face versus virtual meetings

As Guo *et al.* (2009) note, virtual meetings are less effective than face-to-face meetings, especially for tasks that require high levels of coordination. This is linked to the lack/restriction of visual feedback and of the traditional social mechanisms that facilitate communication and decision making in face-to-face meetings. However, many other researchers argue that the increased globalization and advancement in communication technology has made using virtual meetings through computer-mediated communication a necessity (e.g. Adalinskaya, 2013). Virtual meetings are more flexible, especially in relation to allowing people to participate from wherever they are based and at any time, thus helping to reduce the costs and environmental impact of travel and, consequently, widening the networking capabilities (Eztalks, 2019). Thus, video-conferencing technology allows participants in different geographical locations to meet and interact through a viable, environmentally friendly and cost-effective alternative to in-person meetings (Sedgwick, 2009). Guo *et al.* (2009) also posit that the effectiveness of virtual meetings can be enhanced through adopting a dialogue technique to develop relationships among the participants, thus improving meetings' outcomes to be more closely aligned with those of face-to-face meetings.

Virtual meetings regularly facilitate the exchange of knowledge, the sharing of thoughts and the discussion of new ideas and work principles between IUG and its external partners. It needs to be stressed that virtual meetings were and remain almost the only option available for IUG to break the isolation created by the blockade and represent an option to resist the siege and send a message to the world that Gaza is still alive and ready to collaborate and to contribute to the wellbeing of humanity. As a result, they are considered a reliable way to develop cross-border collaborative relations, within the context of the Gaza Strip, under the current circumstances (Fassetta et al., 2017).

The next section discusses the T-MEDA Project as an example of the successful use of both the English language and online tools as ways to engage with international higher academic institutions. It shows how, by joining this programme, IUG managed to lay the grounds for a future in which international travel from/to the Gaza Strip will be possible, and one in which its programmes of study will be recognized internationally. This does more than align IUG's programmes of studies with those of other countries: it keeps alive the hope for a future when people in the Gaza Strip will be able to move freely for study and work, and in which IUG will be able to attract international students from a wide range of countries.

T-MEDA, an Example of IUG Cross-border Collaboration Projects

This section presents the experience of IUG in participating in the T-MEDA Tempus Project (2013–2016), mainly using the English language and utilizing technological means of communication as a substitute for personal mobility. This particular project was selected for discussion in this chapter for various reasons: it was the biggest, to date, in terms of partner countries, universities and associations; it provided a very rich diversity of academic and linguistic backgrounds and allowed a good opportunity for sharing experiences and cultural values. It covered four different subject areas (Architecture, Nursing, Law and Tourism), with relation to developing the curricula in accordance with the Bologna Process. Furthermore, the IUG team for T-MEDA was led by the author of this chapter, who was responsible for directing all local activities and maintaining contacts with other partners, and this allows the writer to offer first-hand experience of the project's details, its challenges and outcomes. Finally, the project is a good example in that it illustrates clearly the impact of mobility restrictions imposed on academics and researchers in Gaza, and their attempts to overcome these through the technological communication means that are available.

Tuning methodology

The *Tuning Educational Structures in Europe* methodology is a universal process for modernizing curricula to achieve professional competences, i.e. knowledge and experiences, and enhancing the quality of education (González & Wagenaar, 2008). It was initiated in 2000 as a project based on the Bologna Declaration of 1999, in order to support the continuous reform of the European higher education systems. The objective of the Tuning methodology is 'to build compatible and comparable descriptions of degrees that are relevant to society and that are intensively focused on maintaining and improving quality' (Tuning Academy website, 2019). Originating from the need for recognition of study-abroad periods and qualifications, the Tuning methodology has evolved into a tool that can facilitate the convergence of degree programmes in different countries. Over time, many universities worldwide have adopted the Tuning methodology to build new study programmes of a high quality in terms of structure, competences and learning outcomes (Huisman *et al.*, 2012). The programmes developed are mainly designed to meet the needs of the labour market, society and the academic community to solve specific tasks. Accordingly, the Tuning methodology has been gradually transformed into a global system covering educational sectors in many regions of the world. It does not aim to unify programmes and curricula, nor seek to restrict or determine local and national academic institutions, but rather it looks for points of reference, convergence and to create a common understanding. As Hakky (2016: 10) notes, 'the protection of the rich diversity of European education has been paramount in the Tuning Project from the very start and the project in no way seeks to restrict the independence of academic and subject specialists or undermine local and national academic authority'.

About the T-MEDA Project

The *Tuning Middle East and North Africa* Project (T-MEDA) is an international project which was funded by the EU via the Tempus Programme. It aimed to promote the use of the Tuning methodology in the practice of higher education in the Middle East and North Africa region. It focused particularly on applying the Tuning approach to develop reference guidelines in four subject areas, namely Architecture, Law, Nursing, and Tourism. The project mainly concentrated on building comparable, compatible and transparent study programmes in the target fields.

An international collaboration project

In addition to the academic and research aims, T-MEDA was designed to promote regional and international collaboration between universities in the Middle East, North Africa and the EU. For this purpose, the project involved 30 different universities, plus three associate organizations from eight EU countries and nine Arab countries from the Middle East and North Africa (see Table 8.1). The lead institution for the project was the University of Deusto in Spain, which was responsible for directing and managing all activities of the project (Hakky, 2016).

The wide range of universities involved permitted a rich diversity of educational systems and responses to many of the concerns of local,

Table 8.1 The partner countries, universities and associations in the T-MEDA Project

	Country		Universities and associations
1	Spain	1	Universidad de Deusto
2	Netherlands	2	Rijksuniversiteit Groningen
3	United Kingdom	3	London School of Economics and Political Sciences
4	Greece	4	Aristotle University of Thessaloniki
5	France	5	Universite d'Angers
6	Italy	6	Universitá Degli Studi Di Padova
7	Malta	7	University of Malta
8	Cyprus	8	University of Cyprus
9	Algeria	9	Université d'Alger 1
		10	Université Mouloud Mammeri de Tizi Ouzou
10	Morocco	11	Université Moulay Ismail
		12	University Mohammed First
11	Egypt	13	Cairo University
		14	Suez Canal University
12	Palestine	15	Islamic University of Gaza
		16	Palestine Ahliyeh University College/Bethlehem
13	Syria	17	Arab International University
		18	International University for Science and Technology
		19	The Syrian Consulting Bureau for Development and Investment
14	Jordan	20	Hashemite University
		21	Yarmouk University
		22	Jordan University of Science and Technology
		23	Association of Arab Universities
15	Tunisia	24	University of Tunis
		25	University of Jendouba
		26	University of Monastir
16	Lebanon	27	University of Balamand
		28	Modern University for Business and Science
		29	Beirut Arab University
		30	Holy Spirit University of Kaslik
		31	Directorate General Of Higher Education, Lebanon
17	Libya	32	The Libyan International Medical University
		33	University of Omar Almukhtar

Source: Reproduced from T-MEDA (2013).

regional and international institutions. All the partner universities were involved in a step-by-step development process based on continuous discussions and the carrying out of individual and collective tasks. Each partner was represented by a group of specialists in the various subject areas, who were delegated by their institutions to undertake the tasks required and to participate in the project's meetings. Throughout the lifetime of the project, five meetings were organized in four different countries, namely Jordan, Spain, Malta and Cyprus. The meetings formed the main pillars of the project and were organized in correspondence with the project's developmental stages, allowing in-depth discussions following up on progress or concerning new findings.

IUG participation in T-MEDA

As a partner in the project and the only university from the Gaza Strip, IUG strived to collaborate actively with the project leader and partners to contribute to the success of the project and benefit from its outcomes. IUG's representatives responded positively to all the required tasks and were one of the most active teams, according to the certification of the project manager, Dr Ivan Dyukarev (personal communication, 2015). However, as noted earlier, the IUG team could not participate personally in any of the organized meetings, and this represented a considerable challenge in relation to keeping up to date with the project development, presenting IUG's achievements and interacting personally with the other delegates. For the IUG team, it was very disappointing to be denied the possibility to leave Gaza in order to attend the meetings, having prepared themselves fully all five times to participate – including, for example, obtaining visas, permits and all the documentation required for travel, a process which, for people in the Gaza Strip, is very expensive and time consuming. Despite these significant constraints, IUG approached this project as an important opportunity to develop its educational programmes, to exchange knowledge and experiences and to establish academic and research relations with the universities involved. Therefore, it adopted the use of alternative means of communications to overcome the blockade and go beyond the physically closed borders.

Means of Communications

English language

In addition to the limited access to travel for personal meetings, there were language concerns. The participants were from various linguistic backgrounds, speaking eight different languages (Spanish, Dutch, English, Greek, French, Italian, Maltese and Arabic). Although the leader of the project was from Spain, English was chosen as the official language for communication among all participants. All meetings, discussions, presentations, calls, emails, documents, etc. were therefore conducted in English. The focus on English proficiency that characterizes IUG's approach was one of the success factors in IUG's participation in the project. It facilitated an easy interaction with the European partners, and served as a common language for sharing thoughts, knowledge and cultural understanding. The IUG team used English to communicate with the other partners by email, text messages and during virtual meetings and calls. All the required tasks were carried out in English, including the evaluation of the current programmes at IUG, questionnaires to evaluate different issues including the selected competences, the study loads of modules, and presenting information about IUG and Gaza.

To ensure knowledge transfer was accessible to all participants at IUG, including students and staff, some translation into Arabic was performed by the IUG team. The discussions and meetings at IUG were carried out in Arabic and then translated, documented and finally submitted by the IUG team in English to the project leader. For example, to evaluate the IUG curricula in the targeted fields, each of the T-MEDA IUG team met a group of specialized staff in their department to discuss the components of the study programme. The discussion focused mainly on the availability of generic and specific competences that should be incorporated at the level of the full degree course, based on the Bologna Process. Arabic was the language of discussion with staff, to make it more inclusive of those who were not fluent enough in English and to avoid any misunderstanding due to language barriers. The same also happened with the students who were targeted to evaluate the study loads of some specific modules. The English questionnaire prepared for this purpose was translated into Arabic in order to help the students understand the questions and answer precisely to reflect the real situation. The responses to the questionnaires were then translated back into English to be shared with the project's partners.

This process of translation from Arabic to English – and vice versa – was necessary to facilitate effective communication and to create a common understanding. However, this process required some extra effort and more time on the part of the IUG team who took responsibility for this task. The translation, conducted by each member of the IUG team, helped to convey the required information in an efficient way, taking advantage of the fact that each member combined subject-area expertise with a very good command of subject-specific English in addition to Arabic. This contributed to achieving the project's objectives and disseminating its principles and methodology to a wide audience.

As a joint project, each university team was required to carry out allocated tasks to be collated for each subject area and later presented at the meetings. In most cases, this required using the national language with each team member to discuss and implement a specific task before submission or presentation, as happened, for example, with the IUG team. All teams then presented their work at the main five meetings in English. They did this as a necessary step in order to transfer knowledge and experiences in an understandable language for the majority of the project's participants. The findings and outcomes of the project were published at the end of T-MEDA in three different languages, namely English, French and Arabic. This choice aimed to disseminate as widely as possible the project's insights, and to make them more accessible and understandable for various groups of people in different regions of the world.

Technological means of communications

Another success factor of IUG's participation was in the use of technological means for communication. As noted above, this was the only available way to keep the IUG team updated on the project development and to allow all members to respond actively and effectively to the various requirements of the project. Emails, phone calls, text messages and Skype were needed to ensure the presence of the IUG team in all of the project's activities. Through emails, all information was transferred to and received from the other partners, while Skype facilitated meetings with the T-MEDA Project leader and other partners, to exchange knowledge and be informed of the latest news. Text messages and phone calls were also among the various technological means used by the IUG team to communicate with the other delegates and to share materials.

If technology served to overcome many of the constraints resulting from the blockade, this response was not always straightforward. Most of the other teams were present personally at the meetings, except in some individual cases when people were unable to attend due to personal circumstances. The IUG team, however, faced specific challenges, such as the difficulty of maintaining constant contact due to the frequent disconnection of the internet because of power cuts. In addition, there were some technical problems resulting from a mismatch in technology used by the various partners such as, for example, using different versions of the Skype program, which caused the IUG team to miss a meeting or to join a meeting late.

Results of IUG's Participation in T-MEDA

The project, which ended in 2016, fulfilled its objectives, met its stated targets and served to establish a platform for a continuous development of the educational systems in the targeted region. It provided a practical methodology to assess the quality of the educational programmes to meet specific needs. To this end, it developed both generic and specific competences that the graduates of the selected academic subjects should have, in addition to evaluating the current educational programmes and comparing them with agreed profiles. The competences were developed by the project team for each of the targeted subject areas and carefully articulated to be suitable for the Middle East and North Africa region and in line with European standards.

Following the development of models, local academic programmes were then compared to find out the degree of correspondence. For example, the comparison result showed that the Architecture programme at IUG meets about 70% of the targeted level. This helped IUG to concentrate more on redressing the gap to meet the target in the development process of the Architecture programme. An analysis of study loads for students and staff was also among the outcomes of the project. This was carried out with the aim of estimating the actual volume of work hours needed by a student to pass a module, from the point of view of both students and teachers.

For IUG, the project was also an opportunity to collaborate with regional and international universities as a way to overcome the blockade and continue the development process of the university. The project served to develop IUG's educational programmes and the capacity building of its staff, and to exchange knowledge and experiences. It also facilitated expanding IUG's relations and networks with a relatively large number of regional and international universities. A significant result was the signing of a bilateral collaboration agreement with the leader of the project (University of Deusto in Spain) to work jointly on mutual fields of interest, including conducting academic and research activities and exchanging staff and students.

There were also less obvious outcomes, with equally important ramifications in the context of the Gaza Strip. First, the project helped to increase the academic and cultural interaction between the European and Arab universities in the Middle East and North Africa region, allowing the exchange of cultural and social values and an appreciation of the local, regional and international diversity of the participants. Secondly, insights into the hardships and challenges facing Gazan universities under the blockade were also transmitted to the regional and international universities. IUG's participation contributed to shedding light on the mobility restrictions that all academics in Gaza have been suffering from. This helped to raise awareness of the situation in the Gaza Strip and to advocate for the rights of the local people to live normally and move freely. As a result, an understanding of the local situation, sympathy with Gazan universities, and interest in supporting them were promoted and spread, especially among the project partners. This has not only benefited IUG, but also all Gazan universities, which have been experiencing the same difficulties. Although the Arab partners were already aware of the difficult situation in Gaza and come from countries that are generally sympathetic to the Palestinian cause, the participation of IUG helped to gain solidarity from the European partners, especially the Spanish university leading the project, which was, at each step, in direct contact with the IUG team in its work and in its failed attempts to leave Gaza to attend the project's meetings.

Conclusion

The blockade imposed on the Gaza Strip has badly affected all aspects of life, including the education sector. This situation is abnormal and is widely considered as a form of collective punishment (Amnesty International, 2017), which is illegal according to the Fourth Geneva Convention (UN, 1949). Due to the blockade, the economic situation has deteriorated considerably in recent years, and local people, including academics and researchers, have been virtually trapped in Gaza with very limited access to the outside world. Universities in Gaza have been struggling to keep running and to provide a good quality of educational services. One of the most promising solutions is to develop cross-border collaboration as an alternative method for local universities to keep up to date and integrate into the international academic community.

IUG has embraced distance collaboration with external universities worldwide in order to bypass the blockade and open new horizons of knowledge transfer. Using the English language and available technological means of communication have been the two main pillars of IUG's plan. This has helped to keep IUG in a continuous relation with the international academic and research community and to integrate into the global academic conversation. It has also provided a partial source of funding to continue the development process. Moreover, it has served to enhance the international reputation of IUG through the various projects, agreements and memberships in many networks that IUG has become involved in. In addition, cross-border collaboration has helped to promote cultural understanding, and to convey Gazans' message of hope and desire to live peacefully. It is a kind of peaceful resistance to the unbearable conditions that the universities and people in Gaza have been experiencing for many years.

IUG has achieved a considerable success in breaking the isolation, collaborating with partners worldwide to gain new insights, skills and knowledge. This has been shown particularly through the experience of joining the T-MEDA Project, as described in this chapter. IUG's participation in the project has served to establish long-lasting academic and research relations, developing IUG educational programmes and promoting cultural understanding. Furthermore, it has resulted in the development of academic programmes in line with the Bologna process, future-proofing its offer for a time when Gaza's students will be able to travel freely and when IUG will be, like many other universities worldwide, a desirable destination for international students.

The experience of IUG in cross-border collaboration proves that a combination of the English language and technological means of communication can contribute significantly to bypassing the blockade and providing an acceptable way for continuous development in places with similar circumstances of unstable political and security situations. It also confirms that nothing can stop people from searching for freedom and opening closed doors.

References

Adalinskaya, Y. (2013) Face-to-face meeting or video conference? Factors influencing organisational choice of communication media. Unpublished Master's thesis, University of Stavanger.

Amaratunga, D., Liyanage, C. and Haigh, R.P. (2018) A study into the role of international collaborations in higher education to enhance research capacity for disaster resilience. Conference Proceedings, 7th International Conference on Building Resilience. *Procedia Engineering* 212, 1233–1240.

Amnesty International (2017) Looming humanitarian catastrophe highlights need to lift Israel's 10-year illegal blockade. See https://cutt.us/GAZAcatastrophe/ (accessed 1 April 2019).

Anderson, B. (2006 [1983]) *Imagined Communities*. London: Verso

Baramki, G. (1996) Palestinian university education under occupation. *Palestine-Israel Journal of Politics, Economics and Culture* 3 (1). See http://pij.org/articles/569 (accessed 4 April 2019).

British Council (2013) The English effect. See https://cutt.us/TheEnglishEffect (accessed 18 June 2018).

Cloete, N., Maassen, P. and Pillay, P. (2017) Higher education and national development, meanings, and purposes. In J. Shin and P. Teixeira (eds) *Encyclopedia of International Higher Education Systems and Institutions*. Dordrecht: Springer.

El-Namrouti, S. (2013) *The Story of the Islamic University of Gaza*. Johannesburg: Helen Suzman Foundation.

Eztalks (2019) Virtual meetings vs face to face meeting: Which one to choose? See https://cutt.us/VirtualMeetings (accessed 12 November 2018).

Fassetta, G., Imperiale, M.G., Frimberger, K., Attia, M. and Al-Masri, N. (2017) Online teacher training in a context of forced immobility: The case of Gaza, Palestine. *European Education* 49 (2–3), 133–150.

Gellner, E. (2006 [1983]) *Nations and Nationalism*. Oxford: Blackwell

González, J. and Wagenaar, R. (2008) *Universities' Contribution to the Bologna Process: An Introduction*. Bilbao: Deusto University Press.

Guo, Z., D'Ambra, J., Turner, T. and Zhang, H. (2009) Improving the effectiveness of virtual teams: A comparison of video-conferencing and face-to-face communication in China. *IEEE Transactions on Professional Communication* 52 (1), 1–16.

Hakky, R. (ed.) (2016) *Reference Points for Design and Delivery of Degree Programmes in Architecture*. Bilbao: Deusto University Press.

Huisman, J., Aldeman, C., Hsieh, C.C., Shams, F. and Wilkins, S. (2012) Europe's Bologna process and its impact on global higher education. In D.K. Deardorff, H. de Wit, J.D. Heyl and T. Adams (eds) *The SAGE Handbook of International Higher Education* (pp. 81–100). Thousand Oaks, CA: Sage.

Imperiale, M.G., Phipps, A., Al-Masri, N. and Fassetta, G. (2017) Pedagogies of hope and resistance: English language education in the context of the Gaza Strip, Palestine. In E.J. Erling (ed.) *English Across the Fracture Lines* (pp. 31–38). London: British Council.

IUG EAST News (2018) The graduation ceremony of EAST project graduates in collaboration with UofG. See https://cutt.us/IUG-EASTnews (accessed 1 December 2018).

IUG Internationalization News (2018) Internationalization of the Palestinian universities. See https://cutt.us/IUG-INTERNATIONALIZATIONnews (accessed 18 June 2018).

IUG Zurich news (2016) IUG environmental engineering students meet with their peers from Zurich University of Applied Sciences. See https://cutt.us/ZurichNews (accessed December 2018).

Mugizi, W. (2018) The role of higher education in achieving Uganda vision 2040. *Elixir International Journal* 115, 49831–49837.

Ndaruhutsehigher, S. and Thompson, S. (2016) *Literature Review: Higher Education and Development*. Oslo: Norwegian Agency for Development Cooperation (Norad).

Paas, L. (2008) *How Information and Communications Technologies Can Support Education for Sustainable Development*. Winnipeg: International Institute for Sustainable Development. See https://cutt.us/InfoComm (accessed 12 June 2018).

Sedgwick, M. (2009) The use of videoconferencing as a medium for the qualitative interview. *International Journal of Qualitative Methods* 8 (1), 1–11.

T-MEDA (2013) T-MEDA partners. See http://tuningmeda.org/ (accessed 12 December 2018).

Tuning Academy (2019) What is Tuning? See https://cutt.us/Tuning (accessed 16 October 2019).

United Nations (1949) Geneva convention Relative to the protection of civilian persons In time of war of 12 august 1949. Available from: See: https://www.un.org/en/genocideprevention/documents/atrocity-crimes/Doc.33_GC-IV-EN.pdf (accessed April 2019).

Zagonel, J. and Fatrous, T. (2018) University internationalization through collaboration with industry. Master's thesis in Business Administration, Linköping University.

9 From the Kitchen to Gaza: Networked Places and the Collaborative Imagination

Chantelle Warner and David Gramling

> *Se wo were fi na wosankofa a yenkyi*
> It is not wrong to go back for that which you have forgotten
> – Ghanaian proverb

> اليَوْمَ لا يفصلنا حصار
> Today, may there be no siege between us
> – 21st century Arab-American meditation

Collapsed Contexts and Cages

Chantelle: *I woke up Monday to a debate being waged across the international media, and the social media sites that fuel them, concerning the political efficacy of the new US embassy in Jerusalem and the appropriateness of the use of force displayed by Israel, and my first thoughts are with my friend and colleague Nazmi in Gaza. After several attempts to formulate a response that feels even remotely adequate, I post without comment a news story from Democracy Now, entitled 'Gaza: Israeli Soldiers Kill 50+ Palestinians Protesting Nonviolently as U.S. Opens Jerusalem Embassy.' It is shared almost immediately by an acquaintance in Phoenix – just over 120 miles north of where I sit. Outside of my online echo chamber of progressive academics who tend to agree with me, and relatives who have stopped reading my more political posts long ago, the news story sparks a more contentious discussion on an acquaintance's Facebook page. The debate raged complete with embedded videos of the US's UN ambassador Nikki Haley, whose question to the UN Security Council 'Who among us would accept this type of activity on your border?' draws a rhetorical line to my current home in Tucson, which – with sixty miles of the Sonoran desert in between – is the closest metropolitan area to the Arizonan stretch of US-Mexico border.*

The next day, Nazmi reaches out, posting and tagging me and others on a personal commentary from the Scottish paper The National, co-authored by himself and Alison Phipps, 'Let's break the bars of the cage of Gaza so, like a bird, I can fly and sing songs of freedom.' Through the words of Nazmi mediated by Alison, this piece introduces the readership of The National to a person and a place I have come to know through a series of collaborations and conversations over the past few years, as part of the AHRC-sponsored project Researching Multilingually at the Borders of Language, the Body, the Law, and the State (RMly). *Professor Nazmi Al-Masri, whom we've always called 'Nazmi' in our work together, speaks of a vibrant scene of creative non-violence along the Palestinian border, which stands in contrast even to the darkened grey photos of protesters carrying signs demanding an 'End of the Siege of Gaza' in the National Scot. I am reminded of the first time I met Nazmi. It was the first symposium for the collaborators of the RMly project. David and I had landed in Glasgow, tense with excitement, anticipation and some amount of uncertainty as to what expect from the band of collaborators that had been brought together through Alison's leadership. Nazmi, the only other core collaborator on the project who was not based in Europe, had been prevented from physically attending that first meeting in 2014 by travel blockades and visa hurdles, and yet was with us through the entire day through Skype – moving between home and office, when electricity generators alternatingly failed.*

When it was Nazmi's turn to introduce himself and his case study site, he contrasted two images. The first was in black and white with red elements depicting Gaza under siege. It resembled flyers and posters wielded by pro-Palestine groups I had encountered many times on college campuses. The second image was a sunny photo of the Islamic University of Gaza, where Nazmi is Associate Professor of TEFL and Applied Linguistics. Blue skies framed an impressive peach-colored building with mirrored windows reaching up almost the full height of the facade. 'This too is Gaza.' Nazmi told us. He concluded with a plea that has stuck with me, that we as collaborators could best support him and other academics in Gaza by acting as colleagues, equal in dignity and intellect. The unpassable borders around Gaza that have left him unable to join us in Glasgow need not default to intellectual barriers as well. Collegiality, Nazmi's talk taught me, can be an academic but also a humanitarian duty, when scholarly exchange is de facto embargoed.

David: *In large part because of my congenital visual disability, called 'ocular albinism', I saw and remember Nazmi's self-introduction differently. I do not remember the poignant visual and online interactional details Chantelle has just described. What I do remember was what I could actually see, hear, and thus invest with meaning, from my vantage point in that small conference room in Glasgow: not any of the images of IUG or Nazmi onscreen, but rather the physically present and larger-than-online-life figure of Dr Mariam Attia – whom I had also barely met* *back then – bending over the networked laptop at the head of the room, chatting respectfully, but in intimate solidarity, with Nazmi. Attia (whom we refer to within the RMly group as 'Mariam') was bowed over the computer laterally throughout most of the interaction, caretaking the conversation (and its affordances and constraints), a conversation which was my own first-ever introduction to Nazmi and the Islamic University of Gaza. Now, seven years on, this memory of Mariam's figure leads me to believe that the age of real-time online interactive talk has ushered in newly improvisational and newly conventional semiotic forms of posture, bending, bowing, and conveying deference by way of the body, facial musculature, and embodied voice (see also Imperiale, 2018).*

When the prospect of this particular international partnership was first presented to me in 2013, I had for five years carried various titles with 'professor' in them. Whatever uncertainties about my own academic training I still felt at that juncture, I nonetheless believed that, with my doctoral studies behind me, I had seen all the formal education I was going to see. (Surely, more seasoned colleagues will smile abidingly at this simplistic view of 'training'.) Of course, I assumed, there would be continuing education 'events', of various scope and seriousness, but I was not expecting an opportunity for profound reeducation. Such as it was, my vocational identity at the time (2013) was that of a pre-tenure Germanist, who had dutifully engaged in the kinds of interdisciplinary discourses expected of someone at, and in, his age: inquisitive neighborly forays, for instance, into methodologically commensurate fields, or perhaps a willingness to ponder equivalences and divergences between, say, German histories of migration and their Turkish parallel discourses. I'd felt sufficiently responsible for, if not exceedingly competent at, my home field of 'German Studies' – which was itself an odd and recent historical construction, a remedy that had been adopted amid the discipline skirmishes of the 1980s and 1990s, and served as an agreeable enough locus amoenus among literature, culture, political science, and history. My safe and enterprising interdisciplinary identity circa 2013 did not, and had no apparent reason to, prepare me for the kinship feast that was germinating at the time under the title Researching Multilingually at Borders. *Like most of my colleagues who quickly or slowly became involved in that project, I approached its title with a quizzically affectionate glance, knowing yet little of what it meant or comprised.*

It turns out that the dauntingly comprehensive title of the project 'projected' for me then less of a rhetorical or hermeneutic puzzle to solve – as had been my first hunch about it – than a sheer dramatization of my own deficit of general knowledge (see, on such 'incompetence', Phipps, 2013b). Unpopular as 'deficit models' are for portraying the position of any learner, including tenured professors like me, my personal feelings of deficit nonetheless rippled through my position in 2013, and – lest I sketch out the wrong sort of picture here – those ripples of deficit feeling have not since settled; they've rather become a more active and acknowledged part of the positionality I seek to account for. And they now cross and collude with ripples – no, waves – of plenty and of friendship.

Here are some of the things I knew little or nothing about in 2013: the reformed higher education landscape of the United Kingdom, the meaning and predicament of 'modern languages' in the UK in the face of neoliberal audit cultures, the contemporary struggle for Scottish self-determination, European and EU refugee law, the border-brokering institutions of Southern and Southeastern Europe, West African language diversity and creative arts, pan-African poetics and African multilingual solidarity movements, UK early career research development programming and its effectiveness in responding to the casualization of young and multigenerational academic labor, and immigration and multiethnic society in Belgium and the Netherlands. If all of this not-knowing-about doesn't itself add up to an impeachable deficit for an academic, there's also the fact that I knew virtually nothing about Palestine in 2013 – before Dr Mariam Attia brokered an online group introduction that day with Dr Nazmi Al-Masri, who could only make our acquaintance, and ultimate friendship, by online means.

Despite my currently deepened sense of deficit and, indeed, of longing for a beloved Gaza I have never seen, there is now in the having-been of this RMly project a beginning, and a reason, for courage and accountability. To say that this beginning feels adequately foundational for future work does not mean it brings a sense of satisfaction or achievement. Sometimes you have to go with a beginning feeling and a desire for stamina of an uncertain kind, when other disciplinary methodologies and prospects fail to provide these. Being unmoored, as Chantelle and I wrote of our 'beginning feeling' in the founding documents of our Multilingual, 2.0? project in 2011, turns out – we think – to be a necessary condition, not only of human epistemic finitude in our age, but also for the kind of research methods that are increasingly becoming our home idiom. Amid this unmoored feeling (see also Phipps, 2013a), amid the ripples of deficit and the waves of friendship and plenty, accountability is something I can and will offer now – to those precaritized in my home interdiscipline, including the faculty at IUG whom I met so singularly through online interaction. Such accountability is now a small gift – handed back and forth up into the webwork of social relations, into which we were invited and projected in 2013–2014.

In the remainder of this contribution, we reflect further on the experience of participating in the UK-based project *Researching Multilingually at the Borders of Language, the Body, Law, and the State* as constituents of one of the two non-European hubs of the project – Tucson, AZ (the other being Gaza City, Palestine). In particular, as these two opening reflections above suggest, we are concerned with accounting for what we learned through the largely remote, digitally mediated collaborations with our now colleague and friend Nazmi Al-Masri, who is a Professor in Applied Linguistics at the Islamic University of Gaza (IUG). We consider how the RMly research network, which was facilitated through symposia held at multiple sites related to the project as well as through telecollaboration, took the shape of what Marwick and boyd (2011), referring to social media, have termed 'context collapse', i.e. phenomena by which various offline networks with different sociodemographics and hence different relations of selfhood become co-present in virtual space. For our purposes, virtual space will refer not only, and not even primarily, to digitally mediated environments, but also to the ways in which particular physical spaces became common referential ground for the imagined community, and for the always emerging imagined collaborative history that we 'projected' together. In this way, particular sites related to the project took on the shape of chronotopes, in the sense conceptualized originally by Mikhail Bakhtin (1981). As its two Greek base words (*chronos* = time; *topos* = place) suggest, the term expresses an intrinsic connectedness of temporal and spatial relationships, but central to Bakhtin's operationalization of the notion is the aesthetic effect of the chronotope as a means of coalescing meaning around a place and a moment. By focusing on three sites, where project events were hosted and which took on significance for our understandings of what it means to research *researching multilingually*, we show how international research networks are shaped through place in the chronotopic sense, even in the age of digital communications tools that may seem poised or designed to overcome such topographies.

A particular but not unique feature of the three-year project was how such a conceit of 'overcoming' borders in online space, to whatever extent such was viewed as credible or desirable, was always structurally offset by racialized and geopolitical border-patrolling offline, in consequence of which some – predominantly White and global North/West – participants could travel with relative ease to the physical locations of our meetings, while our Global South colleagues of color rarely were so enfranchised. (Indeed, many of these offline border-patrol modalities came online too, as Gazans were prejudicially excluded during the project period from receiving GoFundMe support payments, etc., which other collaborators were able to receive.) In this sense, we believe that researching multilingually cannot be a meaningful topic of critical reflection without accounting for broad and minute features of racialization, dis-citizenship and de-development (Roy, 1995) which have been reproduced and indeed reinvigorated under conditions of globalistic online interactivity.

At the same time, the collaborative activities of the project – including extended digitally mediated dialogues, telecollaborative talks, and visits with walks along one another's well-trodden pathways – shaped the places that were the project's hubs and case sites. These physical locations, mapped out in the original conceptualization in a visual gesture of stability, hovered shiftily from the start. Shifty because of the changing possibilities of access and interest which, for example, prohibited us from meeting in Gaza as a group and brought us to Ghana. But also potentially shifty, because the continual experience of being digitally mediated into one another's lives left us dis-placed.

In order to think about how places are made and unmade through human activity, anthropologist Tim Ingold (2013) offers a thought exercise, in which a sneaky elf switches your favorite cookbook from the kitchen shelf and replaces it with an equally beloved book of theory (in his example, Pierre Bourdieu's *Outline of a Theory of Practice*). While Ingold's fictional actor is at home in both the kitchen and in the study, the displacement of the books from the contexts within which they are typically housed creates a sense of confusion that at the time put things in their place, by making salient the relationships between these objects and their placement. By visiting places within which we do not normally dwell – in Gaza, in Glasgow, in Accra, in Brussels, in Tucson – and by inviting others into local, familiar places, we were *put into place*. We were made more aware of our relationships to the places we tend to occupy and the potential for reimagining those places, moving in and out of them in new ways.

Place as Case

To see what connects the research of two German Studies professors from the USA and the efforts of an applied linguist at the Islamic University in Gaza, it will help to understand a little about the local context of Tucson and how it shaped our role in the project. The University of Arizona rests on the traditional land of the Tohono O'odham people, in a city some have claimed is the longest continuously inhabited place in the United States. When Spanish settlers arrived in the late 17th century, they found that the Tohono O'odham already had established villages with irrigated gardens (Ortero, 2010: 2). Although the United States acquired most of the Arizona Territory in 1848, this excluded the southernmost part, which was home to the border-crossing O'odham, other nations and bands including the Yaqui, and the tuconenses, the early Mexican pioneer families of Tucson. The rest of this region accrued to US territorial possession five years later, as part of the Gadsden Purchase, but Mexican troops remained until 1856, around the time when the 'Kitchen' referenced in our chapter's title was first built. After this followed a more than century-long colonial culture war over the heritage and future of Southern Arizona, which many would argue still wages on today, with recent battles fought over language rights and about whose history gets to be taught (see O'Leary & Romero, 2011; Otero & Cammarota, 2011). As of the latest count in 2015, more than a quarter of Tucsonans speak Spanish, and around 40% identify as Latinx. In the 2000s Tucson became a frequent destination for refugees being resettled in the United States and, between 2007 and 2011, 10% of newcomers to Pima County were refugees. In due course, languages of Africa have collectively become the third most common language group spoken at home in Tucson, following Chinese and displacing French and German.

Within the Researching Multilingually Project, Tucson was conceived as one of five case studies, each located in different geographical, as well as disciplinary, contexts. The history that had shaped Tucson into a multilingual border city of refuge formed the backdrop of our shared set of research questions, which centered around the ways in which borders make worlds (e.g. Lechner & Solavova, 2014: 376; Mezzadra & Neilson, 2012: 59), by imposing a binary logic upon the physical, ecological and social worlds they purport to divide. We were inspired by previous work by some of our local colleagues in Tucson, which considered how the bipartite conceptual structures that emerge in border zones also shape practices which at first appear tangential or marginal to those discussions, in particular a paper by Mary Carol Combs and Sheilah Nicholas (2012), two colleagues from the School of Education at the University of Arizona, which examined the largely unanticipated and unintended effects of Arizona language policies on Arizona Indigenous students. They ascribe to Arizona policy makers 'the imperious immediacy of interest' which, as they state, 'describes an action so deeply desired by certain individuals or groups that they willfully ignore its potential for unintended consequences' (Combs & Nicholas, 2012: 102). Through ethnographic inquiry and classroom-based research, we considered how walls and borders become reproduced more or less metaphorically in official and unofficial communications that occur in institutional settings, such as university committee meetings, refugee centers, foreign language classrooms, and outside of these in learner testimonies and reflections (see Gramling & Warner, 2016; Warner & Gramling, 2014).

While Tucson was the locus of our project in the traditional sense of a case study, our node of the research network was more exactly situated in David's kitchen. Nestled in the neighborhood south of Tucson's modern downtown, in the once bustling center of daily life for tucsonenses, David's house was once home to a Sonoran state senator and judge named Carlos Ygnacio Velasco (1842–1914), who witnessed the transfer of the Gadsden Purchase from Mexico to the United States, and published a Spanish-language newspaper called *El Fronterizo, the Frontier.* Of course, the border had moved, in the course of Velasco's life, from approximately 50 miles north of Tucson to 65 miles south of it. The 'border' thus comprised temporally as well as spatially experienced divisions. Here, in the Velascos' kitchen, we deliberated for hours about concerns emanating explicitly from our research studies and academic work, but also on the various political and social dynamics around us that were themselves sometimes more revealing of the ways in which borders make worlds.

Glasgow stood as the epicenter for the project – a second home in our 'invisible college'. The largest contingent of collaborating scholars and artists associated with the project was situated there, and the inaugural symposium and eventually the final symposium of the three-year project took place there. The Velasco kitchen in Tucson, then, sometimes felt like a distant satellite, tethered to the rest of the network through the meetings and encounters that took place at other sites and sustained through online communications. Gaza, another satellite, remained an unfulfilled (and under current circumstances unfulfillable) promise throughout the duration of the project. Unfulfilled were the prospect of group travel to Gaza City, when the location of the final meeting necessarily shifted from Gaza to Glasgow amidst security and logistical concerns; the promises of peace, justice and freedom, born by Gaza as an occupied city; and the promise of Nazmi and his Gazan colleagues' physical presence in our deliberations elsewhere.

The following section reflects on several of the meeting places that shaped the trajectory of our participation in the project. Beginning with Gaza, we reflect on our practices of imagining a space which was for us unreachable and for Nazmi often unleavable; we then reconsider Tucson as it was imagined through the presence and practices of collaborating colleagues from the project. Finally, we consider Accra and Dodowa, Ghana, as an (unexpectedly) imagined and imaginable space, where we worked together in the last year of the project. If project means 'to throw forth', a visit to Ghana had not been 'thrown forth' in 2013 in the way travel to Gaza had been, and geopolitical circumstances shifted what was possible and how.

The complexity and complications of possibility and mobility in a three-year period involving nationals of 15 or more states are captured by one delirious contingency affecting our Scottish-Ghanaian colleagues, who were able to receive multi-year US entry visas upon their travel to Tucson in 2016 because the Ghanaian government had in previous years agreed to 'take' 'enemy combatant' detainees from the US extraterritorial prison at Guantánamo Bay, Cuba. Likewise, our visit to Ghana was facilitated by both a domino effect of geopolitical events and by two of our collaborators' bonds of friendship and kinship to the village of Dodowa, outside Ghana's capital of Accra. Through prose, poetic and photographic reflections, we consider the effects of performed locality. We consider the chronotopes, that is, the 'field[s] of historical, biographical, and social relations' (Morson & Emerson, 1990: 371), that emerged through our experience of particular sites during the project. The practice-led nature of the project allowed the sites of research, the places within which we as a research network dwelled, to expand and emerge in response to new questions, collaborations and developments.

Places as Sites of Shared Stories
Gaza

In the original proposal for the three-year grant, the final symposium had been scheduled to take place at IUG. We learned this at the first meeting in Glasgow and immediately began to project ourselves, i.e. 'throw ourselves forth', three years ahead. Would our university, with its strict bureaucratized processes of applying for international travel permissions, even approve it? Would our spouses and children approve of our shifting travel plans? What we had not yet quite begun to adequately ponder was that the very reality of us sitting in Glasgow, Scotland, where we had traveled with relative ease without even the necessity of a visa, while Nazmi sat in Gaza, inhibited by the Israeli blockades sanctioned by our own government, was at the heart of what it meant to research multilingually – more so than any of the individual case studies or projects.

Although we did not undertake a physical journey to Gaza during the three-year span of the project, we each had an opportunity to connect with Gaza remotely: David during a one-day symposium on Language and Arts of Resistance hosted at IUG; and Chantelle as part of a pilot Arabic as a Foreign Language course developed by Nazmi and other collaborators – Drs Mariam Attia, Giovanna Fassetta, Maria Grazia Imperiale and Katja Frimberger.

David: *It was indeed with a very elementary level of education about Gaza that I had an opportunity in 2015 to give a lecture to what was probably the largest audience I'd ever spoken with: the students, colleagues, and community-members of the Islamic University of Gaza. The lecture necessarily took place by Skype, as immigration prohibitions make it next to impossible for me to visit my colleagues in person. In lieu of this prospect of being a guest in Gaza City, one I still hopefully imagine, I stood in my living room at 3am Pacific Standard Time and spoke about the German-Jewish language compiler Viktor Klemperer and his arts of creative resistance while living under Nazi rule. Not an Arabic speaker, another predicament I must face every day in my personal and professional life, I asked my Jordanian husband whether he could share with me an appropriate and meaningful phrase of solidarity with Palestine, which I could utter in Arabic. We debated several options – though I knew little about the advantages or pitfalls of these – and we soon settled on one wish, prayer, or greeting:* Aliyom la yefsiluna hisar Today, may there be no siege between us. Hisar, *the word for siege, I knew from my years living in Turkey, and it was the only word of the four I was somewhat confident I could say successfully to this audience. I practiced and practiced. I knew my interlocutors were professional users of English, just as much as I, but I felt behooved to seek ways to denaturalize my own professional monolingualism in English in this interaction nonetheless.*

When speaking to the audience at the Islamic University of Gaza, I could not see my colleague Nazmi Al-Masri. I did not hear myself introduced. I was not familiar with any of the hundreds of people in the audience. And of course I did not know if they could hear or understand what I was saying. I was able to see Mona Baker, the other Skype speaker for the panel. Standing there in my own living room, where I had scrubbed up for the occasion. Other than my voice, it was silent in my house at 3am, and speaking as loud as I was speaking felt somehow untoward. Despite the substance of the topic at hand, I felt deeply uncosmopolitan, unworldly, wrong-footed. And yet: It was likely the most meaningful thing I had done in this rented house, Carlos Ygnacio Valesco's house, built when Tucson was still Mexico. And it was perhaps the first time Gaza City and Tucson had interfaced in this public and academic fashion.

Chantelle: *My colleagues have put out a call for guinea pigs. Non-Arabic speakers wanted (see Imperiale, 2017). I seize this chance to research multilingually with a language I lack and I add my name to the list. A few weeks later, I am contacted by Ethar[1] who introduced herself as my Arabic Trainer. After a few rounds of emailing back and forth negotiating time differences and exchanging Skype addresses, Ethar and I set a date and time. The ten-hour time difference between Gaza and Arizona has me waking up at dawn. I sneak off to a quiet corner at the front of the house, so as not to rouse the kids with my Arabic lesson. Ethar has sent me a PowerPoint presentation in advance, which I open on my laptop, before launching Skype and waiting for her call. She is already waiting for me online. As we connect my screen becomes an image of her sitting in her living room in Gaza with a smaller image of my living room in Tucson embedded in the bottom right corner, like Russian doll salons. At Ethar's suggestion, I minimize our faces and places and open the PowerPoint.*

In just a couple of weeks I will be welcoming a new cohort of new teachers to the German Studies Department for a week-long orientation and one week later they will stand before what for many of them will be the first class that they teach in their career. Thinking of them, I am struck by both the specificity of my and Ethar's Arabic lesson, as well as the similarities. The topic of her first day lesson, like our first day lesson, is 'greetings,' التحية. She teaches me both the greetings for the day and for the night, and indeed we need both because my morning is her late afternoon. These expressions, born out of shared physical moments, feel threadbare across the video chat, but at the same time, living room to living room, the digital presentation feels more clearly like a vehicle for linguistic input which exists slightly adjacent to the human contact that is going on in the joined windows on the left side of my screen where Ethar faces me. Several times the internet connection cuts out, making it hard for me to hear the words and phrases Ethar is introducing, but she has already anticipated this by embedding audio files with the key phrases into the PowerPoint, so that I can replay the sounds when I feel the need. I am reminded of Nazmi's seemingly unwavering resilience for finding a plan B. At one point, a small child runs into the room captured by the webcam and climbs upon Ethar's lap for a portion of the lesson. At the end of the lesson, my own daughter wanders into the room, still groggy with sleep, to tentatively peer around the edge of the laptop and see who is feeding me the unfamiliar sounds she hears my mouth speaking. While the digital-mediatedness takes away certain physical elements that I try to ask my new instructors to consider when teaching, such as seating patterns, and gesture, and mimic, it introduces new possibilities, such as the potential for two women to sit across from one another worlds apart as they share a few phrases and a small glimpse of each other's lives.

Tucson

> … through the desert
> Where rare gifts of water nourish stories
>   that resist
> Being counted
> As they branch and grow and reach out
> Stories
>   that end in flowers.
>
> – Chantelle, 'Desert Survivors' (Tucson, 2016)

For the fourth symposium in the project, we hosted almost the entire RMly team in Tucson. We chose the week of our university's spring break, so that we would be freed from other academic responsibilities, and it turned out that other colleagues on campus with the same idea were scheduling the annual conference of the National Association for Ethnic Studies during the second half of that same week. This gave colleagues on the project an opportunity to present at the conference and all of us a chance to participate in some of the non-academic events they had planned – including a guided visit to the courtroom proceedings of Operation Streamline, an initiative of the US Department of Homeland Security and the Department of Justice, which was introduced in 2005 to deter illegal entry. The 'streamline' refers to the unconstitutionally fast-tracked prosecution of those arrested with the charge of illegal entry in hearings during which as many as 80 defendants may be tried simultaneously, with public defenders representing multiple individuals at the same time (see also Schatz, 2017).

Chantelle: *On the Sunday before the official events of the Tucson symposium would begin, many of our guests have already arrived and we decided to take this as an opportunity for them to get to know Tucson, this location that had primarily featured in the life of the project as that place David and Chantelle come from, a little better. While some* *groups set off to hike through the nearby canyons or to explore the downtown, a small group of us consisting of Nazmi, our mentor and mediator from the funding agency Charles Forsdick, one of our graduate students from German Studies, Martina Schwalm, and myself headed towards the University of Arizona campus to stroll through the annual festival of books, an annual community book fair that happened to be in its final day. This was the first time that Nazmi had been able to join us in person, so between his presence and the ways in which the clusters of white tents of the book festivals transform the landscape of campus, what are for me well-trodden pathways took on a somewhat dreamlike quality. This was heightened when Nazmi made us pause at the far west end of campus, in a grove of trees just beyond the festival, to examine the quality of olives on the ground. High quality was the estimate. Much to Nazmi's obvious shock and perhaps even dismay, I had never even noticed that these were olive trees. (Confession: Although I enjoy the outdoors, I am not very taxonomically minded when it comes to the flora and fauna that reside in them and the difference between an oak and a birch or a sparrow and a starling is often lost on me.) Nazmi told us about his olive trees back home and about the process of curing them.*

It was Martina's suggestion to take a detour on the walk back to the hotel, so that we could visit the Islamic Center of Tucson. We entered to find a group of women organizing snacks along a table. When we explained who we were and introduced Nazmi, one of the women began to speak with him excitedly in Arabic. It turned out that she was from Palestine and after only a brief exchange they were able to identify common acquaintances. He asked her about the olive trees, chiding her jokingly for the fact that so many had fallen to spoil on the ground and she reassured him that they already had jars-full soaking in brine at home.

I bike by the grove of olive trees almost daily on my way into campus, but in the process of writing this article, I recently took an opportunity to return there on foot, so that I could capture a photo of the spot. I'm lost in my own thoughts about what I will write and so I can't help but feel directly addressed when I look up and notice the word 'Gaza' posted in bold white letters across a black background hanging from a yellow magazine box across the road. The box had already been emptied of whatever free periodical had once been stored inside but someone had affixed the following note to the front.

It's difficult to take issue with a single statement in the letter, especially in the absence of the original article it responds to, and yet the calls for research and cautions of complexity bear little of what I have learned from speaking with Nazmi and from seeing the effects of occupation at multiple levels, for example in the constraints on Nazmi's ability to participate fully as a colleague on our project. This disembodied debate

Figure 9.1 Periodical box on the University of Arizona campus

around the 'conflict' would have once been my own mode of access, but – although our interactions have also been fleeting and largely mediated through telecollaboration – Gaza for me is now so vividly Ethar's living room; Nazmi's office space and his home from which he has skyped into the many meetings he could not attend; Nazmi's students, whose strength becomes clear in the stories that he tells; and the olive trees, whose cousins stand before me here in Tucson.

Streamed Lines
Who they are and where they are,
And who you are and where you are,
Who I am and where we are,
Converge.
All we can do is stand together,
When ordered to rise.
Until we rise up on our own.

– Chantelle, Tucson

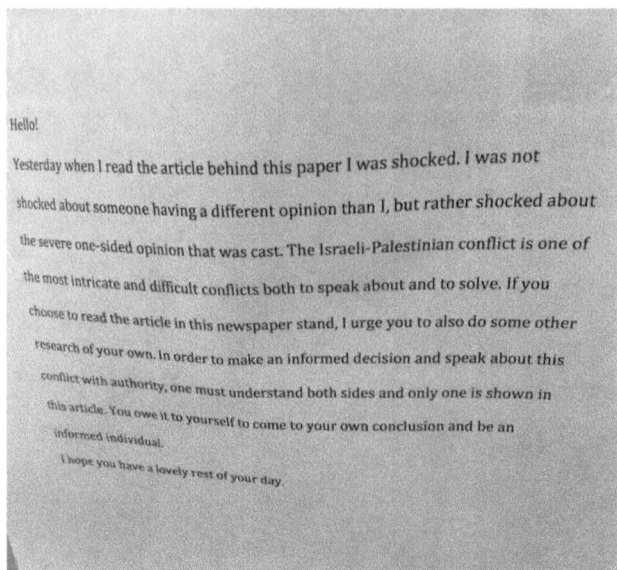

Figure 9.2 Open letter on Gaza

Chantelle: *Every morning for the past four days, I have hopped on my bike, cruised down the final two blocks of my street, made a left turn and then pedaled up the sloping street that runs along the eastern edge of downtown before turning across the highway towards the hotel where my colleagues await me. Right as the road starts to veer away from the center of the city, the Federal Court Building stands erect with two broad towers joined by a bridge of windows. Within my everyday life, this building functions as little more than a landmark – a sign that Granada Ave. will soon be merging into Cushing St. and that my path will soon be veering either towards the Barrio Viejo, the old urban center of Tucson, or towards the fast-growing new developments sprawling off the edge of town. Today I will pause here and go inside.*

Our day began at the at the Global Justice Center, a community organizing and activism center located on the southern edge of Tucson, where we would attend a panel of talks, in which academics and activists introduced us to Operation Streamline through statistics and stories, before we moved to the courthouse. There was a sense of peace among many of my colleagues in this place. Perhaps a familiarity? A sense of alliance? Of having already made good on the invitation from the cartoon cactus featured on a wall-length hand-painted tapestry, 'Occupy Tucson'? As we were all filing through the entryway, Nazmi immediately directed my attention to the photos from Palestine displayed together in a small installation, which he seemed to view as a sign of welcoming. As he talked me through the photos, I was once again struck with wonderment that Nazmi was standing beside me here in Tucson, rather than projected through a large screen, even as there was something quite natural and appropriate about the fact that my colleague of two years now was here with us.

A few hours later we are standing in a wide corridor outside of the courtroom, waiting to be admitted. Silver-haired women move among the crowd, handing out flyers with critical information about Operation Streamline. *They are part of a group committed to ensuring that there is a presence at every court proceeding, so that someone can keep records and bear witness. I am told this by one of the women who has accompanied us from the Global Justice Center, who also tells me that there had been murmurings a few years back about the possibility of moving the hearings to a courthouse on the military base outside of Tucson, but they had dropped the idea after public outcry. The distance and security between most people and the court would have made it almost impossible for witnesses to attend in this way. And yet, here in the center of town, for many of us it remains largely hidden in plain sight.*

When the heavy wooden double-doors of the courtroom are shoved open, I stand close to Nazmi and Naa Densua, one of our colleagues from Ghana. As we are ushered into the narrow corridor which leads to a matching set of heavy wooden double-doors, Nazmi looks visibly shaken. He leans in and tells us quietly that it feels like the border crossing checks he has to pass through when leaving Gaza. The clerk shoves open the doors and we are thrust into a large courtroom. The magistrate already sits at the raised bench at the front beneath an emblem of the American eagle and we are directed to sit in the rows of pews in the back corner of the room. From the right side of the room enter around 40 men and a smaller number of women, with their feet and hands shackled. They appear to me criminalized before they have had a right to stand trial – and this has been a longstanding critique of the proceedings.[2] *From next to me, Naa Densua shares a slightly different impression. 'They are chained together like slaves.'*

David: *The grim fact about visiting the Wednesday-afternoon workings of* Operation Streamline *was how relatively easy it was to prepare for, from an event-organizer's point of view. On this weekly basis, 99% of up to 80 incarcerated border-crossing persons are judged guilty simultaneously of a civil immigration offense in Federal Court – often without effective interpreters or a credible fear interview. As a group, the RMly colleagues filed into the Courthouse in March 2016 and sat together in the back of the gallery, in quiet rows, having agreed to refrain from photographing, commenting, or otherwise expressing political and moral agency in the room. Our guests were witnesses now, participants in a much different sense than they had been a few hours earlier. One of the legal experts in our group imagined aloud whether she had been* *intuitively identifying more with the defense lawyer or with the women detained – with the officer of the law or the subject of it. The unapologetic regularity of the proceedings corresponded with the stoic self-evidentness with which we conveyed our colleagues to the Courtroom. Debriefing in the afternoon, simultaneously as the defendants were being processed through 'expedited removal' from the United States, the RMIy group struggled about whether to be more angry with the proceedings or with ourselves for having witnessed them without protesting.*

David: *In the course of our project, Nazmi rarely spoke about Israel or the Israeli state. He spoke about Arabic as a Foreign Language programs, telecollaboration, the beauty of Gaza and Gazan people. And yet, I learned gradually how important it was for him to build institutional connections with universities like mine. This was primarily about a politics of recognition, of getting colleagues at my university to say 'Islamic University of Gaza' as readily and enthusiastically as they said, for instance, 'The Sultan Qaboos University of Oman.'*

Nazmi had come to Tucson along with 20 other colleagues from our project, many of whom undertook at our bidding truly dispiriting and disquieting processes of application for entry to the United States. Nazmi's attendance was the most logistically improbable, and when we greeted him at the hotel in Tucson after his journey of many weeks from Gaza to the West Bank to London and Glasgow and then to the United States border, it felt like a truly historical accomplishment in an age that otherwise seems eager to make assumptions about 'transnational mobility'. Knowing the hurdles he and others had contended with, Chantelle and I shied away from planning a trip even to the US-Mexico border, let alone across it. We pictured scenarios in which someone – maybe not the most likely geopolitical scapegoats, but someone – would get stuck on the Mexican side of the border for some miniscule and punitive reason of paperwork compliance. I myself had stopped going anywhere near the border in recent years since my Jordanian husband, the driver in the family, began expressing concern for his personal safety in a region patrolled by trigger-happy Border Patrol agents, who did not know Arizona particularly well and felt emboldened to readily suspect Muslims of wrong-doing.

From an event-organizer's point of view, skipping the border seemed a rational and worldly calculation. As a group, we would attend hearings of Operation Streamline, which is a material extension of the border. But we would not travel to 'the border' in the traditional fashion. And nonetheless, on the last day of our retreat together, I came back to the hotel in the afternoon to find out that two of the colleagues who had faced the most peril gaining access to the USA and UK had indeed taken themselves to Mexico for the day and were standing before me with shopping bags full of gifts from Nogales, Sonora. This was a two-pronged lesson

Figure 9.3 With some of our colleagues absent, we performed their presence as part of our collaborative community through signs such as this

for me: we had probably had the right idea to not cavalierly compel the group to traverse another border together. Although doing so is in many senses an important symbolic performance of political provocation, intercultural communication, and experimental solidarity, such a venture ought not be managed by a White US citizen who faces few of the violences that routinely constrain the movement of my colleagues of color. But secondly, I learned how it was precisely *those colleagues who faced likely consequences for border-crossing whose spirit moved them to do so in a jovial, unremarked, and impromptu fashion. This was one of the ways that my colleagues rekindled their spirits and their political imagination, after having witnessed the devastating, violent drama of Operation Streamline.*

Earlier in the week, I had learned an absurdly simple lesson too regarding online and offline meetings, which apparently had eluded me for decades. Hospitality and hosting are far more meaningful to a potential friendship than any other proposition or gesture. Surely, and despite being a private person to a fault, I'd hosted many gatherings over the years, but having these 20 colleagues at my house in downtown Tucson was transformational. In the overall context of the collaborative RMly project – this 'together being thrown forward' – I was no longer the satellite stranger, the American cousin, or even the David of Chantelle-and-David. I was a person whose home my becoming-friends – Ghanaian, English, Scottish, Dutch, Zimbabwean, Danish, German, Egyptian, Belgian, Romanian, Palestinian – had visited and relaxed together in. Ultimately, they could find it again when the power went out, when the Skype went off, or when the borders ceased to exist in their current forms. Were they able to walk far enough, they could find my home, and me in it. They saw the kitchen, where we had first written and said their names.

They knew they were truly welcome there, always. Meeting my husband, whose home it was also, sealed this deal.

But still, an indefinitely long period of time needed to be spent in the house together; there had to be phases and variations of togetherness, a small simulation of a life. All of our Skype meetings had primed and necessitated this kind of a physical convergence, but the Skype meetings were not able – whether because of necessity or convention – to house such spatial variation, the meandering of occasions, the room-to-roomness of it. But without the Skype meetings and email exchanges, there would have been no need for our laughter here, our collaborative and triumphal construction of locality anew. Tawona playing the Mbira on the porch allowed us to settle in to our lives together, to feel together a gratitude for this reprieve from our various precaritizations.

The logo of my home university means little to me. I've always felt some disaffection and alienation from the blocky corporate podiums that come with rented rooms in the vast Student Union conference center on my campus; oversized like SUVs, they are unportable and unalterable, unlike the rickety stand I often present from in my home department, which I ordered through the mail a few years ago and often carry across campus with me, just to be sure. But there was one moment so far in my eight-plus years at my home university when the oversized podium and oversized university logo meant something to me: the day my colleague Nazmi Al-Masri presented behind it at the National Association for Ethnic Studies conference in 2016.

That following morning, Nazmi stood in front of our University's logo-branded podium in Tucson, beginning his research presentation with the salutation 'In the name of Allah, the most Gracious, the most Merciful.' His previous exclusion from project meetings, an exclusion that ran coterminously with Palestinians' exclusion from academic institutional exchange in general, meant that Nazmi's invocation and praisegiving had also not yet been able to be offered in such a secular, capitalist, offline educational setting until that day in March 2016. (Again, Skype and online interactive culture seem to have quickly developed divergent conventions around speaker introduction and invocation, even when an online speaker is giving a relatively traditional academic 'talk'.) The difference his invocation of Allah made was palpable and singular to me, having witnessed hundreds of such academic-talk-giving performances already in my short career.

Ghana

In 2016 we were invited to visit two sites of collaboration in Ghana. The first was the University of Ghana in Accra, where Chantelle assisted with a week-long symposium for junior scholars organized by Alison

Phipps and Gameli Tordzro. The second was the Noyam African Dance Institute in the village of Dodowa – a dance academy for young dancers and choreographers, which had been founded by Professor Francis Nii-Yartey in 1998. Before Nii-Yartey's passing in 2015, Alison, Gameli, Naa Densua and our colleague and resident poet for the project Tawona Sithole had been working closely with the group of dancers and had enlisted them as co-interpreters, choreographers and performers of the Researching Multilingually Project's findings. This resulted in a production entitled 'Broken World Broken Word', which was documented by Gameli in a film with the same name (available online at https://vimeo.com/202427382).

Chantelle: *In a courtyard outside of the University of Ghana I sit with my two collaborators, Judith Reynolds – a postgraduate member of the RMly team from Durham in the UK – and Rashida Resario – then a graduate student scholar in Dance at the University of Ghana. As part of the workshop, we have been tasked with writing an article together. To Alison's great amusement, we have been huddled together at this plastic patio table for hours now with three identical silver Mac laptops set before us. Among the unexpected effects of technologization and globalization is now a working draft of an article on intercultural communication and/as dance written by three women from three distant countries. Distant but connected by histories with multiple and long lasting effects – including not least of all the common language we are speaking.*

One of the highlights of the visit to the University of Ghana was a lecture by poet and literary studies scholar Professor Kofi Anyidoho. He devoted much of his talk to the poetry cycle 'Zong!' by NourbeSe Phillips. The poems tell the story of the slave ship Zong and the death of 150 Africans, who were murdered by drowning so that the ship's

Figure 9.4 A painting from the University of Ghana campus depicting the sankofa bird, an Asante Adinkra symbol, which expresses going back into the past and taking what is good to use back towards the present. Sankofa in Twi translates as 'to go back and get it'

owners could collect insurance monies. The slaves came from Ghana and other parts of West Africa, destined for an involuntary journey in the reverse direction of the one I made by plane only three days before. And I have had to come to here to Accra to be put in the position of ethical secondary witnessing which the poem, performed for us by Professor Anyidoho, challenges us to. As I am sitting there again with my colleagues from the project, connections between the other rooms we have sat in together and imagined sitting in together emerge in my mind – Glasgow, Brussels, Tucson, Gaza. Our shared histories and friendships overlapping but not quite mapping onto the larger, collective histories, which we are a part of or represent, sometimes proudly and sometimes in spite of ourselves.

I find myself wondering how a project like RMly would have looked differently if it had been set in a single local context like Tucson or Accra. Both places have long histories of multilingualism and movement of borders and people, which we could trace and analyze. But through the expanding web and travel trajectories of this project, not only our concepts but also we have become unmoored. I felt this more in Accra at the University of Ghana than in other places we shared along the way. This university and its practices were both familiar and defamiliarized in this setting with its pace. I think it was first here that I began to understand that researching multilingually isn't only or even most importantly about the languages you are or are not using in your data collection, analysis, and publication procedures, but about the ways of displacing ourselves, our tongues, and our bodies in time and place that allow us to reimagine that which we think we know – an ability that we often unlearn as we establish ourselves in a comfortable relation with our expertise, proficiency, and professional position.

David: *The first time one of the young dancers brought me a calabash, I was half asleep in the balcony of Noyam, fighting the jetlag from Phoenix. A muddy sleep pierced by outreached arms, I began to note how most of the work here in Dodowa would be the work of border crossings and of transformations of status and position. The cooks in our crew, equally regarded as participants as were the dancers, took me in to the kitchen and taught me how to stir the peanut stew with a meter-long wooden paddle. The dancers, accordingly, nicknamed me* David Soup *and raced around spreading this new name in my midst. At the Dodowa Market, women berated my friend and chaperone Naa Densua for allowing her foreign husband to carry all the shopping – on his head! Naa Densua corrected our hecklers in Ga, noting that we were working together at the 'National Theater' in Dodowa, a correction that satisfied her market acquaintances, and I learned to trade the mutually encouraging adjacency pair 'Ayekoo/Yaye'. Upon departing, Noyam, Mariam Attia and I wished to compose a farewell lyric in a Ghanaian language, and though* *we ultimately succeeded, our interlocutors spent copious amounts of our preparatory chats telling us why we ought to present the lyric in Ewe and not Dangbe, or in Ga and not Twi. Mariam and I ran around the yard at Noyam, from teacher to teacher, learning and practicing what we could for our time-limited salutation task. Although occasional internet access was possible, none of these occurrences above had any sort of online equivalent, at least in my limited imagination.*

Collaborative Imaginations

I tell you this because this is likely the last time
We will meet in this fashion.
In the course of this project
I have traveled 55,348 miles to see you
To listen to you.
You have met me in my tired
Bedraggled, unfurled state
At airports, breakfast tables, and reception desks.
Three years ago, I followed Mariam's light blue-coated
Lead across Kelvingrove Park.
Mariam is a fast walker
And I feared then, as I do now, that I would lose her.
Each time it is as if I am traveling backward
As if I need to travel backward against the chronos wind
Into stories that are simple, small, contrary, and amply silent
No one else will ask
No one else will ask me about those stories but you.
No one will ask me about those stories outside of Durham,
Glasgow, Nejmehen, Gaza, Dodowa, Sofya,
Loch Lomond, Copenhagen.

I'm not sure if this is our first symposium
Or our last symposium.
I feel as if I am still about to introduce myself
It's as if we are indeed on a threshold of knowing
And it's as if I feel compelled somehow
to pull myself back to the cislingual side of things
Compelled out of fear of sentimentality, fear of dissolution,
Fear of vicious and viscous excess
Of goofiness and messiness
Of loss of face and the indexterities of accentedness
Of wrong-footing and insecurity
Fear of being compromised by the languages
That might command us.
As the multilingual researcher Franz Kafka wrote 100 years ago:
ich wage nicht
an die Küchentür zu klopfen,
nur von der Ferne horche ich,

nur von der Ferne horche ich stehend,
nicht so, dass ich als Horcher überrascht werden könnte.
Und weil ich von der Ferne horche,
erhorche ich nichts,
nur einen leichten Uhrenschlag höre ich
oder glaube ihn vielleicht nur zu hören,
herüber aus den Kindertagen.
Was sonst in der Küche geschieht,
ist das Geheimnis der dort Sitzenden,
das sie vor mir wahren.
Je länger man vor der Tür zögert,
desto fremder wird man.
Wie wäre es,
wenn jetzt jemand die Tür öffnete und mich etwas fragte.
Wäre ich dann nicht selbst wie einer,
 der sein Geheimnis wahren will.³

See Kafka knew what it was to research multilingually
And his whole collected works are an absurd monolingual write-up
On that knowledge.
This, too, is the story I am still traveling backward in search of.
So I am inclined to think this is our first symposium,
And the one here in this very city in 2014
will have been our last.

– David, Glasgow (2017)

Over the course of the three-year project, *Researching Multilingually at the Borders of Language, the Body, Law, and the State,* we met as a group, and always as an incomplete group, only a handful of times. Without the affordances of digital communications media – emails, conferencing software, a shared website – the collaborations that developed through this project would have certainly been impossible. But our sense, which we have sought to convey through this set of reflections, is that the networked nature of the collaborations was an extension of and extended into moments of shared physical co-presence or imaged co-presence, which more than any of the case studies alone, shaped our understanding of what it means to research multilingually.

At the same time, it must be noted that the lingua franca English was as instrumental as digital media in allowing us to stay connected. At most of the borders we crossed, English negotiated our ability to cross. It is likely that Nazmi would have had even greater difficulty joining us in Tucson and our colleagues in the UK, if it were not for his background in English as a foreign language teaching and his PhD degree from the University of Manchester. It would be easy to lodge a critique that very little that we have described here has to do with multilingualism at all. Without downplaying the importance of recognizing that the majority of our shared public discourses, organizational emails, conference talks, public-facing documents and proceedings were in English for understanding, and the institutionally ingrained English language hegemony that perhaps made this so, through our reflections on the role of place in the constitution of a collaborative imagination, a sense of shared experience, history and endeavor, we hope to offer a bit of caution against the fetishization of multilingualism as simply the presence or absence of utterances in multiple languages at a given moment of social interaction and instead to begin to think our way into a more intersectional sense of multilingualism that considers the multiple scales upon which multilingualism might be refracted in a given moment or exchange.

In some instances, this was revealed in moments of rupture through translanguaging, code meshing and code play – uttering *inshallah* at the mention of Nazmi possibly joining us at the next gathering, observing that the weather in Glasgow is *dreich*, learning and rejoicing at a few words and phrases of Ewe or Twi, or letting the words of the Tohono O'odham blessing by Miguel Flores in Tucson wash over us. But in addition to these moments of explicit multilingualism there were the many moments of absurd monolingual enactment: the professor from Gaza speaking to us about Arabic as a foreign language teaching under siege; the official, publicly audible proceedings of Operation Streamline, which obscure the small headsets worn by each of the defendants and the interpreters' voices feeding through them; the academic publications shared with us by colleagues at the University of Ghana, where the insertions of Twi, Akan, Hausa and Ewe that have become familiar to us from our conversations feel like a conspicuous omission from the English prose. These moments and many others give us a chance to shift the focus somewhat from monolingualism/multilingualism, English/non-English language, as if these were toggled on or off like a switch, and instead to reflect more on the complex shades of modality between 'having to' and 'getting to' speak another language that become visible.

Even now, when critiques of simple equivalencies of geographical space and linguistic community are a standard trope in academic writings on multilingualism, place and movement are often used as analogies and metaphors for monolingualism and multilingualism, respectively. The context and premise of the project allowed us to 'unmoor monolingualism and multilingualism' in ways we had only begun to imagine in 2011, when we first began to conceptualize the field of inquiry that has developed into 'critical multilingualism studies'.[4] Writing in response to that same event, Alison Phipps captures the ambivalence of this:

> Monolingualism and multilingualism as anchors being raised and raising both anchors means movement, a possible loss of control, a move into what may be unknown, however charted. It may be a movement that is chosen or it may be the frightening, enwinding drag of a storm. To be unmoored suggests possibility – potential pain, insecurity, escape, freedom, hope, danger, release and a sea-ward flow. (Phipps, 2013a: 98)

Throughout the three-year project, we as a collective of intellectual and creative collaborators were in many senses unmoored, without a core epicenter or a common home base. And yet the places where we convened or felt ourselves tethered created sites of memory and imagination, chronotopes where we could put down tentative and temporary anchors that held us together as a group. On the one hand, this is a testament to the power of the digitally networked communications media that enabled us to connect with one another, and to get to know Nazmi while borders remained unsurpassable for him; but at the same time the salience and poignancy of place-based experiences point to what is at stake when we put up borders between academic collaborations through languages, laws and other apparatuses of state securitization, and the regulation of bodies and their movement. The crucial distinction here isn't between the physical and the virtual, another binary that tends to erase time, movement and history, but rather between connectivity as a flattened-out medium of communication and connectivity as an embodied and enlanguaged invitation to take part in the places one another inhabit.

Notes

(1) In this instance, the name here has been changed to protect the research participant.
(2) A more recent 2017 decision from the US Circuit Court of Appeals overturned the policy that all federal defendants be shackled, which has also impacted this aspect of the Operation Streamline proceedings.
(3) In the English translation by Tania and James Stern: And I don't dare knock at the kitchen door, / I only listen from a distance, / I only listen from a distance / standing up, in such a way that I cannot be taken by surprise as an eavesdropper. / And since I am listening from a distance, / I hear nothing but a faint striking of the clock passing over from childhood days, / but perhaps I only think I hear it. / Whatever else is going on in the kitchen / is the secret of those sitting there, / a secret they are keeping from me. / The longer one hesitates before the door, / the more estranged one becomes. / What would happen if someone were to open the door now / and ask me a question? / Would not I myself then behave / like one who wants to keep his secret?
(4) The journal that was founded as part of this initial project bears this name, *Critical Multilingualism Studies*, and has developed into a site for defining and expanding this field. See cms.arizona.edu.

References

Bakhtin, M.M. (1981) 'Forms of Time and of the Chronotope in the Novel.' *The Dialogic Imagination: Four Essays by M.M.* (trans. C. & M. Holquist). University of Texas Press.
Combs, M.C. and Nicholas, S. (2012) The effect of Arizona language policies on Arizona Indigenous students. *Language Policy* 11, 101–118.
Gramling, D. and Warner, C. (2016) Whose 'crisis in language'? Translating and the futurity of foreign language learning. *L2 Journal* 8 (4), 76–90.
Imperiale, M.G. (2017) A capability approach to language education in the Gaza Strip: 'To plant hope in a land of despair'. *Critical Multilingualism Studies* 5 (1), 37–58.
Imperiale, M.G. (2018) Developing language education in the Gaza Strip: Pedagogies of capability and resistance. Unpublished PhD thesis, University of Glasgow.

Ingold, T. (2013) *Making: Anthropology, Archaeology, Art and Architecture*. London: Routledge.
Kafka, F. (1972) Home-Coming (trans. T. Stern and J. Stern). In N.N. Glatzer (ed.) *The Complete Stories*. New York: Schocken Books.
Lechner, E. and Solovova, O. (2014) The migrant patient, the doctor and the (im)possibility of intercultural communication: Silences, silencing and non-dialogue in an ethnographic context. *Language and Intercultural Communication* 14 (3), 369–384.
Marwick, A. E. and boyd, d. (2011) I tweet honestly, I tweet passionately: Twitter users, context collapse, and the imagined audience. *New Media & Society* 13 (1), 114–133.
Mezzadra, S. and Neilson, B. (2012) Between inclusion and exclusion: On the topology of global space and borders. *Theory, Culture & Society* 29 (4/5), 58–75.
Morson, G.S. and Emerson, C. (1990) *Mikhail Bakhtin: Creation of a Prosaics*. Palo Alto: Stanford University Press.
O'Leary, A. and Romero, A. (2011) Chicana/o students respond to Arizona's Anti-ethnic Studies Bill, SB 1108: Civic engagement, ethnic identity, and well-being. *Aztlan: A Journal of Chicano Studies* 1, 9–36.
Ortero, L. (2010) *La Calle: Spatial Conflicts and Urban Renewal in a Southwest City*. Tucson, AZ: University of Arizona Press.
Otero, L. and Cammarota, J. (2011) Notes from the ethnic studies home front: Student protests, texting, and subtexts of oppression. *International Journal of Qualitative Studies in Education* 24 (5), 639–648.
Phipps, A. (2013a) Unmoored: Language pain, porosity, and poisonwood. *Critical Multilingualism Studies* 1 (1), 96–118.
Phipps, A. (2013b) Linguistic incompetence: Giving an account of researching multilingually. *International Journal of Applied Linguistics* 23 (3), 329–341.
Roy, S. (1995) *The Gaza Strip: The Political Economy of De-development*. Washington, DC: Institute for Palestine Studies.
Schatz, B. (2017) A day in the 'assembly-line' court that prosecutes 70 border crossers in 2 hours. *Mother Jones*, 21 July. https://www.motherjones.com/politics/2017/07/a-day-in-the-assembly-line-court-that-sentences-46-border-crossers-in-2-hours/
Warner, C. and Gramling, D. (2014) Kontaktpragmatik: Fremdsprachliche Literatur und symbolische Beweglichkeit. *Deutsch als Fremdsprache* 51, 67–76.

Afterword. 'I am Here': Savouring the 'Selfie Moments'

Alison Phipps

And then, as we put the finishing touches to this volume in which the challenges of leaving the Gaza Strip loom so large, we get a message.

'I am here.'
'In Glasgow'

Nazmi is here. He really is. He is here. Our colleague has been able to leave Gaza and is now in Glasgow. In the flesh. Years of pixilation and that wheel on the screen going round and round and ... years of 'Can you hear me?', 'Wait a minute', 'I'll try calling you', 'Can you hear me now?' After untold frustrated attempts, Nazmi is here.

Despite being linguists, these moments of meeting in the flesh elude words, or perhaps more precisely, require tangible accompaniment. We can hug or shake hands, we exchange gifts, we laugh a lot and shake our heads in amazement. We begin to tell stories of how it happened, what happened at the border and with visas, and we do it over food, lovely Palestinian food, in Glasgow. Everything is in flow. There are no technical glitches, no patient waiting for the digital world to reappear or generators to kick in, just hummus, warm pita bread, olives and laughter, and another story, and another, and yet another. And more laughter.

In the digital age, the physical meeting must be recorded. And shared digitally. Here is Nazmi, on Level 6 of the School of Education, University of Glasgow (Figure A1). Yes. Really. In the flesh.

Throughout this volume we have stressed different dimensions of the online and digital teaching which have been part of the multiple projects underlying our research as presented in this book. We have stressed the material dimensions, the tactile elements involved in collaborating online through that notoriously intangible aspect of human expression, language. It is these material dimensions that we have found inserting themselves, almost as tangible signs of defiance, and signs of resistance when miracles happen and those in mutual research relationships have been able

Figure A1 Glasgow selfie smiles

to meet, against all the odds. To date, only I have been able to visit Gaza, in 2011, before the last terrible aggression. Since then security and border protocols have meant no return visit could be made, despite funding being made available through UK and EU funded projects, for the specific purpose.

Nazmi has been able to visit on two occasions over the last 10 years of our collaboration, and in doing so the tangibility of our presence has been a time of unparalleled joy. While we can undertake many things through Skype, Zoom, email and WhatsApp, we are still embodied creatures and our presence close to one another, when so much work has been shared, matters greatly.

In the long stretches of absence between us, we make the relationships materialize in a variety of other tangible ways. When Nazmi has been absent from our work, we have held up signs in a group photo that say 'Salaam Nazmi' and filled a whiteboard with words of peace in all our languages around his name and the world 'Gaza'. A retreat with postgraduate students on an island off the coast of Scotland saw Nazmi's name written in the sand (Figure A2), the tangible symbolism of an absent presence and of a present absence, these contradictions in terms being the only way to express what happens when working online with Gaza colleagues (see also the reflections by Warner & Gramling, this volume).

This practice of connecting and memorializing does not just move one way. It also includes similar moments of mutuality recorded by Nazmi,

Figure A2 Absent presences and present absences (1)

not least when he was in Durham and found that I was a former student there, by bumping into my photograph on the wall, in the college where his son was now studying too (Figure A3).

The digital connections have formed relational connections which social media has now made possible, digitizing our contact as a way of making what is longed for, frustrated and intangible, digitally tangible. There is, in short, nothing 'virtual' about these moments. They stand as a sign of endurance and of overcoming the impossible conditions of the blockade.

This, we hope, is what this volume also does. It is produced in very different sets of material conditions and with very different sets of access

Figure A3 Absent presences and present absences (2)

to academic resources, but it is an attempt, nonetheless, to do what scholarship and equity and justice require: to bring work together, multilingually and interculturally, despite all the separations, failed connections, bombings, power cuts, visa refusals and physical privations. Here it is, a testimony to a certain *sumud*. A testimony, to hold in your hands or read online, to the way borders may be overcome – with immense resilience and endurance – even when they seek violently to prevent these encounters.

So that we can carry on 'here-ing' each other.

After the Afterword

And then the world changed.

The afterword was meant to be the last word. The happy miracle, the moment when we stopped being 'can you hear-ers' and became 'here-ers'.

The world of our collaboration pixelated again, only this time most of the world pixelated with us. Through the global COVID-19 pandemic, online learning in the isolation of 'lockdown' became the experience of everyone, not just of those singled out for years and years of blockade and segregation.

The pandemic restrictions to movement caught us right at the start of a new collaboration which includes our partners at IUG. During our online calls to Gaza from our confinement in Glasgow, we heard our colleagues – this time smoothly – wrap confident and experienced arms around us, as we struggled. Via new and much improved platforms, we heard them say:

'in Gaza we have nearly 15 years' experience of this.'
'We send you all our solidarity.'

This book has therefore become much less of a niche event, or just a record of our work in exceptional circumstances, and it is now a timely testament to something all of us are experiencing.

Solid.
Here.
Can you 'here' me?

This book is for the here and now. A solid testimony to a changed world.

Index

absent presence 191–192
Abu Aylan, Abedrabu 39
Abu Rahma, Safaa 136
Abu-Lughod, I. 38–39
academic hospitality 5
academic solidarity 125
academic travel
  being unable to travel home 44–45
  difficulties of 2–4, 11–12
  online communication instead of 154
  Researching Multilingually at the Borders of Language, the Body, the Law, and the State (RMly) 169, 172, 176, 180
  SDTCCD Project 57, 67, 68
  SHE-GE project 40–41, 42–43, 48
  T-MEDA Project 158
academic writing 5
Accra 182–185
Accreditation and Quality Assurance Commission (AQAC) 43
accreditation of teachers 125
acculturation 18
Achilli, L. 62
action research 124
active learning 95–97, 104, 112
active listening 99, 112
administration 24, 45
affective issues 29, 34, 98, 101, 103
Ahmed, R.A. 119
air-conditioning 24
Al Mqadisi 41
Al Nakba 4
Al-Busheikhi, E. 120
Alexander, J. 59
Alhabahba, M.M. 60, 68
Al-Hilali, Z. 125
Al-Masri, Nazmi 136, 166, 168, 169, 172, 173, 174, 176, 178–179, 180, 182, 186, 187, 188, 190–191

Al-Quds Open University 39–40
Alsaleem, B. 78
Alsattari, Yaser 136
Alsulami, S. 79
Amnesty International 162
anthropology 134, 170
anti-terrorism laws 33
Anyidoh, Kofi 183
Aouragh, M. 121
APPEAR 41, 42, 45, 46
applied linguistics 132, 135–136, 143, 144, 169
appropriacy 98
apps 62, 66, 67, 68
Arabic
  English for Academic Studies Telecollaboration (EAST) 20, 26
  in Gaza 38, 39, 41
  as global language 117, 119–120
  idioms of distress 134–135, 138
  in Israel 119
  at IUG 52, 153
  as medium of instruction in Gaza 41
  online teaching in Gaza 117–130
  postgraduate programs at IUG 43
  Researching Multilingually at the Borders of Language, the Body, the Law, and the State (RMly) 173, 174
  SDTCCD Project 57, 63–64, 66
  SHE-GE project 47, 50
  T-MEDA Project 159
Arabic Center, IUG 117–130
Arbaugh, J.B. 22
arrests 40
Arts and Humanities Research Council (AHRC) 118, 123, 131, 166
arts-based methodologies 131
assessment 44
asynchronous communication 23, 32, 124
Attia, Mariam 166–167, 168, 173, 184

audio feedback 24
audio materials 79
audio-quality issues 23, 24
authentic reasons for communication 19, 23, 102, 104
authentic teaching materials 19, 79, 96
autonomy, learner 76, 77, 80, 82, 89

back-up strategies 24, 124, 174–175
Bahour, S. 39
Bahrani, T. 79
Baker, Mona 174
Bakhtin, M.M. 169
Barber, B.K. 134, 135, 141
Barnett, Ronald 2–3, 5, 11, 125
Belenky, M. 102, 112
Bernaus, M. 78
bilingualism 73–93
biomedical science 17, 25, 28–29, 32
blended learning 44, 121
blockade
  bypassing 80, 85
  as collective punishment 162
  effects on academic travel 57
  English as medium of communication to circumvent blockade 149, 152–154
  English for Academic Studies Telecollaboration (EAST) 22, 32
  historical context 1, 3, 4, 6, 7
  Idioms of Distress, Resilience and Wellbeing Project 131–145
  IUG plans to circumvent 152–155
  limitations on students studying abroad 151
  and motivation for learning 74
  RM Borders Project 118, 121, 123
  T-MEDA Project 149–164
  using international collaboration to circumvent 151, 152–155, 162
body language 140, 167
body metaphors 132
Bologna Process 149, 155, 159, 162
bombing raids xii–xiii, 3, 5, 7, 127, 138
bonding 24, 27, 63
Bonwell, C.C. 95
borders *see also* blockade
  border openings 4
  Gaza's 6, 190
  metaphors 171
  opening of 11
  overcoming 169
  Rafah border controls 4, 48
  US-Mexico 180–181
boundary-crossing 63
Bourdieu, P. 3, 119, 170
boyd, d. 85, 121
Braille 41
Branch, W.T. Jr 105
'breathing, unable to' idioms 140–143
bricolage 3
British Association for Lecturers in English for Academic Purpose 28
British Council 25, 33, 57, 60–62, 153
'Broken World Broken Word' 183
'broken/destroyed' idioms 134–135, 138, 140–143
Brophy, J. 75, 81, 87
Bubbers, J. 62
Bulos, N. 63
Burde, D. 58
Burden, L. 77
Butler, J. 12
buy-in 21

Cameron, D. 119
'Can you hear me?' 2–3, 6, 190–193
Canagarajah, S. 31, 84
capabilities approach 4, 126, 135
capacity building 118, 161
certificates 22
certification of teachers 125
charitable aid 126
Charitonos, K. 60, 68
Chile 27–28
chronotopes 169, 172
citizenship 60, 81, 126, 169
Clark, M.C. 101
classroom activities 73, 78
classroom atmosphere 80–81, 82, 86
Cloete, N. 150–151
co-creation 57, 59, 126
code meshing 187
code play 187
Codner, G. 95
collaborative imagination 165–189
collaborative writing 97
collective trauma 7
Combs, M.C. 171
communication skills 28–29, 96, 97–99
communicative acts 31
communicative competence 79, 82, 96

communicative language teaching methodology 19
communities of practice 102
competitions 83–84
comprehensibility versus accuracy/appropriateness 98
confidence 25, 80, 81, 82, 89
conscientization 102
constructive feedback 22–23, 97
contact zones 11
context collapse 169
conversational analysis 144
cooperative supervision 44–45
costs
   of academic travel 41
   English for Academic Studies Telecollaboration (EAST) 24, 26–27, 32–33
   face-to-face versus virtual meetings 154
   library resources 3
Coursera 87
COVID-19 2, 11, 193
critical consciousness 102
critical discourse analysis 144
critical multilingualism studies 187
critical thinking 12, 81, 85, 169
Csizér, K. 75, 77, 78
cultural capital 3
cultural mediation 57
cultural revitalization 74 *see also* intercultural communication
culture of academia 18
curriculum development 155–156

Daly, S.R. 100
dance 131, 183
Darwish, Mahmoud 84, 127
de Jong, J.T. 134
De Wit, H. 36
deadlines 50, 98
deaf students 41
Deci, D. 76
decolonization 11
de-development 1–2, 8, 40, 169
defending a thesis 44–45
Densua, Naa 179, 183, 184
detentions 40
dialogic education 102
dialogue journals 78
dictionaries 79
differentiation 65

Digital Capabilities Framework 96
digital literacy 23, 25, 28, 97
digital natives 79
Dillenbourg, P. 37
dis-citizenship 169
disorienting dilemmas 101, 102–103, 104–105, 110
dis-placement 170
distance learning models 62
distress, expressions of 131–145
Dix, M. 103, 111
doctoral programs 43
Dörnyei, Z. 73, 75, 77, 78, 81, 82
Du, X. 76
Dwaik, R. 76
Dyukarev, Ivan 158

EcoLink 44
Economic & Social Research Council (ESRC) 56
Edmonds, W. 80
Egypt 6, 48
Eison, J.A. 95
electricity cuts 24, 32, 88, 121, 124, 137, 160
Ellinger, B.S. 79
Elsevier Science Direct 44
ELTRA 25
email
   English for Academic Studies Telecollaboration (EAST) 20
   Idioms of Distress, Resilience and Wellbeing Project 137
   intercultural communication 85
   Researching Multilingually at the Borders of Language, the Body, the Law, and the State (RMly) 182, 186
   SDTCCD Project 57, 61
   SHE-GE project 47
   T-MEDA Project 154, 160
Emerald 44
Emerson, E. 172
emotional intelligence 111
empathy 102, 104, 111, 112
employment
   and English skills 153
   as goal of foreign language instruction 60
   as goal of HEIs 39
   international job markets 80
   in online technologies 79

online technologies offer 118, 120, 121, 123, 127
skills for future employment 23, 81, 100, 153
engineering 17–35
English
  cultural power 76
  defending a thesis 44–45
  developing positive attitudes towards 81
  as foreign language in Gaza 75
  in Gaza 38, 75, 136
  as global language 76, 81, 83, 88–89
  hegemony 187
  at IUG 52
  in Jordanian education system 59, 68
  as medium for intercultural communication 89
  as medium of communication to circumvent blockade 149, 152–154
  as medium of instruction in Gaza 39, 42–45, 76
  as medium of instruction in Jordan 60
  in multilingual collaborations between HEIs 38, 149–164
  Palestinian context 76–77
  postgraduate programs at IUG 43–45
  Researching Multilingually at the Borders of Language, the Body, the Law, and the State (RMly) 186
  SDTCCD Project 56–70
  SHE-GE project 47, 48–49, 50
  for Syrian refugees 59–60
  T-MEDA Project 158–160
English as a Foreign Language (EFL) 73–93
English as a Lingua Franca (ELF)
  collaborative imagination 186
  English for Academic Studies Telecollaboration (EAST) 20, 31, 97–98
  Idioms of Distress, Resilience and Wellbeing Project 138
  motivational strategies 75–76, 89
  T-MEDA Project 150, 153, 159
English clubs 85
English for Academic Purposes 38
English for Academic Studies Telecollaboration (EAST) 17, 19–34, 94–114, 153

English for Academic Study (EAS) 19
Erasmus 26–27, 28, 34, 48
Erasmus Mundus 41
Erasmus+ 26, 28, 41, 42, 46
e-resources 48, 79
Ernst, C.W. 117, 119
ethics 137–138, 143
ethnography 104, 131, 136, 143, 171
European Credit Transfer and Accumulation System (ECTS) 48
European Union 33, 41–42, 46, 122, 149
evaluation 25, 26
Expanding Circle Englishes 31
experiential learning 101
exploration-integration-application approach 22
extremism 119
extrinsic motivation 76

Facebook
  English for Academic Studies Telecollaboration (EAST) 20, 24, 97
  Idioms of Distress, Resilience and Wellbeing Project 137
  motivation for learning 84, 88
face-to-face interactions 2, 24, 190
face-to-face versus virtual meetings 154–155
face-to-screen interactions 117, 124
Fassetta, G. 38, 80, 85, 121, 124, 136, 137, 149, 151, 154, 155, 173
feedback 77
Feldman, I. 127
female teachers 120
First Intifada 4
focus groups 63, 64
Forsdick, Charles 176
frames of reference 103, 112
Freadman, A. 112
freedom of choice 4–5
Freire, P. 102, 124
friendships, online 87, 121, 168, 181, 191
Frimberger, K. 173
Fromme, J. 84
funding applications 32–33

game-like activities 83–84
Gardner, C. 75, 78
Gardner, J. 121
Garfinkel, H. 104
Garrison, D.R. 22

gatekeeping functions 21, 22, 25, 29
Gaza city 13n(1)
Gaza Great March of Return 13n(4)
Gaza Strip history 1, 6–8
Gender Studies, interdisciplinary 47–52
German 47, 49
Ghana 131, 136, 165, 170, 172, 182–185, 187
Global Challenge Research Fund (GCRF) 67, 131–145
global citizenship 81
global languages 76, 81 *see also* Arabic; English
global mental health studies 132–135, 144
Global South 2, 3, 103, 169
globalization 79, 154, 169
goals, learners' 81–82, 86, 88–89
Godwin-Jones, R. 84
GoFundMe 169
Gonzalez, M. 81, 136
Gonzalez, R.G. 38
Good, T.L. 81
Google Docs 97
Graddol, D. 79, 117, 119
grades, as incentives 83
Graduate Attributes Matrix (UoG) 96
Grandi, Filippo 57
Gray, P. 85
Graz University, Austria 47
group work 82, 87
Guariento, W. 19, 22, 25, 85, 95, 111, 153
guest speakers 44, 85, 182
Guilloteaux, J. 77, 78
Guinea Bissau 134
Guo, Z. 154

Hadfield, J. 73
Hadith 51, 120
Hakky, R. 156
Hallam, E. 3–4
hamm 134
Hannides, T. 60
Hassan, G. 135, 140
Hattie, A. 87
hear-ing 11–12, 190–192
HEI ICI 41
here-ing 12, 190–192
high-stakes tests 59
HINARI 44
holiday periods 50, 66
Holmes, B. 121

home internet access 121
Horizon 2020 42
hospitality 181
human capital 150
human rights 150
Human Rights Watch 58
humanitarian relief 7, 126

ice-breakers 27
identity 38, 87, 95, 96, 101, 111, 112, 133, 167
Idioms of Distress, Resilience and Wellbeing Project 131–145
IELTS 18, 21, 23, 52, 53, 87
imaged co-presence 186
imagined communities 169, 172
Imperiale, M.G. 38, 80, 84, 135, 136, 137, 151, 153, 167, 173, 174
imports 40
improvisation, of resources 3–4
incentives 21–22, 83
Independent Commission for Human Rights 126
India 133
inductive methods of learning 30
informal schools 58–59
information gap 19, 26, 32
infrastructure 7 *see also* internet connectivity; power cuts
Ingold, C.W. 125
Ingold, T. 3–4, 170
in-house teaching materials 19
inquiry-based learning 95
instrumental motivations 76, 81
insurance 28
integrative motivation 75–76
intercultural communication
  English as medium of 76, 89
  English for Academic Studies Telecollaboration (EAST) 21, 25, 28, 29, 30, 31–32
  Idioms of Distress, Resilience and Wellbeing Project 131
  and internationalization 36
  and language teaching generally 5, 119
  motivation for learning 75, 80, 85, 88
  multicultural collaborations as general trend 37–38
  Researching Multilingually at the Borders of Language, the Body, the Law, and the State (RMly) 123, 183

SDTCCD Project 60
  teachers sharing cultural experiences 83
  T-MEDA Project 161
intercultural communicative competence 79, 85
intercultural language teaching 81
intercultural studies 135–136, 143, 144
interdisciplinary conversations 5, 47–48, 144, 167
international aid 7
International Association of Universities (IAU) 36, 37
International Credit Mobility (ICM) programme 26–27, 34, 42
international job markets 80
international students 18, 31–32, 48, 122, 124, 153
internationalization 36–55, 151–152, 161
internet connectivity
  EFL in Gaza 88
  English for Academic Studies Telecollaboration (EAST) 24, 32, 100
  Idioms of Distress, Resilience and Wellbeing Project 137
  Researching Multilingually at the Borders of Language, the Body, the Law, and the State (RMly) 124, 174–175
  SDTCCD Project 62
  Syrian refugees in Jordan 66–67, 68
  teaching Arabic online 120–121, 127
  T-MEDA Project 160
interpersonal skills 96
intrinsic benefits 21, 22
intrinsic motivation 76
Islamic values 45
isolation, breaking
  becoming members of the international community 127
  English for Academic Studies Telecollaboration (EAST) 17, 22, 28, 30
  internationalization 37, 41, 45
  internet provides a means for 121
  motivation for learning 80
  RM Borders Project 118
Israel 6, 48
IUG (Islamic University of Gaza)
  collaboration with University of Glasgow 19
  English for Academic Studies Telecollaboration (EAST) 17, 19–35, 94–114
  financial struggles 126
  Idioms of Distress, Resilience and Wellbeing Project 136
  internationalization 36
  motivational strategies 80–88
  online teaching of Arabic 117
  overview 41–42
  partnerships 4–5
  Researching Multilingually at the Borders of Language, the Body, the Law, and the State (RMly) 166–167, 173
  SDTCCD Project 56, 63, 66–67
  Strategic Plans 122
  'Strengthening Higher Education Capacities in Palestine for Gender Equalities' (SHE-GE) 46–52
  T-MEDA Project 149–164

Jackson, J. 76
Jebril, M.A. 40
Jenkins, J. 75–76
Joint Information Systems Committee 96
jointly constructed artefacts 37
Jordan 56–70
Jordan Response Plan for the Syria Crisis (JRPSC) 57–58, 59
journals 44, 137
JSTOR 44

Kachru, Braj 31
Kegan, R. 102, 112
Kennedy, T. 80
Kilmas, A. 82
Knight, J. 36
knowledge cascading 68
knowledge construction
  and academic travel 3
  collaboration 95–96, 105, 111
  peace-seeking 12
  team-working skills 99
  transdisciplinary modes of knowledge production 3, 5
knowledge forms, 'more grievable' 12
Kolb, D. 105
Kramsch, C. 75, 96, 98, 103

language assistance provision 22, 31
language proficiency 28, 43, 50, 64, 65, 81
languaging distress/wellbeing 136
LASER Project 60, 61
Lauridsen, K.M. 38
Lee, J. 63
lesson planning 59, 66, 124
Lévi-Strauss, C. 3
libraries 3, 44, 79, 137
lifelong learning 122
Life-long Learning in Palestine (LLIP) TEMPUS Project 122–123
Ligorio, M.B. 100
Lillemose, M.K. 38
linguistic capital 3
linguistic readiness 21
linguistic resistance 84
listening practice 21
Lorente, B. 20

Machel, G. 59
Maitland, C.F. 62
Makerere University, Uganda 131
Mandarin 20
Marie, M. 17, 74
marketing 34n(4)
Marshall, C. 80
Marwick, A.E. 169
Matar, D. 6–7, 118
Mayordomo, R.M. 95
McCloud, T. 38
McKay, S.L. 81
measuring outcomes 99
media coverage, as data source 132, 138
mental health and wellbeing 7–8, 74, 131–145
metaphors 132, 141, 171
Mezirow, J. 94, 101, 102–103, 110, 111, 112
mindmaps 111
Ministry of Education and Higher Education 39, 40, 41, 43
miscommunications 111–112, 137, 159
mistakes, learning from 82, 98
mixed-methods research 134
mobile technologies
  authentic teaching materials 79
  and internet access in Gaza 121
  motivation for learning 84
  and refugees 60–61
  SDTCCD Project 65

monitoring 24, 25
monolingualism 187
MOOCs (Massive Open Online Courses) 121, 126
Moodle 44, 47, 49, 50, 86, 121
Morley, J. 19
Morson, G.S. 172
motivation for learning
  Arabic 120
  English for Academic Studies Telecollaboration (EAST) 28, 31
  extrinsic motivation 76
  information gap 19
  instrumental motivations 76, 81
  integrative motivation 75–76
  intrinsic motivation 76
  motivational strategies 73–93
  multidimensionality of 77
  and native speaker interlocutors 31
  online technologies 78–80
Motteram, G. 56
Moughrabi, F. 39
multicultural collaborations as general trend 37–38
multiculturalism 73, 75
multilevel textbooks 65
multilingual collaborations as general trend 37–38, 187
multilingual education 37
multilingualism
  decolonization 11
  EFL in Gaza 73–93
  Researching Multilingually at the Borders of Language, the Body, the Law, and the State (RMly) 165–189
music/songs 65

Nair, C.S. 96
'Nakba' 6
Nasir, A.A. 134
national development and higher education 150–151
native speaker interactions 31 *see also* authentic teaching materials
Ndaruhutsehigher, S. 150
networked places 165–189
NGOs 59, 61, 64, 67, 68
Nicholas, S. 171
Nichter, M. 132, 133–134, 138
Nii-Yartey, Francis 183
non-verbal communication 140, 167

Northern Ireland 4, 12
Noyam African Dance Institute 183
Nussbaum, M. 126, 127, 135

Ó Tuama, Pádraig 12
Occupied Palestinian Territories 6
offline, materials able to be used 62, 65
online educational software 121
Onrubia, J. 95
Open University (UK) 60
open-source training materials 61, 62
Operation Streamline 175, 179, 180–181, 187
Oslo 4

Pacetti, E. 121, 122
pair work 82
Paranjape, A. 105
participatory research 124
parties, online 97
partnerships 42
Patil, A. 95
peer mentoring 97, 100
permits 63, 66, 67, 158, 173, 180
personalization of teaching 83
PhD programs 43, 44–45
Philippines 20
Phillips, NourbeSe 183
Phipps, Alison 2–3, 5, 11, 39, 40, 81, 125, 131, 136, 140, 149, 167, 168, 183, 187
phone calls 160
place as case 170–172
places as sites of shared stories 173–185, 187–188
plays 87
poetry 84, 183
politeness strategies 29
politics of recognition 180
postal services 44
postgraduates 40, 43, 47–52
post-traumatic stress disorder 133
poverty in Gaza 6, 94, 150
power balances
    English for Academic Studies Telecollaboration (EAST) 20–23
    structural imbalances 22
    symbolic power 22, 33, 119
power cuts 24, 32, 100, 124, 137, 160
PowerPoint 84–85, 174

pragmatics 29 *see also* non-verbal communication
Pratt, M.L. 11
Prensky, M. 79
present absence 191–192
pre-sessional English courses 18–19, 21, 32 *see also* English for Academic Studies Telecollaboration (EAST)
private universities 39
problem solving 25, 28, 99–101, 102–103, 104–105
problem-based learning 95
professional development 66, 167
protocols 63
Psathas, G. 104

Q and A sessions 24
qualified teachers 125

race 169
radicalization 63
Rafah border controls 4, 48
rapport building 63, 80–81, 86
reading lists 82
reading materials, electronic 48
RecoNow-TEMPUS 122
recorded classes 85
reflective practice 103, 104, 105, 111, 112, 124, 169
refugees 6, 56–70, 171
Reis, R. 134
relationship building 167–168, 181, 190–191 *see also* bonding; rapport building
religious differences 83
Resario, Rashida 183
Researching Multilingually at the Borders of Language, the Body, the Law, and the State (RMly) 118–128, 166–189
resilience 17, 34, 60, 68, 74, 100, 111, 131–145, 175
respectful communication 137
revitalization 74
Reynolds, Judith 183
right to education 59
Roberts, C. 21
Rolinska, A. 25, 34, 85, 153
Rossman, G. 80
Rothenberg, C.E. 134

Roy, S. 53n(3)
Ryan, M. 76

Saffarini, G. 39
Said, E.W. 52
Scarry, E. 132, 139
Schaeffer, D. 99
Scholare 3
Schwalm, Martina 176
Second Intifada 4
Second Life 79
self-beliefs 75
self-confidence 80, 81, 82, 89
self-determination theory (SDT) 76
self-directed learning 111, 112
self-evaluation 77
self-examination 103
self-study 79, 89
Sen, Amartya 4, 74, 126, 127, 135
Shehadah, A. 76
Siege
   and academic travel 48
   bypassing 86
   effect on higher education 40
   forcing monolingualism 38
   historical context 4, 17
   and motivation for learning 74
   RM Borders Project 123
sign language 41
Sithole, Tawona 183
Situation-Problem-Response-Evaluation (SPRE) 103, 112
Skype
   authentic teaching materials 79
   defending a thesis 44–45
   English for Academic Studies Telecollaboration (EAST) 20, 24, 27, 97
   Idioms of Distress, Resilience and Wellbeing Project 137
   multicultural collaborations 44
   multilingual collaborations 44
   Researching Multilingually at the Borders of Language, the Body, the Law, and the State (RMly) 124, 173–174, 176, 182
   SDTCCD Project 57, 61, 63, 64, 67
   SHE-GE project 47
   T-MEDA Project 160
   visiting speakers via 85
social justice 5, 126, 127

social networks 60
social practice, language as 75
social-emancipatory transformation 102
socio-constructivist frameworks 100
soft skills 96
speaker introductions 182
speaking skills 21, 78, 85
staff diversity 45
Stockwell, G. 79
storytelling methodologies 131, 132, 136, 137–138, 143
'Strengthening Higher Education Capacities in Palestine for Gender Equalities' (SHE-GE) 37–53
study abroad 44
'study of work' 104–105
subject-specific content 98
summer schools 18
sumud 17, 34, 111, 193
supervision 44–45
Supporting and Developing Teachers in Contexts of Conflict and Disturbance (SDTCCD) Project 56–70
sustainability 118, 128, 150
symbolic power 22, 33, 119
symposia 169, 172, 173, 175
synchronous communication 21, 27, 97
   see also face-to-face interactions
Syrian refugees 56–70, 135

Tawil-Souri, H. 6–7, 118, 121
Taylor, E. 101, 102
teacher development 57, 58, 61–68, 167
teacher personality 87
teacher training 58, 61–68, 89, 123–124, 125, 128, 175
teacher-led methods 96–97
Teachers for Teachers 61
'teachers of meaning' 96
Teaching Arabic to Speakers of Other Languages (TASOL) 117–130
teaching loads 24
teaching materials
   English Language Learning 19
   imports of 40
   improvisation, of resources 3–4
   relevance to students' lives 84, 87
   RM Borders Project 125–126, 128
   SDTCCD Project 59, 66
   Syrian refugees in Jordan 57

team-working skills 21, 25, 28, 96, 99
technological infrastructure 126–127
technological issues 160
technology failure 50
Teeler, D. 85
TEMPUS 41, 46, 122, 149, 155
text messages 160
textbooks 44, 59, 65
thesauri 79
thesis writing 44–45
Thompson, S. 150
time-zone differences 27, 121, 174
T-MEDA Project (Tuning Middle East and North Africa) 149–164
TOEFL 43, 52, 53
Tohono O'odham people 170, 187
Tordzro, Gameli 183
transdisciplinary modes of knowledge production 3, 5
transformative learning 101–113
translanguaging 28, 187
translation 50, 135, 138, 144, 159
transparent, open communication 137, 138
trauma 7, 74, 132, 134, 137–138, 139–143
travel *see* academic travel; visas/passports
treats as incentives 83
triangular contacts 27
Tuhiwai-Smith, L. 138
Tuning methodology 155–156
Tuscon, AZ 168, 170–172, 174, 175–182

Uganda 131
UK Research and Innovation (UKRI) agency 67
unemployment 7, 11, 23, 118, 121, 123
UniGraz 47–52
United Nations
  Arabic as official language 117
  Conference on Trade and Development 7
  Country Team in the Occupied Palestinian Territory 1
  Geneva Conventions 162
  Office for the Coordination of Humanitarian Affairs (OCHA) 7
  Sustainable Development Goal 16 3
  UNESCO Mobile Learning Week 128n(4)
UNHCR (High Commission for Refugees) 57, 59, 60
UNRWA (Relief and Works Agency for Palestine Refugees) 6, 7–8, 13n(4), 56, 66, 126
University of Deusto 156, 161
University of Ghana 131, 182–183, 187
University of Glasgow
  English for Academic Studies Telecollaboration (EAST) 17, 19, 95
  Idioms of Distress, Resilience and Wellbeing Project 131, 136
  international students 18
  networked places 172
  Researching Multilingually at the Borders of Language, the Body, the Law, and the State (RMly) 118, 173
  T-MEDA Project 153
University of Liverpool 131
University of Manchester 56, 57, 61, 63, 66–67, 131
unspeakability of pain and trauma 139–140
Ushioda, E. 75, 77, 81, 82
Ustad Mobile app 62, 66, 67, 68

Velasco, Carlos Ygnacio 171, 174
Versteegh, K. 117, 119
video-conferencing 85, 86, 97, 154 *see also specific platforms*
videos 66, 79, 85, 97
Vimeo 79
virtual classrooms 121
virtual learning environments 44, 47, 79, 121
virtual meetings 154–155
virtual mobility 121
virtual professional development 85
visas/passports 4, 158, 172, 180
visits to Gaza 28, 40
visually impaired students 41
vocabulary acquisition 78, 79
Voice over Internet Protocol (VoIP) 79 *see also specific programs e.g. Skype*

Wagoner, David 12
Walker, M. 126
Wall, M. 60
Wang, S.C. 125

webinars 28
webs of affiliation 112
well-being 7–8, 74, 131–145
Wenger, R. 102
WhatsApp
　English for Academic Studies Telecollaboration (EAST) 20, 24, 27
　Idioms of Distress, Resilience and Wellbeing Project 137
　motivational strategies 78
　SDTCCD Project 57, 58, 61, 63, 64, 66
　Teachers for Teachers 61
whiteboards 65
Wiki 47
Williams, M. 77
Wilson, A.L. 101
Winter, Y. 6, 7
WiziQ 97, 121
Women's Studies Centre (WSC) 47
World Bank 23
World Englishes 31

xenophobia 119
Xu, Y. 62

YouTube 79, 82, 85

Zaatari Camp Management Council 62
Zagonel, J. 151
Zoom 79
Zurich University 153

For Product Safety Concerns and Information please contact our EU Authorised Representative:

Easy Access System Europe

Mustamäe tee 50

10621 Tallinn

Estonia

gpsr.requests@easproject.com